DIVINE REBEL

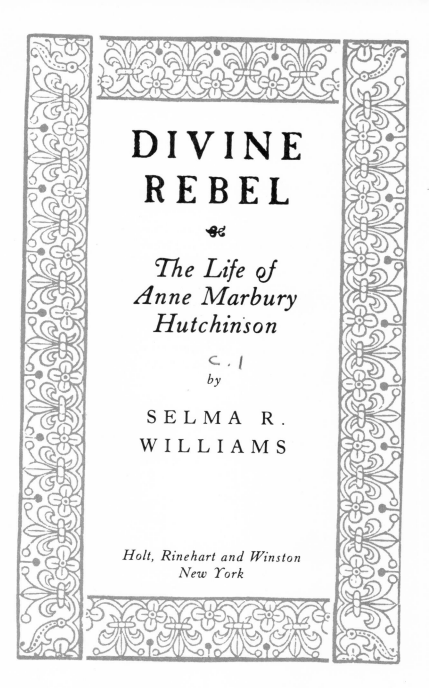

DIVINE REBEL

*The Life of
Anne Marbury
Hutchinson*

c. 1

by

SELMA R.
WILLIAMS

*Holt, Rinehart and Winston
New York*

TO BURT

❧

Published by Holt, Rinehart and Winston,
383 Madison Avenue, New York, New York 10017.
Published simultaneously in Canada by Holt, Rinehart and
Winston of Canada, Limited.

Library of Congress Cataloging in Publication Data
Williams, Selma R
Divine rebel.
Bibliography: p.
Includes index.
1. Hutchinson, Anne Marbury, 1591-1643. 2. Massa-
chusetts—History—Colonial period, ca. 1600-1775.
3. Antinomianism. 4. Puritans—Massachusetts—Biography.
I. Title.
F67.H92W54   280 .4 [B]   80-20109
ISBN: 0-03-055846-8

First Edition

Designer: Amy Hill
Printed in the United States of America
1 3 5 7 9 10 8 6 4 2

Contents

Author's Note

This book owes a great deal to the expert criticism and encouragement of several people. John Anderson, my agent, first saw the dramatic possibilities inherent in the life of Anne Hutchinson, and his excellent feel for language and literature proved indispensable. The enthusiasm and skill of Jennifer Josephy, my editor, made the writing a continually exhilarating experience. My friend, Dr. Joyce Miller, a specialist in seventeenth-century history, made many helpful suggestions. Similarly, Edwin Sanford of the Social Sciences Research Library of the Boston Public Library, a descendant of Anne Hutchinson's widowed son-in-law John Sanford and long interested in the life of Anne, was kind enough to read the entire manuscript and suggest changes. As always, my husband Burt gave full support and encouragement and, no matter how exhausting his schedule, was willing to help in the search for the *mot juste*. The original inspiration for the book came from Tammy Ziskind of Pittsburgh who was excited by the legend of Anne Hutchinson only to be disappointed by the lack of substantive material on this new-found heroine.

At Alford, England, the birthplace of Anne Hutchinson, historian Geoffrey W. H. Hatfield spent the better part of a day providing invaluable information on local lore.

The unmatched resources and highly knowledgeable staffs of various libraries provided immeasurable assistance. In the Boston area, I am most grateful for the privilege of using works available at the Boston Public Library's Research Library and Department of

Rare Books and Manuscripts; the Massachusetts Historical Society; Harvard University's Widener Library and collection of rare books and manuscripts at Houghton Library. In my own town of Lexington, Massachusetts, Cary Memorial Library continually adds to its already impressive treasury of early history sources.

In England, I was privileged to use the British Library, the London City Museum, the Greater London Record Office, and the Lincolnshire Archives at Lincoln.

DIVINE REBEL

∿

INTRODUCTION:
A WOMAN FOR ALL SEASONS

"Liar," the Massachusetts Establishment called forty-six-year-old Anne Marbury Hutchinson, excommunicating her from the Puritan church on March 22, 1638, for leadership of the crusade to smash Original Sin once and for all. "Liar," the Mormon hierarchy called forty-three-year-old Sonia Johnson, excommunicating her from the Mormon church on December 5, 1979, for outspoken advocacy of the Equal Rights Amendment to the United States Constitution.

Over and over, Anne Hutchinson's colonial crusade illuminates today's *New York Times* headlines: PLAN TO ORDAIN WOMEN PUT OFF IN FACULTY VOTE, HEAD OF JEWISH SEMINARY CALLS ACTION "A DEFEAT"; CATHOLIC CHURCH DISCIPLINES PRIEST FOR OUTSPOKEN VIEWS ON WOMEN; IN THE RELIGIOUS LIFE A CONFLICT OF FAITH AND FEMINISM.

Under this last headline, there appeared a long news feature on a conference entitled, "How to Survive as a Feminist in a Patriarchal Society." Fascinating though the story is, it is totally inexplicable without reference to the controversy engendered by the words, ideas, and activities of Anne Hutchinson. Over the centuries since the original colonization of America by the English, the issues in-

I

volved and the stands taken—by women clamoring for recognition and employment of their special talents, on the one side, and by the men in power, on the other side—have changed hardly at all. For example, in the early seventeenth century, Anne Hutchinson repeatedly rejected literal reading of the Bible, offering instead her own radically updated reinterpretations. In the late twentieth century, at the conference on feminist survival amid patriarchy, Sister Anne Patrick Ware, activist Catholic nun and associate director of the Commission on Faith and Order of the National Council of Churches of Christ, declared, "The Scriptures are unredeemably sexist," adding that there is "need of correction." And a Baptist member of the faculty at Boston College, Dr. Cheryl Exum, urged the audience to reread the Bible in the light of feminism. In their challenge to exclusively male church hierarchies, they were joined by Episcopalian, Jewish, Lutheran, Mormon, and Presbyterian women also participating in the conference.

Fortunately, for purposes of comprehension and clarification of the conflict, early New England, where Anne Hutchinson held forth, was a compact, miniature society—Western culture in microcosm, its newly planted roots exposed to full view. It is incredible, therefore, that since the murder of Anne Hutchinson more than three centuries ago, the nation's most brilliant and conscientious historians have paid little attention to the substance of her challenge to male authoritarianism. To a man, they have taken note of her activities in early America, sometimes in a paragraph, sometimes in a page or two, occasionally in a whole chapter or section. However, accepting the eyewitness accounts of her nine-year crusade in America as truth from on high, they have in the end dismissed her as a babbling troublemaker. Indisputably, the writers of those eyewitness accounts were the most distinguished men of Massachusetts, dedicated to the establishment of Utopia in the New World. But that was exactly the problem: They were hardly impartial observers. On the contrary, they assured themselves and each other that for the success of their lofty experiment, they had to cut to size this woman they accused of having "rather been a husband than a wife, a preacher than a hearer, and a magistrate than a subject." At the height of the controversy, Anne Hutchinson's chief inquisitor, Gov. John Winthrop, incensed that she had a larger following than he had—almost every man and woman in Boston, and many from the rest of the colony, too—sneered that her behavior was "nor fitting for your sex." Consequently, he insisted, he would have to "reduce" her.

He succeeded better than he could ever have hoped. Historians took their assessment of Anne Hutchinson from the writings of John Winthrop and his colleagues, as well as from official records of her trial and church excommunication. One after another, the historians relied on contemporaneous denunciations of Anne Hutchinson by the colonial fathers; for example: "instrument of the Devil," a "leper," and a proponent of "that filthy sin of the community of women and all promiscuous filthy coming together of men and women, without distinction or relation of marriage."

As for biographers, they totally ignored Anne Hutchinson for a full two centuries after her death. Then, in 1847, her very first biographer, the meticulous and scholarly Dr. George Ellis of Boston, viewing the Puritan fathers as harsh and unbending, tried hard to come down on the side of Anne Hutchinson. At most, however, he wrote as a foe of the Puritans rather than as a friend of Anne. Even so, in his concluding pages, he worried that as a result of his bias against the Puritans, he might have "conveyed an impression contrary to his own convictions, if it should be inferred from this narrative that Mrs. Hutchinson was an amiable and inoffensive woman, a sage in wisdom, a saint in piety, and a martyr to a patient and faithful testimony to the truth." Warming up to his disclaimer, he added that she had "three great failings and weaknesses: her spiritual pride, her contempt of public ordinances, and her censorious tongue." The last twelve words are a thinly veiled paraphrase of John Winthrop's words at her trial.

Altogether there have been only six formal biographies of Anne Hutchinson. Carrying on where John Winthrop and his coterie left off, her most recent biographer, Emery Battis, in 1962, updated the list of insults to assail her as a menopausal neurotic. The biography that comes closest to understanding and explaining the goals and frustrations of Anne Hutchinson is the fictionalized *Unafraid* by Winifred Rugg. However, the artificial dialogue is unbearably

memo

distracting. Furthermore, though the book was pathsetting in the 1930s when it was published, in the 1980s it is disappointing in its lack of attention to the influences on Anne of her first forty-three years in England, as well as to the reasons why she presented such a threat to the men in charge of New England. Three additional biographies published about the same time are both superficial and careless with historical facts and dates: *Anne Hutchinson* by Edith Curtis, 1930; *An American Jezebel* by Helen Augur, 1930 (fictionalized); and *A Woman Misunderstood: Anne, Wife of William Hutchinson,* by Reginald R. Bolton, 1931.

Over the years, reading everything I could find on Anne Hutchinson, I have been struck by the many questions that have never even been raised, let alone answered. For instance, if, as most writers contend—some viciously—her leadership abilities were overblown, why have her followers become known as Hutchinsonians? Why were the authorities so frightened by midwives, and what was the connection between midwifery and what the colonial fathers called "the community of women . . . their abominable wickedness?" Was there a connection between Anne's femaleness and her exhorting her followers to supply no men or money to fighting the Pequot War against native Americans? Likewise, was there a connection between Anne's femaleness and her eventual advocacy of anarchy? What was the effect of the newness of New England on Anne's thinking and action?

Furthermore, why was the controversy eventually labeled "Antinomian" (a sixteenth-century pejorative meaning defiance of the laws on which society is based) when at her public trials Anne was repeatedly accused of promoting Familism, accompanied by libertinism and free love? What, in fact, was Familist philosophy and where did Anne hear of it? What connection did Anne's inquisitors find between the Munster uprising of 1534–36 and her activities a full century later? Why have all writers, even the few who are sympathetic, accepted Anne Hutchinson's "revelations" and "prophesying" as the reasons for her downfall, without taking into consideration (1) the seventeenth-century meanings of these words; (2) the repeated use of these same revelations and prophecies by men in authority; (3) the need for women, excluded from established religion—and so from politics and power and society itself—to use a direct line to God, a "Voice from Heaven," as justification for their opinions and actions?

Most of the answers to my questions I found from delving deeply into the politics and preaching, as well as the woman question, in the England of Queen Elizabeth and her Stuart successors. Further, I investigated daily life in London where Anne Hutchinson lived from age fourteen to twenty-one, and also visited her home-town of Alford and her home county of Lincolnshire. She had lived in England for forty-three years before leaving to spend her final nine years in the New World. Similarly, her opponents were men born and bred in England, who migrated to New England in middle life. Obviously, the thinking and behavior of both Anne* and her inquisitors in primeval New England can be best understood only by setting their lives and times firmly in the context of their long years in old England.

On behalf of early American women, Anne urged removing the stigma of Eve-induced Original Sin. For businessmen, she pointed the way to freedom from constant supervision imposed by the church and enforced by the government. Her twice-weekly meetings tested the waters for freedom of speech, assembly, and religion.

Seduction, charged the all-powerful men of Massachusetts. Salvation, responded their worn-out wives defiantly. Good for business, added the newly prospering merchants of Boston.

Gov. John Winthrop and his cohorts decided to put Anne on public trial. But their move backfired. Her intellect, ideas, and

---

*Frequently, Anne Marbury Hutchinson will simply be called Anne. Calling her Marbury in her early years would confuse her with her father, as would calling her Hutchinson following her marriage confuse her with her husband, brothers-in-law, or sons. Besides, I have come to know her too intimately to address her formally as Mrs., Mistress, or Ms., forms repeatedly used by her onetime idol John Cotton in writing about her. Conversely, so many of the men involved in this story are named John (Cotton, Eliot, Endecott, Wheelwright, Wilson, Winthrop) that it seems more sensible to shorten their appellations by using last names.

stamina proved more than a match for the court—and gave her a forum to address the entire colony, England, and posterity. John Winthrop wrote one account of her trial; an anonymous, mildly sympathetic reporter, another.

Following the trial, Anne lost first her freedom and then her life. And her opponents congratulated themselves, and proclaimed their victory publicly and on the printed page.

Here, after almost three and a half centuries, is Anne's side of the story, pieced together from the history of her forty-three years in England, her words at her General Court trial and excommunication hearing, and her actions that spoke louder than words.

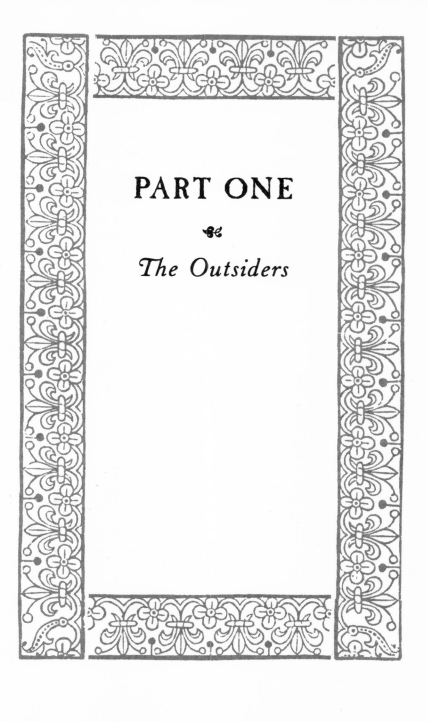

PART ONE

The Outsiders

I

"THOU ART A VERY ASS"

Anne Marbury Hutchinson learned early to challenge old ways. As her model she could look to the tradition-toppling Elizabeth I, the queen who forced the strongest men of Europe to come crawling, kneeling, and yielding at every confrontation. And as her coach and teacher she had her own doting father, the impudently iconoclastic Francis Marbury.

From birth she was swathed in the continuing euphoria of post-Armada England. Her christening in the summer of 1591 marked the third anniversary of Elizabethan England's emergence as master of Europe and mistress of the seas, the direct result of the defeat of the invading Spanish Armada in 1588. Reviewing the new situation, Mary Sidney Herbert, the thirty-eight-year-old countess of Pembroke, exulted poetically:

> Kings on a Queen enforced their states to lay;
> Mainlands for Empire waiting on an Isle;
> Men drawn by worth a woman to obey:
> One moving all, herself unmoved the while.

Cults emerged, worshiping Elizabeth as the savior who had snatched the nation from the foreign fangs of the pope at Rome and his chief military ally, the once omnipotent Philip II of Spain. While the Continent largely continued to adore the Virgin Mary, England substituted obeisance to the Virgin Queen. In an age that reveled in clever nicknames, anonymous subjects dubbed their monarch "the North Star," "Queen of the Sea," and "Diana" (after the Roman goddess of virginity and the moon, fiercely independent, beholden to none). Highly original, and thus considered especially appropriate for this unique ruler, was "Gloriana," the name bestowed on her by England's leading poet in the 1590s, Edmund Spenser.

From the very beginning of her reign in 1558, the Queen had made frequent royal progresses up and down the countryside, mingling with her subjects as no previous monarch had ever done. Now approaching sixty and on the throne for more than thirty years, this tall, dark-eyed, redheaded queen and her nation enjoyed an intimate, almost family-like relationship.

Characteristically, at the height of the invasion threat, Elizabeth had ridden her white horse through the lines, dismounting to walk all around the encampment meeting her soldiers. Her message to them, written down to be read aloud by officers, raised the morale of the military immediately—and subsequently, when circulated throughout the nation, transformed her forever into an idol for all her male subjects and an ideal for her female subjects: "I know I have the body of a weak and feeble woman, but I have the heart and stomach of a king, and a king of England too, and think foul scorn that Parma or Spain or any prince in Europe should dare to invade the borders of my realm."

Small wonder it was no longer practicable to indulge in the centuries-old sport of denouncing women—without casting aspersions on the Queen herself. Politicians and poets fell all over themselves praising the female sex effusively. They produced a constant flow of small books top-heavy with the long titles so much in vogue. For example, courtier Anthony Gibson came up with *A Woman's Worth, defended against all the men in the world. Proving them to be more perfect, excellent, and absolute in all virtuous actions than any man of what quality soever.* Not to be outdone, the highly popular poet Nicholas Breton turned to prose to contribute a work titled *The Praise of virtuous ladies. An invective against the discourteous discourses of certain malicious persons, written against Women, whom Nature, Wit, and Wisdom (well considered) would us rather honour than disgrace.* Women, too, got into the act. True to her own name, Jane Anger wrote a scathing attack against man (always wicked, she concluded), and a soothing defense of woman (always virtuous).

Young Anne never met Queen Elizabeth personally, but she observed firsthand, on both sides of her own family, the prerogatives of power wielded by this purposeful woman in command of an entire nation. For example, there was Sir Anthony Cope, member of Parliament and maternal uncle of Anne's mother, Bridget Dryden Marbury. He was forever in and out of prison for leading the opposition to Elizabethan mandates. One time he and three of his closest associates were thrown into the Tower of London for almost a month after introducing legislation—Cope's Bill and Book—to authorize the Puritan revision of the royally sanctioned Book of Common Prayer. (As her very first move, one year after ascending the throne, Elizabeth had promulgated the Act of Settlement of 1559, designed to restore seething England to religious harmony and political stability. The English Reformation, set in motion by Elizabeth's father, Henry VIII, in the years 1530–34—following the break with Rome—had been badly undermined by the five-year reign of her staunchly Catholic half sister, "Bloody Mary," 1553–58. Elizabeth's compromise solution was to borrow ritual from the Catholics and rejection of the pope from the Protestants, and establish the Church of England with herself as Supreme Governor. Beginning in the late 1560s, a newly developing sect, the Puritans, articulated opposition to this compromise, urging the Queen and her bishops to "purify" the Church of England by abolishing all vestiges of Catholic ritual.) Elizabeth had forcefully given notice that she would tolerate no criticism of her middle way, whether from the Catholics at one extreme or from Puritan reformers at the other. The spectacle of impugning the bishops, by either group, she considered an exhibition of extreme disloyalty to her person, and a threat to her office as queen. In the late 1580s, she pretty well took care of the Catholic opposition, executing Mary Queen of Scots, the beautiful cynosure of Catholicism, in 1587; and in 1588, scattering and shattering the Spanish Armada, her royal navy had administered a resounding defeat to the foreign allies of England's homegrown Catholics. Subsequently, to the end of her reign in 1603, she regularly jailed, suppressed, or—on occasion—executed Puritans who publicly questioned her religious policy.

Under these circumstances, Anne watched her beloved father, Francis Marbury, conduct his life according to the dictates of Elizabeth or her surrogates. As with all fathers, his word was law at home. But when he spoke out against officially declared policies of the Queen, he lost his job and lived in fear of imminent imprisonment. Conversely, when he deliberately curbed his tongue and temper, he edged his way back into the Queen's good graces and was granted the right to work again.

After some ten years as a popular master of Alford Grammar School and preacher at the 250-year-old church of St. Wilfrid—center of the town's social, political, and religious life—Francis found himself in serious trouble around the time Anne was born. Loudly and frequently, less than a year before Anne's christening on July 20, 1591,* he began denouncing the almighty Church of England—and so by indirection Queen Elizabeth herself. Self-seeking soul murderers he called the powerful bishops, reviving the refrain he had used unsuccessfully in the late 1570s in his crusade for ecclesiastical reform. Impudent Puritan, the bishops responded, reaching out from London, 141 miles away, to strip their defiant schoolmaster and curate of his living in the tiny market town of Alford.

Now thirty-five, Francis Marbury was feeling too old to go to prison again. Before turning twenty-three, he had been locked up for three uncomfortably long periods, each time for the same reason: rebellion against the status quo as he single-mindedly campaigned to raise the standards of preaching in the Church. Repeatedly he had demanded that rigorous training and improved education be required for the clergy, and had further insisted that the Church must

*Church and religion were so all-pervasive in society that christenings rather than births were entered in official records. Usually the christening took place three days after the birth.

provide for the ordination of many more ministers to ensure a rector for every parish church. This time, adding the cautiousness of maturity to his still-undiminished zeal for reform, he carefully protected himself and his right to speak out—and also took pains to have his lost respectability restored by putting an end to the constant barrage of threats and accusations leveled at him anonymously. (He had even been erroneously accused of being the mysterious "Martin Marprelate, gentleman," the devilishly effective author of some seven underground tracts, widely circulated between the summer of 1588 and the fall of 1589 and aimed at demolishing the Church hierarchy with mortal mockery: e.g., "profound, proud, paltry, popish, pestilent, pernicious, presumptuous prelates.") He called for help at the very top echelons of government, specifically Queen Elizabeth's lord treasurer and chief adviser William Cecil, Lord Burghley.

Carefully rejecting the label of Puritan, he emphasized his credentials as a member in good standing of the Church who, unlike his wife's uncle, subscribed to the Elizabethan Book of Common Prayer "and none other, in our churches." Bemoaning the injustice of his expulsion "for cause to me utterly unknown, by information . . . never prevailing till now that both cause and accusers are concealed . . .," he appended to the letter three petitions from fellow preachers in the area and from his neighbors, all asking for his reinstatement.

But he was forced to wait a painfully long time for any official reaction. And in the meantime his restless intelligence could find no outlet in tiny isolated Alford—described by a contemporary as a church and marketplace surrounded by a cluster of thatched-roof houses. The only way to pass the time was to work the fields and putter around the house, typically too small for privacy, too noisy for serious study.

In this situation, when Anne was born, her father could shower her with all of his attention and most of his time. Since it was not until 1594 that Francis Marbury finally recovered his license to preach, the first three years of young Anne's life coincided with her father's years of enforced idleness and smoldering anger—which, quite unconsciously, he could easily mix with awe for femaleness as incarnated in the person of his monarch and master, Queen Elizabeth. After all, he had been less than three years old when Queen Bess ascended the throne, back in 1558, so that she was virtually the only ruler he had ever known. And despite his personal treatment at the hands of the Queen and her religious entourage, he could still bring himself to credit her with leading the country from chaos to magnificence.

Baby Anne turned out to be Francis's most attentive audience in all of Alford, including the rest of his family. And from her point of view the benefits were infinite. In fact, she probably should have been grateful that she began life at a time when her father had no sons. Anne's three living siblings were also girls. By his first wife, Elizabeth Moore, whom he married around 1580, Francis Marbury had had three daughters, of whom only Susan, born in 1585, would survive him. (Elizabeth, his first child, born in 1581, would live only to 1601, when she was twenty; and Mary, born in 1583, was buried at Alford, December 29, 1585.) Sometime around 1587, following the death of his wife, he married Bridget Dryden who, before the arrival of Anne, had given birth to Mary in 1588, and in 1590 to John who was never again mentioned in either family or official records, presumably because he died at an early age. Besides Anne, the only other child to be born during Francis's enforced leave of absence from the Church was Bridget who was christened in 1593 but died in 1598. The first long-surviving son, Francis, was born in 1594, the year the elder Francis finally won reinstatement.

In this family full of females, only Anne and her father were free of responsibility during the years of her infancy and his unemployment. By centuries-old custom, society regularly promoted daughters to the status of miniature adults at around the age of four, complete with appropriately sized, grown-up clothing and a long daily list of domestic chores. By the time Anne was six months old, this arrangement took care of her four-year-old sister Mary, her seven-year-old stepsister Susan, and her eleven-year-old stepsister Elizabeth. As for her mother Bridget, in addition to performing a full schedule of housewifely duties, she was constantly weighed down by pregnancy—forced to ensure the future of her family in a world where fewer than half of all children born could be expected to live to adulthood. In fact, not much more than twelve months following the baptism of Anne, Bridget was pregnant for the fourth time in five years of marriage.

Francis was the ideal teacher and Anne the perfect pupil, a member of that fast-growing sect of Elizabethan bookworms, female division, who spent more time reading than sewing samplers. And both father and daughter had only to look to the example of the Queen whose intellectual accomplishments were the toast of all Europe. Elizabeth had mastered ancient Latin thoroughly and Greek moderately well; used English faultlessly (so that in this era of the nation's still developing and potentially confusing language any listener or reader could easily understand her meaning); and could converse fluently in French, Italian, Spanish, and Welsh (the language of her Tudor ancestors). She wrote pleasant poetry and delightful music, played the harpsichord competently, and composed her own political speeches in a fine, round, legible hand. Reflecting the brilliance of his adored Queen, William Shakespeare, whose plays burst onto the London theater scene in 1589, endowed all his women characters with the gift of literacy. And in fact, female literacy was higher in Elizabeth's reign than ever before in England—or ever again, till the late nineteenth century.

Additional impetus for Francis to tutor his daughter—if indeed he needed any more—came from the writings of Richard Mulcaster, headmaster of the Merchant Taylors' and St. Paul's School in London. In print for all to see and read, this leading English educator reasoned: "That young maidens can learn, nature doth give them, and that they have learned our experience doth teach us. . . . What foreign example can more assure the world than our diamond [Elizabeth] at home?"

For her early reading assignments Anne had at hand her own father's writings. He was a born dramatist with an irreverent sense of humor who amused his audience even as he abused his opponents.

He published his magnum opus just about the time he was removed as schoolmaster and preacher in 1590. This was his own recorded version of his trial by the Church back in 1578. In the intervening years neither he nor the Church had budged an inch, making the trial record a still surprisingly relevant account of their opposing positions. Even the adversaries in the early 1590s were the very same men who had been on opposite sides of the judge's bench in November 1578.

Representing the Queen, God, and the Church of England was the formidable John Aylmer, consecrated bishop of London in 1577, when he was fifty-six, and known from that time forward as an uncompromising prosecutor of all opponents, whether papist or Puritan. He would retain all his power and authority up to his death in 1594, at age seventy-three. (Interestingly, the year of his death—1594—would be the same year Francis Marbury was restored to his living.) The sole speaker for reform at this early hearing was the defendant, Francis Marbury, by comparison to the venerable bishop a green stripling of only twenty-three at the time of the proceedings. The High Commission in London was the body officially designated to use any and all means necessary to enforce conformity to the Church of England.

Ensuring wide though underground circulation was the language of this particular hearing record, irreverently spiced with the young rebel's sharp-tongued ridicule. This was his only way of attracting attention. And he had nothing to lose. As everyone knew, the sole purpose of a public trial was to set an example for other potentially wayward subjects. Justice was never the issue; the verdict was always decided before the proceedings began.

Like a proper playwright, Francis Marbury began the pamphlet by setting the stage for the confrontation and listing the cast: "The conference between me and the Bishop of London in the presence of Sir Owen Hopton, D. Lewys, M. Recorder, and Archdeacon Mullins, high commissioners, in the consistory in [St.] Paul's Church, the 5 of November last past, anno 1578, many people standing by."

Then followed Francis's own careful record of the hearing, designed in part to ensure that posterity would know his side of the story, as well as the officially released version. As it turned out, the member of posterity most strongly affected was his own daughter Anne, who, for her own reasons, would similarly challenge officialdom a generation later.

Perhaps to save space or typesetting, the speakers' names are, with few exceptions, reduced to initials: "B" for Bishop Aylmer, "M" for Francis Marbury, and so on.

In the beginning, a scolding, unbending bishop heard a sarcastic, unrepentant Marbury:

B.   Marbury, where were you since your last enlargement?

M.   At Northampton.

B.   That was the place whither you were specially forbidden to go, for there you did all the harm.*

M.   I neither was, nor rightly may be inhibited the place; neither have I done harm there, but (I trust) good.

B.   As you say, sir.

M.   Not so, but I refer me to the judgment of God's Church there.

B.   The last time you found more favour than you deserved, and more than (possibly) you shall find hereafter, and yet you vaunted that you had rattled up the Bishop of Peterborough, and so you would me.

Objecting, as always, to the employment of anonymous smears, Francis exploded:

M.   Sir, if your ears be open to every sycophant, you shall have such slanders enough, but for proof bring forth mine accuser, for if bare words will serve, you may as well accuse me of high treason.

The bishop continued, ignoring the interruption:

B.   Well, sir, now you are come, what have you to say to my Lord of Peterborough or to me?

---

*The year before this confrontation young Marbury had, in quick succession, been (1) ordained a deacon at Northampton; (2) dismissed for insubordination within a few months, but allowed to remain free on condition of never again showing his face at Northampton; (3) sufficiently defiant to return to Northampton where he continued his crusade publicly.

M. Nothing but God save you both.

B. Nothing? Why you were wont to bark much of dumb dogs. Are you weary of your part?

M. I come not to accuse, but to defend, but because you urge me for advantage, I say that the Bishops of London and Peterborough and all the bishops in England are guilty of the death of as many souls as have perished by the ignorance of the ministers of their making whom they knew to be unable.

B. Whom such have I made?

M. I accuse you not particularly, because I know not your estate [status]. If you have, you shall bear this condemnation.

Finally, Francis succeeded in making the bishop lose his temper. A sound tongue-lashing followed—which only raised Francis's impudence quotient.

B. Thy proposition is false. If it were in Cambridge, it would be hissed out of the schools.

M. Then you had need to hire hissers.

B. If I finding one well qualified with learning admit him, and he after play the truant and become ignorant, and by his ignorance slay souls, am I guilty of their death?

M. This is another question, I distinguish. I speak of them which were never able.

B. Distinguish? Thou knowest not a distinction. What is a distinction?

M. It is a severing of things which seem to be the same. . . .

Anomalously, at this point the bishop and the defendant battled over a discussion of the Latin origins of the word "distinction" and such synonyms as "difference" and "ambiguity," till Francis, determined to get back on the track, expostulated: "Why do you ask me questions so impertinent?"

The recorder looked up from his note-taking to intervene with a scolding: "Marbury, use my Lord more reverently. He is a peer of the realm. I perceive your words are puffed up with pride."

The oral duel then resumed:

B. Thou speakest of making ministers. The Bishop of Peterborough was never more overseen in his life than when he admitted thee to be a preacher in Northampton.

M. Like enough so (in some sense) I pray God those scales may fall from his eyes.

B. Thou art a very ass, thou art mad, thou art courageous [spirited], nay thou art impudent, by my troth I think he be mad, he careth for nobody.

M. Sir, I take exception against swearing judges. I praise God I am not mad, but sorry to see you so out of temper.

B. Did you ever hear one more impudent?

M. It is not (I trust) impudence to answer to myself.

B. Nay, I know you art courageous, thou art foolhardy.

M. Though I fear not you, yet I fear the Lord.

REC. Is he learned?

B. Learned? He hath an arrogant spirit, he can scarce construe Cato I think.

M. Sir, you do not punish me because I am unlearned. Howbeit, I understand both the Greek and Latin tongues. . . .

The bishop again fell back on name-calling, while Francis went right on contending that the Church was riven with incompetence and stupidity:

B. Thou takest upon thee to be a preacher, but there is nothing in thee. Thou art a very ass, an idiot, and a fool.

M. I humbly beseech you, sir, have patience, give this people better example. I am that I am through the Lord. I submit the trial of my sufficiency to the judgment of the learned, but this wandering is not logical.

SIR OWEN HOP. Master Marbury, how prove you all the bishops in England to be guilty of the death of as many souls as have perished by the ignorance of the unable ministers which they have made?

M.   If it please your worship, if they order unable or unmeet ministers, they give imposition of hands over hastily to those men, which to do, the Apostle saith [I Tim. 5:22] is to be partaker of other men's sins. . . .

Over and over, Francis Marbury returned to his insistence that by failing to demand a well-educated, caring ministry, the bishops were guilty of the "sin" of "soul murdering." The bishop was not convinced:

B.   How provest thou that?

M.   They are in a manner the words of the Prophet: "My people are destroyed for lack of knowledge, but who should teach them knowledge? [Hosea 4:6]

B.   Knowledge? Have they not the homilies and the catechism? It is more than they will learn methinks.

M.   Yea, or their parish priest either to any purpose in many places. . . .

The bishop and Marbury sparred, until D. Lewys interrupted impatiently:

D. L.   Go to the purpose. If I put a man to my Lord, whom I take to be true, and he prove a thief, am I guilty of his theft? No, neither is the bishop guilty of the faults of the ministers, whom when he maketh there is good hope of.

Lewys and Marbury argued back and forth, making little progress till Marbury summed up his views by contending:

M.   You may try him that would be a spiritual thief before you trust him. . . .

The hearing then got a second wind as the disputation became more substantive:

D. L.   What trial would you have more than this? He is an honest man, and like to prove learned in time.

M.   But in the meanwhile the people perish. You will not commit your sucking child to a dry milch nurse, be she never so honest.

D. L.   A good life is a good sermon, and such slay no souls though they be not so exquisite.

M.   To teach by example only is good in a matron whom silence beseemeth. . . . The Apostle telleth Titus they must be able . . . to convince the gainsayers [Titus 1:5]. These are but evasions.

B.   This fellow would have a preacher in every parish church.

M.   So would Saint Paul [Titus 1:5].

B.   Where wouldst thou have them?

M.   In Cambridge, in Oxford, in the Inns of Court, yea and some in prison, if there wanted more, we doing our part the Lord would do his part.

Here the money issue intruded and was met head on with ridicule by Marbury:

B.   I thought where thou wouldst be, but where is the living for them?

M.   A man might cut a good large thong out of your hide and the rest would not be missed. . . . If living be the default, they are to blame which have too much, whatsoever is the cause the Church feeleth the smart.

Archdeacon Mullins offered an official explanation for poorly qualified ministers:

MUL.   Sir, in the beginning of her majesty's reign, there was defect of able men, and the Church was constrained to take such as it could get upon commendation of noble men.

M. I speak of a later time, as for noble men they are no sureties for us, as for the defect it cannot dispense with the absolute word: He must be able to teach, there is no such clause (except there be a defect).

MUL. Why then you have a preacher or else none, and so the Church shall be unserved.

M. It is better to have nothing than that which God would not have.

B. How proveth thou that God would not have them, when we can get no better.

M. Doth he not say, "Because thou hast refused knowledge, I will also refuse thee, that thou shalt be no priest to me" [Hosea 4:6].

Pejoratively the bishop spat out the most insulting label he knew and condemned the accused Marbury:

B. Thou art an overthwart proud Puritan knave. Thou wilt go to Northampton, and thou will have thine own saying to die, but thou shalt repent it.

M. I am no Puritan. I beseech you be good to me. I have been twice in prison, but I know not why.

B. Where was he before?

KEEPER OF THE JAILHOUSE. With me, my lord.

B. Have him to the Marshalsea [a notorious London prison]. There he shall cope with the papists.

M. I am to go whither it pleaseth God, but remember God's judgments. You do me open wrong. I pray God forgive you.

[Signed] Francis Marbury

Like father, like daughter. These parting words seared their way into the consciousness of young Anne, the child of Francis's rebellion. She would come to resemble him more nearly than any of his other children who eventually survived him.

As a matter of fact, in the future Anne would be excellent proof of St. Ignatius's dictum (repeatedly reconfirmed by modern philosophers and psychiatrists): "Give me the child till he is seven, and afterwards anyone may have him." By the time her father returned to full-time professional teaching she could begin looking beyond her own home—to view her Queen providing a dazzling demonstration of successful female rule.

2

"HERS TO OBEY"

Anne was eleven going on twelve when Queen Elizabeth died on March 24, 1603. Brazenly swooping down from Edinburgh came James VI of Scotland, a foreigner who stomped heavy-footed onto the throne as James I of Great Britain. King by divine right, this coarse, misshapen monarch proclaimed himself, calling on God as his partner in stifling dissent, innovation, and the Elizabethan elevation of women.

All too easily, Anne could write off the King as thoroughly bad. Her father, of course, she worshiped as thoroughly good. Yet, like a bolt from the blue, there the two men were, in the summer of 1605, seemingly in complete agreement. Quite simply, her father, Francis Marbury, had given up. Repercussions from all the nation's troubles, both natural and man-made, had demoralized him into submission: the deaths of three young children from the plague; runaway inflation, which made life's necessities unobtainable, even on the once-ample wealth he and his wife had each inherited; and a long, freak series of crop-killing storms and droughts that turned his lands barren. Sufficiently mellowed at age forty-nine to reject a return to prison, Francis proceeded in the opposite direction. He sought, and finally received, appointment as preacher in the prestigious London church of St. Martin in the Vintry, built around 1399 on Thames Street in the shadow of St. Paul's.

As a direct result, Anne, who had just turned fourteen, was uprooted from sleepy little Alford, the only home she had ever known, a country market town of several hundred hardy souls. Together with all the Marburys she headed south to bustling, bursting London, capital and political cauldron of the nation, and home for more than 225,000 faceless strangers. (In 1605 the Marbury brood included her mother, Bridget Dryden Marbury who was barely forty, and ten children ranging in age from Susan who was twenty to baby Elizabeth, born in January. The others—in addition to Anne—were Mary, seventeen; Francis, eleven; Emma, ten; Erasmus, eight; Bridget, six; Jeremuth, four; and Daniel, three.)

The 141-mile journey from Alford to London took some ten days on horseback over rutted, muddy paths infested with notorious highway robbers waiting to descend on the wagon train filled with family goods and treasures. Unfortunately, England's roads, which had been laid out so precisely by the Romans more than a thousand years earlier, had not been maintained or repaired.

For such journeys there was a regular ritual, covering every detail. First there was the official requirement that the head of the household must obtain documented permission for himself and his family—and servants, if any—to move from one county to another and to travel over the countryside. Next came attention to the special clothing needed, and to the departure breakfast. Men wore boots that could be pulled over the knee while riding and folded down to the calf when dismounting and walking around. For women a so-called safeguard was considered essential: a short coat or cloak designed to protect clothes from the spattering mud or dust, or contact with a sweaty horse. Before setting off, all travelers ate a hearty breakfast of eggs, bread and butter, and milk. There was no telling when or where the next meal stop might be. (At home, the Marburys, since they were neither full-time farmers nor laborers, regularly waited until dinner—around eleven in the morning or noon—for their first food of the day, and ate a second meal, supper, after sundown.)

Security loves company, so that the Marbury troop would stay as close as possible to other groups similarly on the move, especially at times when their route took them through wild country with no landmarks or signposts to indicate direction. On days already made miserable by constant rain and wind, crossing the numerous streams and rivers by horse-ferry or on horseback ranged from dangerous to inhumanly uncomfortable. Travel at night was out of the question; inns along the way offered twenty-four-hour meal service, as well as dormitorylike accommodations, with beds that slept three, four, or even five, depending on the travelers' ages and sizes. Apparently, the Marburys were lucky enough to arrive in London unmolested, though the family coach, in which Anne's mother and the very youngest children rode along with their nursemaid, attracted unwanted attention. Conspicuously embossed in silver on the side was the Marbury coat of arms ("Sable, a cross engrailed Argent between four piles").

It would be a long time before the Marburys would undertake such a move again. But by and large London turned out to be well worth the journey. And certainly, for Anne, life would never again be the same. First of all, she was now set off from most of her compatriots who never left home, who instead spent their whole lifetime seeing no more than one or two hundred other people. Second, she was now resident in one of the great cities of the Western World.

London, though containing no more than six percent of the population of England (variously estimated between three and four million at this time), completely dominated the entire nation. The capital was the largest industrial center in England, making a wide range of goods for sale at home and abroad; the city served as the source of all new ideas and manners and provided most of the news. Anyone having, or pretending to have, wealth and influence kept a London residence—including all English writers, poets, dramatists, and publishers. The royal court remained in the city most of the time (except for the plague years). And symbolizing London's growing financial strength was the nation's only Royal Exchange, established by Sir Thomas Gresham in 1571.

Following their arrival, the Marburys moved into the rectory provided by St. Martin's Church and located nearby. Typically, the rector's living quarters were comfortable, almost commodious, including a storage hall, kitchen, study-library, large bedroom for the parents, and several small bedrooms for children and servants. Furniture would consist of an oak table, settles (long wooden benches with arms and solid backs), cupboards, and chests. This arrangement was similar to the quarters the Marburys had occupied in Alford after Francis had been restored to his living in 1594.

Once settled in London, Anne could easily imagine herself in another country. The weather was milder, the accents quite different, and the crowds and traffic like nothing she had ever experienced. Two- and four-wheeled carriages, imported from Germany and used to carry goods around the city, made one anonymous Londoner explode in exasperation: "In every street, carts and coaches make such thundering as if the world ran on wheels." And another commented ruefully: "There be few gentlemen of any account who have not their coaches, so as the streets of London are almost stopped up with them."

Depending on the mood of a newcomer from the bucolic countryside, the constant cries of hawkers either added to the general din or provided a carnival-like atmosphere. Each day, new ones were heard on the streets:

"Old clothes, any old clothes."

"Buy, sell, or exchange hats, caps, et cetera."

"Any kitchen stuffs have ye, maids?" (The cry of the soap and candle makers.)

"Ballads, Almanacks." (The sales pitch of the itinerant bookseller.)

"What do you lack?" (Shouted by apprentices standing by their masters' shop doors to solicit trade by calling out to passersby.)

However, it had to be the lack of light, air, and space that proved the greatest shock to Anne's sense of balance. Accustomed to wide open fields dotted with trees and windmills, she now viewed a city jammed with tiny shops on top of which nestled narrow, half-timbered houses, with walls of brick or stone, and roofs of tile or lead. The houses, which looked identical, displayed no numbers. Instead they used signs painted on wood or carved in stone to distinguish one from another. Many shopowners hung out over the street their signs of elaborately worked wrought iron suspended from brackets: for example, a huge key for a locksmith, a horseshoe for a blacksmith. Whole families toiled in these shops by day, retiring at night to cramped, crowded rooms upstairs.

All around the city there was a strange new kind of domestic architecture: four, five, even six upper stories, providing additional space by jutting out over the ground floor, which was limited by the small size of the lot. These upper stories, protruding on each side of the invariably narrow street, meant that neighbors could carry on conversation or even shake hands merely by hanging out of windows separated by only a few feet. These same protrusions also succeeded in darkening streets at all hours, blocking out light and causing deep shadows on sunny days.

In the absence of empty land in which to bury garbage and human waste, all city byways stank and produced instant nausea for the newcomer. It was true that the toilet or water closet had been introduced by Queen Elizabeth's godson, thirty-three-year-old Sir John Harington, and installed at Richmond Palace in the outskirts of London back in 1597. But most people continued to use pails if they were poor, or earthenware chamber pots if they were well-to-do. These were emptied into large containers that the housewife or her maid overturned from the window above onto the street below. It was the job of the hired dustmen to sweep away all excrement, trash, and garbage. In addition, every household head was ordered by official statute to build a fire outside his house three times a week in order to cleanse the air. Under these circumstances, some of the capital city's *grandes dames*, intent on preventing their sense of smell from atrophying by constantly holding their noses, began carrying fragrant flowers with them at all times and, according to a contemporary writer, Philip Stubbes, frequently stuck two or three nosegays in their bosoms. Perfumers made a whole new vocation of sweetening the air in the house. Outside, gardens bloomed in any empty space.

There were several other obvious differences between living conditions in London and Alford. For example, London was already taking for granted the luxury of windows made of imported or English glass, almost unheard-of in Alford because of the cost and difficulty of shipping. Also, here in the capital, Anne for the first time in her life could see and taste a long list of exotic imports: fruits such as almonds, apricots, figs, lemons, olives, oranges, and peaches; and plants that included lilies from America, roses from Holland, and marigolds from France—the direct legacy of England's worldwide naval supremacy. And displayed on numerous bookstalls or hawked by peddlers called chapmen were cheap books on every subject from philosophy to travel to bawdy ballads.

Then, too, there was the Thames River, clear and sparkling, with miniature fleets of snow-white swans. The river was used extensively for travel within the city. Depending on the direction desired, people hailed the boatman by calling "Westward ho!" or "Eastward ho!"

But at best a mixed blessing was the coal used to heat London homes—instead of the wood used in Alford. On the one hand, the houses were perceptibly warmer. On the other hand, the resultant billowing black smoke filled even daytime hours with a hell-like atmosphere and stench.

Thrown into this new setting without any preparation, Anne, groping to recapture some semblance of her earlier, simpler life, could find myriad reasons to cling to her worshipful attitude toward her father. Francis's appointment in London, it turned out, was in part the result of his own superlative timing, but even more the result of the Humpty-Dumpty policy the King followed toward the Church. James had first tried to placate Puritan critics and reformers. Then, angrily accusing them of going too far in their demands, he carried out a wholesale purge of nonconformist ministers, imprisoning some, exiling others. Finally, faced with a shortage of ministers, especially in the capital, he pounced on the likes of Francis Marbury who, though he had once been a conspicuous troublemaker, had never openly embraced Puritanism. Besides, in this particular case there was a very practical consideration at work, one that was equally advantageous for the King and for his job-seeking subject. Francis had good family connections, meaning tappable funds for the embarrassingly empty national treasury, in return for the royal bestowal of a baronetcy, as well as some well-placed influence on Francis's behalf at James's court. As a matter of fact, the King had already conferred a title on Francis's older brother Edward in 1603, and further honored him—and extracted additional money—by making him a sheriff in 1605. And following Edward's death, the King would similarly single out his son, Francis's nephew George, placing the title "Sir" before his name in 1606.

Best of all, there was no reason for Anne's father to face much inner conflict over joining the Establishment at this particular time. His prosperous parishioners, mostly wine merchants descended from early-fourteenth-century immigrants from Bordeaux, worried more about taxes than about their minister's ideas on religion. For more than three hundred years their great wealth had given them a lofty status among London's wealthiest and most powerful men.

Furthermore, exactly eleven days after Francis's installation at St. Martin's, Guy Fawkes, leading a group of fanatic Catholics, unsuccessfully attempted to dynamite to death the King, Lords, and Commons, meeting for opening day of the second parliamentary session, on November 5, 1605. The failed plot resulted in uncommon camaraderie and harmony between King and Parliament, and between King and the entire spectrum of non-Catholics. Over the next five years, Francis would obtain increasingly prestigious appointments, each one of them in the City of London, the financial center and heart of the capital (purposely capitalized to distinguish it from outlying London): February 29, 1607, St. Pancras on Soper Lane, the very same church at which he himself had been baptized October 27, 1555; January 15, 1610, St. Margaret's in New Fish Street.

As for Anne, whose heredity and early environment made politics and religion as instinctive and habitual as breathing, these London years proved a bonanza. As a teenager within the walls of her father's rectory, she could see for herself that the Church, by giving important parish appointments to Francis, was effectively allowing him to involve himself in politics on the local level. Since English society was organized by parishes, Francis as minister was chief of the vestry, the select group of the most influential men of his small community or parish.* Charged by King and Church with running the temporal affairs of the congregation, they met each Sunday, when they regularly selected parishioners to serve as churchwarden (ordered to go door-to-door collecting money for the poor of the parish), constable (empowered to make arrests of vagrants and hand them over to the proper authority for jailing, since police did not yet exist), surveyor of land (deciding boundary disputes), and scavenger (responsible during epidemics for killing all dogs and cats, the animals thought to be spreaders of disease).

As an older child, Anne would be allowed to sit at the end of the table when guests were present for meals. She could then hear and see everything—but in complete silence, opening her mouth only to ingest food.

Some of these visitors were the staunchly Puritan relatives of Anne's mother Bridget, opponents of King James, preparing behind closed doors to mount a public fight against him. Dredging up every insult and innuendo they could unearth, they would pour ridicule on this self-styled superhuman monarch who claimed he sat "on God's throne." Gleefully, those who had seen him in person could report that he looked like a roly-poly clown, dressed as he was in heavily quilted doublets and breeches for protection against an assassin's knife. Certainly there was nothing godlike or even kingly in these clothes, which he wore until they fell away into rags. This might be the common practice of ordinary men and women, but it hardly suited a king—and was in stark contrast with Elizabeth who never wore the same clothes twice in public, changing them several times daily for each new appearance. Also, James, calling himself a scholar and sounding off on every subject imaginable—from the evils of tobacco and witches to the blessings of universal peace—was an unmajestic monarch who habitually lapsed into gutter-dirty jokes in his heavy Scots brogue.

---

*Many historians contend that there was a straight line from this parish assembly in old England to the town meeting of New England. In the eight-mile circuit of London at this time, there were 122 parish churches, so that, as rector, Francis Marbury—formerly of Alford, population well under 1,000—presided over the day-to-day concerns of some 28,000 parishioners.

England had begun its long leap into the future, experimenting with that special brand of nonconformity known as Puritanism which, in addition to rejecting the vestiges of Catholicism in religious rites, was beginning to question the infallibility of the King. In the name of individual freedom and dignity, an increasingly Puritan-dominated Parliament flung a massive challenge to a snarling king for inclusion in the ruling circle. Members represented everyone and every area of the nation, they asserted. The King represented only himself.

Arguments and ideas grew heated and frantic. Every point of view and every conceivable suggestion for action emerged—and must inevitably have spilled out onto the meal table where Anne could easily imbibe and readily digest the fine art of disputation.

Anne was her father's principal protégé, but still she was expected to serve as her mother's chief helper. Within a year or so of the Marburys' arrival in London, Anne had become the oldest daughter remaining at home. As soon as her sister Mary and her stepsister Susan reached their twenties, they apparently married. Consequently, Anne was called on to supervise the younger children and help with the cleaning and cooking. And from time to time, other responsibilities arose. Having reached puberty and rapidly approaching marriageable age, she would be asked to assist her mother during the births of three more Marburys during the London years: Thomas, born in 1606; Anthony, in 1608; and Katherine, in 1610. The experience contributed directly to her later career as midwife and nurse—and her rebellion against the idea that innocent infants were all born in Original Sin.

The seeds of this rebellion were planted in London when she came into contact with the ideas of Familism, a radical sect imported from the Continent. Among other attractions for Anne, this sect preached direct communication between each individual—female as well as male—and God. Such communication, of course, made every human being solely responsible for his or her own actions, and exalted respect for the individual to lofty heights. Totally rejected were predestination, which robbed humans of free will, and Original Sin, which carried with it a denunciation of Eve (all women). An alternative name used by the sect aptly described its special appeal to women and men who were society's outsiders: the Family of Love, referring to members bound together by an intimate relationship with God and basking in divine love.

In London, Anne had plenty of female company as she gravitated toward nonconformity. Women had long played key roles not only in such sects as Familism but in other nonconformist religions such as Puritanism and Separatism—both of which Anne at various times would find highly attractive. (Separatism, despairing of success in the Puritan effort to purify Anglicanism, advocated complete separation from the Established Church.) Refused admission to Parliament and the Church hierarchy, London women had been conspicuous in the vanguard of those embracing Puritanism when the movement first appeared in England in the 1560s. In the Puritans' own record of their confrontation with the bishop of London, Edmund Grindal, in 1567, women comprised a majority in the listing of the names of some two hundred nonconformists. Then, in late 1588 and 1589, women had risked heavy fines and imprisonment for their active participation in concealing from the authorities the Martin Marprelate printing presses, responsible for publication of the satanic satires on the Established Church Anne's father had once been accused of promulgating. In some passages taking direct aim at the Church's attitude toward women, these tracts—turning deadly serious—asserted that with proper education, women would be capable of entering the ministry. Mrs. Elizabeth Crane, a widow, allowed her house on the Thames to be used for printing the first tract, and also ran a salon for Puritan intellectuals. Others, though married and thus completely under the domination of their husbands, according to the law, displayed stubborn independence, determinedly pursuing underground activities, while hiding such activities from their spouses.

The very year King James came to the throne, he strongly, though inadvertently, reinforced the alliance between Puritans and women. Acceding to the Millinary Petition, presented by the Puritans on his arrival in London from Edinburgh (supposedly containing a thousand signatures), he had agreed to meet Puritan representatives at his favorite royal residence, Hampton Court Palace, fifteen miles by boat down the Thames. But if the purpose had been conciliation leading to conformity, the result was bitter recrimination, James proclaiming publicly that Puritanism "agrees as well with a monarchy as God and the Devil."

In the course of three days spent demoting the Puritans to inferiority, the King interspersed several casual digressions denouncing women. Reflecting long-standing, anciently expressed fears that women were untrustworthy, conspiratorial creatures who at every given chance would attempt to establish their own devotional cults, James and his bishops reiterated that never must midwives be allowed to baptize the newborn, even when no priest was available, or even when the baby was on the verge of death. Also in passing, the King's party decreed that only licensed ministers could ever be allowed to preach or to participate in any way in the eucharist. No exceptions, no matter what the situation. These proscriptions, at first touching young Anne's life only subliminally, would later affect her both personally and explosively.

The activities of the Separatists first came to Anne's attention also during her London years. These were the men and women affectionately dubbed Pilgrims by their leader and historian, William Bradford. They were particularly active in London, which, as the nation's commercial center and major port, was the first to import and support radical political and religious ideas from the Continent.

The Separatists were local heroes to Anne. Finding no way to reform the royal Establishment, some one hundred of them attempted to leave England for Holland, in 1607. However, they were betrayed by their own shipmaster at Boston, port city of Lincolnshire. Handed over to the authorities, they were all searched—"the women further than became modesty," in William Bradford's words—thrown into jail for a month, released, and after a long year of waiting, finally granted permission to leave the country. Living in London among a whole clique of former Lincolnshire residents, Anne was privy to every detail of the Pilgrim plight and final flight in 1608—her first close contact with the idea of leaving not only her home but her homeland.

Still, despite all these undercurrents of challenge, King James I remained firmly in control. And living near the royal court, Anne could see for herself the lopsided battle over woman's place in society: the new official policy, as set from on high by the King himself, versus the decades-long tradition of female activism, inspired by the late Queen personally.

The moment James had had the crown placed securely on his head, he gave notice that, in pointed contrast to Elizabeth, he would take every opportunity to trample women into permanent invisibility. Anne felt the effects personally when all attempts to improve female education were quashed—while, in her own family circle, she could see even the youngest boys receive educational training designed to prepare them for college. Three of Anne's brothers would subsequently receive degrees from Oxford: Erasmus, six years her junior; Jeremuth, ten years younger; and Anthony, born seventeen years after Anne and so almost representing a new generation of Marburys.

Lest Queen Bess's glorious reign should give women any outlandish ideas about female worth, the very first piece of legislation the King had called on Parliament to enact was a stiff new witchcraft statute, updating Elizabeth's relatively weak law. As a consequence of this 1604 law, witchcraft was redefined in England as a pact with the Devil to inflict infinite harm, and was made punishable by hanging. The number of witches hanged in each of the first fifteen years of James's reign was several times the number executed in each of the last years of the Queen's rule. Equally dismaying, more than forty percent of those hanged under James's law would have escaped death under the Elizabethan statute of 1563.

At the same time, in case there was any lingering doubt as to the sex of witches, James reissued his best-selling witch tract, *Daemonologie*, originally published in Scotland, in 1597. There he had deduced, on the basis of personal observation and careful study, that for every twenty-one witches, twenty were women, only one a man. All women, he insisted, were lustful, weak, and prey to "the snares of the Devil as was ever well proved to be true by the Serpent's deceiving of Eve at the beginning." With James at the helm, witch-women came to be defined as Devil's handmaidens; trouble-seeking, evil-producing outsiders; outspoken nonconformists. Eventually, Anne would come to be subsumed under every one of these categories, as she protested forcefully against the idea she had first heard expressed so clearly and powerfully by the King of

England, Wales, and Scotland that Eve (woman) and evil were synonymous.

In every way possible, James, unable to surpass, equal, or openly criticize one woman—Elizabeth—took to lashing out at all women. Giving his first formal speech to Parliament, he elevated himself to the special status of Almighty Father of England, and in the process relegated women to nothingness. The Bible gave him the final word on all matters, he proclaimed: "I am the husband and the whole isle [England, Wales, and Scotland] is my lawful wife. I am the head and it is my body." Typical of men in authority, he had bent the Bible for support of privately held theories. The King's choice paraphrase had been inspired by I Corinthians, 11:3: ". . . the head of every man is Christ and the head of the woman is the man."

Following up on this idea, James—deliberately ignoring the dazzlingly successful Elizabeth—instructed his son and heir, Crown Prince Henry, in a widely circulated letter: "Teach your wife that it is your office to command, hers to obey." Even in the household, he insisted, "women must never be allowed to meddle in the government."

With misogyny sitting on the throne of England, Anne could see men losing no time rushing to their pens in imitation. In 1606, for example, London writer Barnabe Rich let loose all his woman-hating venom in a pamphlet pithily titled, *Faults, Faults, and nothing else but Faults*. This was the same Barnabe Rich who, in the final years of Elizabeth's reign, had written a tract effusively praising women.

In this same woman-hating vein, a witch tract published in 1608 circulated an ancient saying, "The more women, the more witches." Unhappily for Anne—for all women—it was indisputably true that women outnumbered men. In London alone there were thirteen women for every ten men. Since no one could deny that doom and disaster were engulfing the land, the second half of the epigram must then also be true. (The litany included unemployment, inflation, plague, and the threat of national bankruptcy.) The King, who had from his throne in Scotland looked to England as paradise on earth, translated his utter despair and disappointment into his repeatedly expressed certainty that those witches were in a frenzy of overactivity.

When scourging witches produced no visible results, however, James broadened his definition of troublemakers to include everyone who opposed him. Borrowing an idea long used on the Continent—but totally ignored by Elizabeth—he proclaimed that "kings are justly called gods; . . . they have power of life and of death; . . . are accountable to none but God only." He and he alone would be God's representative on earth, the only one who could speak or act for God and England. Everyone else must shut up and submit. No exceptions, not even for members of Parliament who, under Elizabeth, had prided themselves on providing a voice in government for all areas of England. And when Parliament resisted, he peremptorily put an end to the session in the summer of 1610, angrily sending all members packing.

Anne apparently kept in mind—and later put to her own use—this idea of exercising power on the basis of direct and highly personal communication with God.

In 1610, after Anne had lived in London for five years—a discouraged witness to the process of subjugating women—there was a slight but distinct boomerang. This was the surfacing of the wild legend of Pope Joan, a story that foreshadowed Anne's own later assumption of religious-political leadership. (Separation of church and state, of religion and politics, was an idea for the distant future. There was as yet no distinction between the two.) Alexander Cooke, the Oxford-trained vicar of Leeds, England, published *Pope Joane*, his book retelling the tale of the female pope, which had first made its appearance more than seven centuries before, in 886. Pope Joan, according to early chroniclers, was well educated and an inspiration to her students who, in the words of the thirteenth-century writer, Martin Polonus, included "great masters."

Alexander Cooke, presenting the legend for the express purpose of demolishing Catholicism, managed indirectly in the process to show the effects (bad, from the point of view of male readers; decidedly emulative, in the eyes of female readers) of allowing a woman to occupy the papacy, once the most high and most masculine of all posts of power.

In his final summation, the Reverend Mr. Cooke insisted that this woman, Pope Joan, had fatally undermined the Catholic church:

How can your priests be assured that they were priested by lawful bishops and how can you lay papists be assured that you are absolved by lawful priests, or that your masses are said by lawful priests, seeing we read (as before I showed) that Pope Joan gave orders, Pope Joan made deacons, and priests, and bishops, and abbots? For it may be well enough that the priests of this present age are descended from those who were ordered by her; especially seeing we nowhere read that they were degraded by succeeding popes, who had their ordination by her.

At the very beginning of 1611, Anne, not yet twenty, saw her whole world collapse around her. Her father, Francis, aged fifty-five, died. All at once, Anne had no intellectual companionship or inspiration, no loving encouragement for her strong individuality and stubborn independence.

But her physical energies were on constant call over the next year. Amid all the confusion and sorrow in the newly fatherless home, she was expected to act as surrogate mother to her ten younger brothers and sisters still at home, their ages ranging from one to seventeen. Nor did tragedy grant any respite. On September 19, 1611, just seven months after the death of Francis, the Marburys buried nine-year-old Daniel at St. Peter, Paul's Wharf, London. ("Daniell Marberye s. of Widdowe Marbery, in the churchyard at the furder end by the bones.")

Anne's private memorial to her father was to shower baby Katherine with affection and intellectuality—tenderly treating and carefully tutoring her youngest sister in much the same way she herself had been treated and tutored by Francis during her own earliest years.

In so doing, Anne nurtured her first disciple.

3

"THE ENGLISH HUSWIFE"

Saint Mary Woolchurch Haw and Saint Mary Woolnoth. These thoroughly English combined parishes were Anne's new London address for eighteen months, beginning early in 1611. Following the death of Francis Marbury, the Marbury children and their mother, Bridget, had to leave the rectory to make room for the new minister and his family.

Francis Marbury who had been well-to-do by the standards of his day—he had had a coat of arms and could, when necessary, live on his inheritance without resorting to hard work—bequeathed his children money and independence in his will dated January 30, 1611. Making his wife "sole executrix," he ordered that each of his twelve children receive two hundred marks on reaching twenty-one; that Susan, his daughter from his first marriage, be given an additional ten pounds; and that his "maid servant then in his house" be granted five marks. On coming of age, each child had the choice of remaining with Bridget—who, after the money was handed over to the children, received "all the residue of his goods and chattels"—and paying her whatever sum she deemed necessary, or alternatively, "they should receive their portions and dwell where they would choose."

On reaching twenty-one, Anne's brothers would be allowed to "dwell where they would choose." But not Anne or any of her sisters. All young females were to be under the guardianship of either their father or husband, the seventeenth century decreed. So, a year after her father's death, Anne finally said "yes" to the man she had known since childhood, twenty-six-year-old William Hutchinson, a wealthy sheep farmer and textile merchant from her hometown of Alford. The ceremony took place at Saint Mary Woolnoth on August 9, 1612, when Anne was a month over twenty-one.

This was a marriage that brought together new money and old class. The recently wealthy Hutchinsons could trace their family to the mid-sixteenth century when William's namesake and great-uncle, William, was mayor, in 1552, of Lincoln, England's fourth largest city at the time; and William's grandfather, John, served in the same office in 1556. In contrast, Anne's lineage, on her father's side, went back to 1420 when her ancestors, John Merbury of Gloucestor and Nicholas Merbury of Northampton, received grants making them members of the landed gentry. And on her mother's side, her ancestors went back to signatories of the Magna Carta in 1215, and included such well-known families and peers of the realm as the Raleighs, Copes, and Drydens.*

Despite London's snobbishness when it came to crossing class lines, marriage was quite common between the socially superior and the *nouveau riche* in such rural areas as Alford. In this particular case, the Marburys and the Hutchinsons had lived in close proximity when Anne and William were small, exchanging gossip and greetings almost daily and sharing the community triumphs and personal tragedies of small-town living.

And indeed the marriage of Anne Marbury and William Hutchinson proved to be one of history's all-time great romances—and, rare for the seventeenth century, a marriage of equals

---

*Bridget's father, John Dryden, owner of the large manor of Canons Ashby, Northamptonshire, was the great-grandfather of the seventeenth-century poet laureate John Dryden, who was thus Bridget's grandnephew and distantly related to Anne.

who respected each other's strengths. Several times during the next three decades, husband and wife would take turns sacrificing everything for the other.

Soon after the wedding, Anne left the frenzy of London to return to the silent, windswept plains of her native Alford, the Dutch windmills revolving in the clean, pure air; dykes and an occasional tree dotting the landscape. Happily, she had arrived toward the end of summer, Alford's best season. The coming fall, like spring, would bring downpours of chilling rains and miserably raw weather. And in winter, as she could well remember from childhood, Alford houses were suffused with damp, penetrating cold, so that chapped lips and blue fingers were common by day, ice-white toes by night.

The young couple's new home would be modeled closely on the house of William's parents: framed in wood, with walls of wattle and daub (a mixture of clay, mud, straw, and twigs); the roof thatched with reeds and straw. Inside his parents' house were eleven rooms, each with a specific function: dining parlor, lodging parlor, four bedchambers, kitchen, study, storage chamber, buttery, and little buttery. Outside on the property were a brewhouse, a milk house, a wool house, and a stable.

William, already a man of considerable means, would have no difficulty filling his own home with the luxury items he had known in his parents' house: for example, the canopy-covered beds, which provided privacy as well as protection against the night air (considered poisonous); chairs, tables covered with carpets (cloths), cupboards; pillows, cushions, blankets, sheets, towels, napkins; candlesticks, silver spoons, pewter, brass, and iron pots; and "in the study, books and other hustlements [bric-a-brac]." All furniture was massive, made of oak and constructed with wooden pins or dowels instead of metal nails.

Even the tub used for baths was made of wood. Almost never would Anne or William take a bath, however, partly because of the cold and partly because of the difficulty of drawing water from the well, carrying it into the house, and then heating it. But for special occasions they might place the wooden tub filled with water in front of the fireplace, and perform the rite with a well-soaked, heavily soaped sponge. The soap, made from a mixture of animal fat and lye, would sometimes be perfumed with sweet herbs and spices, a special treat designed to make bathers less conscious of the harshness of the soap on the skin. There was no such thing as a toothbrush, so in the constant and losing battle to preserve teeth (even Queen Elizabeth had had a smile marred by missing and blackened teeth—apparently the result of the national passion for sugar in drinks, cakes, custards, and puddings), everyone vigorously rubbed teeth with the cleanest available cloth. Mint-flavored or fragrant mouth washes were used regularly to combat odor from foul-smelling, unrefrigerated food.

Such food had long been consumed as a duty to the body rather than a delight to the senses. In an attempt to improve the situation, Gervase Markham—just about the time Anne married—wrote his best-selling book, *The English Huswife*. Full of suggestions on raising the standards of cooking, he told the wife that "she must have a quick eye, a curious nose, a perfect taste, and a ready ear; she must not be butterfingered, sweet-toothed, or fainthearted; for the first will let everything fall, the second will consume what it should increase, and the last will lose time with too much niceness." Also, she should know how to cure, smoke, and pickle meat; raise poultry; make bread; churn butter; and prepare cheese.

Dinner, the first meal of the day, would be eaten around 11:00 A.M., or noon. Salad tossed with a combination of cucumbers, lettuce, parsley, and radishes would be the first course, followed by such dishes as fish, fowl, lamb, pork, beef, or venison, accompanied by a variety of vegetables such as artichokes, beans, cabbage, carrots, onions, peas, pumpkins, spinach, and turnips. The drink would be ale, brewed from barley, rye, or wheat; cider; milk; or wine made from elderberries, ginger, currants, oranges, or grapes. Water, long disdained as a liquid fit only for plants and animals—or on occasion for washing the human body—was never considered potable; and tea and coffee had not yet been introduced into England. Dessert would consist of fruits—apples, cherries, pears, raspberries, or strawberries; custard; gingerbread; or perhaps an apple tart. Of course, all menus were completely dependent on availability, which in turn was governed by the season, the whims of weather, and the individual householder's success in meeting or surmounting the cost of living.

Supper, the final meal of the day, would be served before dark, around 5:00 or 6:00 P.M., the table lighted with homemade candles, and would consist mainly of "white meats": bread, butter, cheese, eggs, milk. Sometimes there might be thick, meat soup or the omnipresent partridge pie. ("Brown meats"—beef, game, mutton, pork—were reserved for dinner.)

Food was important, but Gervase Markham who had subtitled his book, "The inward and outward Vertues which ought to be in a compleate Woman," felt called on to give the housewife special advice on her character. She "must be of chaste thought, stout courage, patient, untried, watchful, diligent, witty, pleasant, constant in friendship, full of good neighbor-hood, wise in discourse, but not frequent therein, sharp and quick of speech, but not bitter or talkative, secret in her affairs, comfortable in her counsel, and generally skilled in the worthy knowledges which do belong to her vocation."

Anne had only a short time following her wedding to become accustomed to her new role as keeper of her own ménage. Amid all her responsibilities, she had to prepare herself for still another turning point in her life. She was pregnant. A little more than nine months after the marriage of Anne Marbury and William Hutchinson, the first of their fifteen children, Edward, was born, baptized May 28, 1613.

Like all other women who went down to the well of death with each pregnancy, Anne found that religion had special appeal. So much about the birth process and her own body was unexplainable and beyond her control that she relied heavily on piety and prayer to protect her newborn and save herself. (More than half of all babies born died before reaching age three. One of every five women died of pregnancy-related causes. Churches everywhere, of all denominations, consistently numbered more women than men among their parishioners.)

Anne watched carefully and learned invaluable lessons in the uses of religion as women appeared on the scene as preachers, that most masculine of callings. The practice, it seemed, had originated across the English Channel, in Holland, early in the century. And before long, there were female ministers all over England: London, Hertfordshire, Kent, Lincolnshire, Salisbury, Somerset, and Yorkshire.

Repeatedly, female preachers would introduce their sermons with a tale of having heard a "Voice from Heaven." Prophets they called themselves, meaning that they had the power to reveal, predict, and interpret God's will. This of course was the best—the only—way women could call serious attention to their words and opinions. Anne could not help noticing the hostility of the Established Church to women, compared with the receptiveness of newly developing sects.

Actually, female preaching came to the fore amid the shambles of King James's reign. Between 1611 and 1621, Parliament met for only nine weeks in the spring of 1614, before being summarily dissolved by the King. Consequently, no legislation on any of the problems England faced could be enacted, and there were no parliamentary restraints on the King's disastrous wrongheadedness on taxation, foreign policy, and royal absolutism. In the absence of newspapers, James relied heavily on loyal preachers to spread his word and sway public opinion—and his opponents followed suit accordingly. Mixing politics and religion was the most natural thing in the world at this time. Governments had never been run any other way. In seventeenth-century England, then, the moment a minister died or a new church was gathered, partisans of the King struggled to get there first with a staunchly Anglican preacher, while opponents rushed to fill the same pulpit with their own man. Or woman.

One such woman made a lasting impression on Anne Hutchinson. Years later, Anne continued to speak admiringly of the "Woman of Ely," calling her "A woman of a thousand, hardly any like to her."

Ely, a small town near Cambridge, about sixty miles south of the Hutchinson farm in Alford, at this time was full of Familists, a sect particularly attractive to the rising new class of businessmen—like William—and to women—like Anne—both groups outsiders to the English Establishment. England was still living in its medieval past when the only people who counted for anything, the only people to be trusted with the power to make decisions were, in descending order of importance, the King, his nobles, and the church hierarchy. Of a population numbering at most four or four and one half million at the start of King James's reign in 1603, only sixty-one families belonged to the nobility, and bishops numbered twenty-six.

Strongly challenging traditional beliefs, Familists preached the superiority of the spirit over the letter of the Bible, believed that women as well as men could recapture on earth the state of innocence that prevailed before the Fall, and advocated election of the preacher by the congregation. Raising reason above ritual, they taught that academic education was not necessary to understand the Bible—a particularly attractive concept for Anne who was self-educated and father-tutored. Familists laid themselves open to the accusation of advocating free love by insisting that marriage and divorce should be a simple declaration before the congregation of the church. And they brought down on their heads the accusation of promoting anarchy when they proclaimed that all institutions of society should be constantly opened to review by individual reason and popular consent. Finally, they denied the immortality of the soul and therefore the existence of heaven and hell, or afterlife.

Change was definitely in the English air. And the more the King wallowed hopelessly in his own mess, the more women proclaimed their right to have a go at straightening out society. Some took to direct action, working to correct such local grievances as town corruption or the need for a new schoolmaster, the kinds of problems that dominated day-to-day existence. Other women, obviously encouraged by recently introduced sects such as Familism, expressed radicalism in terms of religion. For example, Elizabeth Carey, in 1613, used the Old Testament story of Miriam to vent strong feelings about female intelligence. The first woman to publish an original play in English, Lady Elizabeth included these lines in her drama entitled, *The Tragedy of Miriam, the Fair Queen of Jewry*:

> When to their husbands [wives] themselves do bind,
> Do they not wholly give themselves away?
> Or give they but their body, not their mind?
> · · · · · · · · · · · · · ·
>
> For in a wife it is no worse to find
> A common body, than a common mind.

A few years later, poet Rachel Speght centered her plea for recognition of female intelligence around the New Testament words of Paul. One stanza in her long poem, "A Dream," implored:

Both man and woman of three parts consist,
Which Paul doth body, soul, and spirit call,
And from the soul three faculties arise,
The mind, the will, the power, then wherefore shall
A woman have her intellect in vain,
Or not endeavor knowledge to attain.

Then, encouraging the use of all intelligence, regardless of the sex of the possessor, she called God to her side:

The talent God doth give must be employed
His own with vantage he must have again:
All parts and faculties were made for use:
The God of Knowledge nothing gave in vain.

Excited by the bold new attitude of women, playwrights began writing one drama after another on the subject, sometimes supporting, sometimes denouncing female independence—but always keeping the issue before the public. Dramatist Thomas Heywood, busily collecting facts and insights for his monumentally researched *General Historie of Women*, continued to write for his first love, the theater. Topically, in one of his plays he gave these tradition-shattering words to a woman character:

This is the fashion that's but late come up
For maids to court their husbands.

Far removed from London, the chief source of information and iconoclasm, Anne could easily find some adequate substitutes. For one thing, Alford served as market town for surrounding farms and villages unable to raise all the food they needed—especially in poor growing seasons when Alford, working through middlemen, would buy the surplus of other market towns or import food from abroad. Of course, such middlemen, with their wide and varied contacts, served as messengers from the outer world. The market was held every Tuesday, a short walk from St. Wilfrid's Church in the center of town. Mixing, mingling, and thronging there were local townspeople and farmers from outlying areas, who, letting their horses rest from the one-to-three-hour ride while they unloaded and loaded their carts and wagons, tittle-tattled and talked all the while. Thus, amid the selling, buying, or bartering of meat, fish (the North Sea was just six miles away), vegetables, fruit, grain, household utensils, and new and used clothing, Anne could easily pick up the latest news, views, and gossip.

And if Anne looked on the weekly market in Alford as a window opening on the countryside that stretched miles beyond her cloistered house, then she certainly viewed the twice-yearly fairs as doors opening to infinity. Regularly, in late May and late October, Alford was the scene of an exotic, exciting, week-long fair. From all over England and the Continent came peddlers and traveling merchants, filling booths with spices for the kitchen and bric-a-brac for the home—as well as current views imported from the Continent, and sensational printed tracts produced domestically.

Among the more provocative writings making the rounds in this fashion was a poem written by Aemelia Lanier, twenty-one years Anne Hutchinson's senior.* Sharply questioning, reinterpreting, and in the end totally dismissing Eve's sole responsibility for the Fall, she sang out, on behalf of Eve, an apology in defense of women, including these lines:

> Let not us women glory in men's fall,
> Who had power given to over-rule us all.
> Till now your indiscretion sets us free,
> And makes our former fault much less appear;
> Our Mother Eve, who tasted of the Tree,
> Giving to Adam what she held most dear,
> Was simply good, and had no power to see,

---

*A. L. Rowse, in the second edition (1973) of his book, *Shakespeare's Sonnets: The Problems Solved*, finds strong evidence that Aemilia Lanier was the dark lady of Shakespeare's sonnets.

The after-coming harm did not appear:
  The subtle serpent that our sex betrayed
  Before our fall so sure a plot had laid.
. . . .

But surely Adam can not be excused,
Her fault though great, yet he was most to blame;
What Weakness offered, Strength might have
    refused,
Being Lord of all, the greater was his shame.
. . . .

  For he was Lord and King of all the earth,
  Before poor Eve had either life or breath.

In conclusion, Aemelia Lanier pointedly cautioned all men:

  . . . You came not into the world without our pain,
  Make that a bar against your cruelty;
  Your fault being greater, why should you disdain
  Our being your equals, free from tyranny?
    If one weak woman simply did offend,
    This sin of yours hath no excuse, nor end.

With no difficulty at all then, Anne Hutchinson could feel that somewhere out there she had company, she was not alone. And when at these same markets and fairs she heard continually about the activities of the Reverend John Cotton, she could easily be convinced that fate must be on her side. By the happiest of coincidences, the Hutchinsons and the then twenty-eight-year-old minister—seven years Anne's senior, two years older than William—had arrived in the area within one month of each other. John Cotton had taken over the pulpit of St. Botolph's in Boston on July 12, 1612, and Anne and William, married on August 9 that same year, had settled down in Alford, twenty-four miles to the north.

Before Anne ever met her idol in person, she knew everything there was to know about him. John Cotton was the third in a line of hard-preaching, descriptively named ministers at the old port city of Boston, known throughout England as a town of "factious people."

The vicar who had started the city on its way to rebellion answered to the surname Worship (the Reverend James Worship). Among other activities, he had led a group of ministers in petitioning the archbishop to abandon the wearing of the wedding ring. After him came two other explicitly named men of cloth, the Reverend Thomas Wooll in 1600, and the Reverend John Cotton in 1612.

Week after week, the marketplace churned out all the details of John Cotton's career—which, as a matter of fact, almost ended before it ever began. The local Boston aldermen had offered him the appointment to the preeminent pulpit of St. Botolph's, a thirteenth-century parish church so large and grandiose that it could almost qualify as a cathedral (the bishop's seat, or church). But the man who would be his superior, crusty old William Barlow, the archconservative bishop of Lincoln, had vehemently objected, contending that he was "a young man and unfit to be over such a factious people." Thoroughly frightened by Cotton's rebelliously Puritan leanings, the staunchly Anglican bishop was not in the least impressed by his brilliant career at Cambridge University: undergraduate in 1597, at the age of thirteen; A. B. 1603, Trinity College; A. M. 1606, Emmanuel College, which was rapidly acquiring a reputation for rabid Puritanism; ordination as priest, 1610; tutor, head lecturer, and dean at Emmanuel. Cotton, who in his fifteen years at Cambridge had won nothing but praise from "the greatest wits in the university," was quite ready to return to the trouble-free scene of his triumphs. On the verge of departing, he was visited by the aldermen, reportedly pleading with utter simplicity: "Come and help us." Cotton agreed to remain.

Actually, the bishop had been right on the mark in his assessment of Boston as a town rife with dissent and faction. There was a long tradition of rebellious Puritanism in Boston, spurred immeasurably by steady economic decline. The town's three hundred years of prosperity as an old Hanseatic port trading in wines and wool had ended ingloriously in the late sixteenth century when the port silted over. Repeatedly, the Corporation of Boston begged the King "for some more than ordinary assistance," pointing out that foreign ships were bypassing their port, and local shipowners were reduced to using "little barks or boats not worthy of the name of shipping to the utter decay of trading here." When their pleas went unanswered, they turned insular, making all decisions on their own and ignoring all official directives, whether royal or religious.

From the very beginning, then, the Reverend John Cotton's ceaseless search for new ways of handling life's problems fell on well-prepared ground. In no time at all, he single-handedly gave Boston the reputation for being "a town so famous for religion." And he himself rapidly gained fame as "one of England's glories," a skillful orator and brilliant preacher whose sermons were outstanding for their "invention, elegance, purity of style, ornaments of rhetoric, elocution, and oratorious beauty of the whole." Tweaking the noses of his superiors, he refused to wear the surplice, use the cross in baptism, or compel communicants to kneel for the sacrament.

Soon John Cotton began attracting hordes of parishioners to the parsonage for additional instruction. Needing more room and loathe to turn anyone away, he began giving extra sermons: early in the morning on Wednesdays and Fridays, Saturday afternoons at three o'clock, and lectures on Boston's market day, Thursday. The regular Sunday morning service he supplemented with an afternoon service. His newly installed superior, Richard Neile—another in the line of archconservative bishops of Lincoln—making his first official visitation in 1614, gloated that this service was "five hours long, where to my observation, there were as many sleepers as wakers, scarce any man but was sometimes forced to wink or nod."

Back in Alford, reports of John Cotton's many activities regularly punctured the Hutchinsons' routine, as William, in economically depressed Lincolnshire, struggled to preserve high profits in his textile business, while Anne coped with the demands of a proliferating family. Married for three years, she had given birth to Edward, now two years old; Susanna, baptized September 4, 1614; and was pregnant with Richard who would be baptized December 8, 1615.

In this same year of 1615, details of John Cotton's latest innovation began whirling around Alford, exciting both Anne and William into making the twenty-four-mile, day-and-a-half-long journey to Boston as often as they could find a good excuse—usually William's business obligations, or sheep markets or fairs. Apparently the minister had taken the unprecedented step of dividing his congregation into a huge outer circle that included everybody and an elite inner circle.

John Cotton who, throughout his career, uncannily managed to defy the authorities with utmost circumspection, later described this potentially subversive group in the mildest of language: "There were some scores of godly persons in Boston in Lincolnshire . . . who entered into a covenant with the Lord and with one another to follow after the Lord in the purity of his worship."

Under the aegis of the Reverend Mr. Cotton, those words, "purity of his worship," had translated not only into his own specially simplified service, but into words in which Anne Hutchinson was certain she heard a radical reinterpretation of Church dogma. And as for William, joining the elite inner circle, even occasionally, did wonders for his self-respect and brought him invaluable business contacts.

Fortuitously, the Hutchinsons had found themselves a veritable godsend that should help soothe the pangs and pressures of being outsiders in their own homeland.

4

"WHEN I WAS IN
OLD ENGLAND"

Pregnant every fifteen to twenty-three months, Anne rejected Church dogma that women, by the very act of giving birth, were adding to the sin quotient of the world. Cuddling her own innocent-looking babies, she refused to believe that they were each inescapably born in Original Sin.

Her reaction—spurred on by the example of her idol, John Cotton—was to hold meetings at her own home, sermonizing and discussing her personal reinterpretations of the Scriptures. As the years went on, her sessions attracted larger and larger audiences, mostly women. They had come to know her intimately, trusting her with their own and their families' lives during critical illnesses and complicated pregnancies.

Well trained during her London years, she was a rarity in the small community: an intelligent, experienced, and skillful nurse and mid-wife. Working beside her mother in the cosmopolitan capital, Anne had learned to compound herbal ointments, salves, and medicines, seeing for herself the effects of Bridget's private recipes for nurturing the family, and her herbal secrets for nursing them back to health. For example, there was the medicinal lily for bile problems; camomile for headaches; a lotion prepared from dog fennel to strengthen weak eyes. To give ale its sharp tang—and medicinal benefit—there was goat's rue (a tall, bushy perennial plant, part of the pea family, with strong-smelling blue flowers). And for less serious discomfort there was mint for colic, parsley for toothache, and the yellow-flowered herb, St. John's-wort, for general aches and pains in the joints.

When acting as midwife, Anne found herself cast into the almost godlike role of Mother Nature's earthly agent, responsible for delivering a miniature human being from the body of a still-living mother. Mothers-to-be, writhing with labor pains and in the grasp of death, repeatedly put themselves in Anne's steady and capable hands, counting on her to call on skill rather than superstition and mumbo jumbo in these prescientific years. Like their contemporary, poet Anne Bradstreet, they mixed truly awful fear with helpless resignation:

> . . . How soon my Dear, death may my steps attend,
> How soon't may be thy lot to lose thy friend.
> . . . .
> And if I see not half my days that's due,
> What nature would, God grant to yours and you.
> . . . .
> And if chance to thine eyes shall bring this verse,
> With some sad sighs honour my absent hearse;
> And kiss this paper for thy love's dear sake,
> Who with salt tears this last farewell did take.

Anne Bradstreet's cry from the heart was addressed to her husband and titled simply, "Before the Birth of One of Her Children."

The large and ever-growing number of women who became Anne Hutchinson's devoted followers attested to her conspicuous success in her chosen calling. John Cotton himself remarked that she was "well beloved in England at Alford in Lincolnshire (not far from Boston)."

Soon, though, there were not enough hours in the week for Anne personally as she switched from one demanding role to another: wife, mother, nurse, midwife, preacher. Thus, it was good to take off for Boston with William as frequently as possible, she to recharge her thinking, he to recapture the feeling of being a full-fledged member of the community. They would have to plan long in advance for this forty-eight-mile round trip, for which they would be gone at least a week: up to three days for travel and as many as four or five days at Boston. On Wednesday, Friday, and Saturday, Anne could listen to John Cotton's supplemental sermons—some of them at his own home—on Thursday to his market-day lecture, and on Sunday to one or both of his long Lord's Day sermons. While Anne apparently spent as much time as she could absorbing the words of John Cotton, William divided his time between God and mammon.

To prepare for their prolonged absence, Anne would have to make special arrangements for care of the young Hutchinsons, and William would have to leave his business in good hands. For the journey itself they would ride together on the same horse—exchanged for a fresh mount from time to time at taverns along the way. William would sit on the saddle, Anne behind him on a pillion or cushion, from which might hang a double stirrup for her feet if she was lucky.

But it was all worth it. Especially when John Cotton in his preaching de-emphasized the idea that humans were born into sin, contending instead that they fell out of grace through their own sinful actions. Here ready-made for Anne's emulation was an excellent example of Cotton's casting out the harsh teaching of the Church, substituting instead his own mild and modern reinterpretation.

There was no church authority saying such things back home in Alford. In fact, St. Wilfrid's in Alford during these years had no pastor at all, relying instead on resident lecturers. (Lack of money, local refusal to accept the minister imposed by the Church, and ecclesiastical disorganization were the most likely reasons for this situation.) All the more reason why Anne and William liked knowing that John Cotton was always present in Boston whenever they could get there.

Unfortunately, however, the course of messiahdom can be quite rocky. On at least two occasions during John Cotton's first decade at Boston, Anne and William could not be sure that at the end of their hard ride they would be able to receive the word from the short, stout, cherub-cheeked minister they had come to idolize. Mr. Cotton's first brush with authority came after he had organized his exclusive clique in 1615. Not surprisingly, those excluded from this elite group reacted strongly, reporting the existence of the special covenant to the Diocesan Courts. Immediately the minister was called to account by his superiors. To his defense came Alderman Thomas Leverett (a parishioner who would devotedly follow Cotton all the way to the New World where he would look to the minister for guidance in the case of *Massachusetts Bay* v. *Anne Hutchinson*). Calming the situation with "pious subtlety," Leverett succeeded in having the matter dismissed.

But his near-expulsion did nothing to silence Cotton or tone down his inflammatory preaching. Another major confrontation occurred on February 16, 1622, when the case of *Thomas Shaw*, gentleman of Boston, v. *Atherton Hough* and others was heard in Boston by the Star Chamber (a royal court requiring no jury and having the power to enforce royal prerogative on the spot by imposing harsh penalties short of death). Hough's behavior was viewed as a direct consequence of Cotton's preaching. The accusations were that Hough and his friends had shattered the stained-glass windows of St. Botolph's in 1621 and destroyed the ornaments and statuary. Also, they had cut away the cross on the mace carried to church every Thursday and Sunday by the mayor. (Atherton Hough, too, would go to the New World as a follower of John Cotton.)

Somehow, though, Cotton's disciples—and so, by implication, Cotton himself—emerged unscathed. The charges were dismissed on grounds that the damage had occurred before Hough and his friends had joined the church, that the deeds were committed by some unknown and undiscoverable persons, and that besides, everything had been quickly repaired and restored. Lightly tapping Cotton on the wrist, London sent new instructions the following year, 1622, demanding strict adherence to Biblical texts, rejecting all attempts at modern interpretation.

Hearing of Cotton's narrow escapes from the pincers of the authorities, Samuel Ward of Ipswich, a fellow minister, exploded in jealous jest: "Of all men in the world, I envy Mr. Cotton of Boston most, for he doth nothing in the way of conformity, and yet hath his liberty; and I do everything that way, and cannot enjoy mine."

The same authorities who had pursued John Cotton—King James and his bishops—were equally determined to trounce nonconformity wherever it appeared. So in their spare time—when momentarily free of the burdens of running church and state—they turned their glare on women.

Recruiting antifeminist fanatics was no problem. For example, in 1615, Joseph Swetnam published a tract that was reissued ten times by 1634 and finally made into a stage play. The self-contained title set the tone: *The Arraignment of Lewd, Idle, Froward, and unconstant women: Or the vanitie of them choose you whether. With a Commendation of wise, vertuous and honest Women, Pleasant for married Men, profitable for young Men, and hurtful to none.* The best wife, Swetnam contended, would be a seventeen-year-old virgin, "flexible and bending, obedient and subject to do anything." Many other similar pamphlets swamped the bookstalls, but this one by Swetnam turned out to provoke the greatest number of tracts in direct response.

Several women came to the defense of their own sex, though first taking the prudent precaution of hiding behind a pseudonym. One calling herself Constantia Munda (Quiet Perseverance) unleashed her punning talents against "every foule-mouthed male-content" who took it upon himself to libel women. She called her answer to Swetnam: *The Worming of a Mad Dog: Or, A Sop for Cerberus, the Jailer of Hell. No Confutation but a sharp Refutation of the baiter of Women.*

Constantia's response spawned an anonymous play in 1619: *Swetnam, the Woman-hater, arraigned by women. A new comedy.* In the play, Swetnam, given the alias "Misogynos," is put on trial and convicted by women who give him this sentence:

> First he shall wear this muzzle, to express
> His barking humour against women-kind.
> And he shall be led, and publicly shown,
> In every street in the city, and be bound . . .
> Then he shall be whipped quite through the land,
> Till he come to the sea coast, and then be shipped,
> And sent to live amongst the infidels.

Another woman, using the pen name Esther Sowernam, described herself as "neither maid, wife, nor widow, yet really all, and therefore experienced to defend all." Her answer to Swetnam she titled *Esther hath hanged Haman: or an answer to a lewd Pamphlet, entitled, The Arraignment of Women. With the arraignment of lewd, idle, froward and unconstant men, and Husbands.* She explained that she had intended to leave the chore of responding to Swetnam's diatribe against women to a minister's daughter, but considered that answer too weak, so decided to take on the task herself. Turning the tables on believers in tales like Adam and Eve, she defied man to name a single offense committed by woman in which man was not the instigator. Then appealing to male chivalry, she addressed herself "to all worthy and hopeful young youths of Great Britain," calling them "the hope of manhood," and exhorting: "The principal point of manhood is to defend, and what more manlike defense, than to defend the just reputation of a woman."

At the beginning of 1620, the King's strong aversion to female independence took the form of outright orders to the Church:

> January 25, 1620: Yesterday the Bishop of London called together all his clergy about this town and told them he had express commandment from the King to will them to inveigh vehemently and bitterly in their sermons against the insolency of our women and their wearing of broad-brimmed hats, pointed doublets, their hair cut short or shorn, and some of them stilettos or poignards, and such other trinkets of like moment, adding withal that if pulpit admonitions will not reform them he would proceed by another course.

With satisfaction bursting from his pen, the man who made this report, John Chamberlain—a lifelong London bachelor in his late sixties whose ample inheritance enabled him to make the receiving and circulating of gossip his only business—wrote more on the same subject on February 12, 1620:

> Our pulpits ring continually of the insolence and impudence of women; and to help the matter forward, the players have likewise taken them to task, and so do the ballads and ballad singers, so that they can come nowhere but their ears tingle.

And if all this will not serve, the King threatens to fall upon their husbands, parents, or friends that have or should have power over them and make them pay for it.

Around this same time, a new, highly effective pamphlet began making the rounds, giving ammunition to the men Anne Hutchinson would have to combat the rest of her life. With malicious glee, the anonymous author set about smashing age-old rules in a flurry of symbolism; in this case, inviolate rules dealing with—of all things—Latin grammar. *Hic Mulier* he called his pamphlet, going out of his way to shock the reader by making a masculine adjective modify a feminine noun, a hilarious joke that only intellectual insiders—all men, of course—would appreciate. The words would be roughly translated as Man-Woman. The full title read: *Hic Mulier: Or, The Man-Woman: Being a Medicine to cure the Coltish Disease of the Staggers in the Masculine-Feminines of our Times.* Then he resorted to verbal attack in plain English, calling women "the gilt dirt" and denouncing them for cutting their hair,* using cosmetics, and wearing extravagant clothes. All this, he asserted, was "bait which the Devil hath laid to catch the souls of wanton women."

In less than a week, someone (gender unknown) responded with a slashing counterattack, this time using a feminine Latin adjective with a masculine noun in the title: *Haec Vir: Or the Womanish Man: Being an Answer to a late Book entitled Hic Mulier.* Defending female freedom of behavior, the writer, quite possibly a woman, pleads for escape from the bondage of silly custom:

Now for me to follow change, according to the limitation of my own will and pleasure, there cannot be a greater freedom. . . . Will you have a poor woman follow such a fixed star that she shall not so much as move or twinkle in her own sphere? That were true slavery. . . . We are as free-born as men, have as free

*This repeated denunciation of women for cutting their hair harks back to the New Testament, I Corinthians 11:15: "But if a woman have long hair, it is a glory to her: for her hair is given to her for a covering."

election and as free spirits; we are compounded of like parts, and may with like liberty make benefit of our creations.

Back in Alford, life was proceeding on a straight onward-and-upward course for Anne Hutchinson. Celebrating her ninth anniversary, she could look on the healthy and happy faces of her devoted husband and three sons and three daughters, ranging in age from eight years to eight months. Again pregnant—in her third month that August of 1621—she had never lost a single child and was herself bursting with vitality. (Her seventh child, Elizabeth, would be baptized February 17, 1622.)

Furthermore, the appointment in 1621 of the politically sophisticated and religiously moderate John Williams as bishop of Lincoln—England's largest diocese—was good news for John Cotton, and therefore highly pleasing to the Hutchinsons. Word circulated that the bishop, though not himself a Puritan, repeatedly "went to King James and speaking of Mr. Cotton's great learning and worth before him, the King was willing, notwithstanding his [Cotton's] Nonconformity, to give way that he should have his liberty to go on without interruption in his ministry; which was very marvellous, considering how the King's spirit was carried against such men."

But all good times must come to an end apparently, and sometime around the mid-1620s Anne suffered a terrible personal crisis. It lasted "a twelve month together," she later recalled, rekindling her emotions in one pithy sentence: "When I was in old England, I was much troubled at the constitution of the churches there, so far as I was ready to have joined to the Separation, whereupon I set apart a day for humiliation by myself, to seek direction from God."

Taking this extreme step would have presented her with the choice between two living hells: fleeing England, thus abandoning her homeland to those who would destroy it; or going underground, defying King and Church while attempting to stay one hiding place ahead of the authorities. The Separatists, the best organized of the radical groups seeking to improve society through religious reform, had abandoned Holland after a twelve-year stay there and crossed the Atlantic to Plymouth in 1620. Overwhelmed by starvation, disease, and death during their first few years in New England, they could at long last by the mid-1620s point to sufficient success and stability to urge other English men and women to join them.

Anne never revealed the exact date of her year of anguish and indecision over joining the Separatists, perhaps because in the end she could not quite pinpoint it. Some of the worst ordeals she experienced this decade were somehow consigned to oblivion without dates—like the death of her son William, her eighth child and the first to die. He had been baptized on June 22, 1623, a date William and Anne had dutifully recorded in the Alford parish register. Then mysteriously there was nothing more: Anne and William never publicly discussed, mentioned, or recorded his death anywhere. Yet, on September 28, 1631, they gave his name to another son, their thirteenth child, baptized that day in accordance with the custom of giving the name of a deceased child to a newborn baby.*

In her sorrow, Anne could expect no comfort from the Church that insisted that child death was punishment for parental sin. (Expressing this idea in his memoirs, her contemporary, the Reverend Thomas Shepard, the future minister of Cambridge, Massachusetts, wrote:

> The Lord saw that these waters [referring to an ocean voyage] were not sufficient to wash away *my filth and sinfulness*, and therefore he cast me into the fire. . . . My first-born child, very precious to my soul, and dearly beloved of me, was smitten with sickness. . . . Yet the Lord would not be entreated for the life of it, and after a fortnight's sickness, at last it gave up the ghost and was buried. . . . [Italics added]

Always before, a soothing alternative to the implacable teachings of the Established Church had been available to Anne, first in the

---

*The first son William had undoubtedly lived to be at least eighteen months old, since another son was baptized on December 17, 1624, and given the name Samuel. The next three Hutchinson births, however, provide no clues. They were all girls, so that even if the first William had died, baptismal names would not have revealed this: Anne, baptized May 5, 1626; Mary, baptized February 22, 1628; and Katherine, baptized February 7, 1630.

scholarly recalcitrance of her father, and when he died, in the inflammatory challenges to accepted beliefs she heard in the words of
her new hero, John Cotton. Now, however, there was every indication that he was about to be silenced—or worse.

In a power struggle, Cotton's protector, John Williams, bishop of
Lincoln, had lost out to William Laud who was intent on forcing the
Church back to Anglo-Catholicism. This all happened in the spring
of 1625 when King James died and was succeeded by his son
Charles I. Laud, the new King's favorite, secured his own appointment to a succession of increasingly prestigious bishoprics, and with
Charles's support began harassing Williams without letup, pressing
a series of charges against him in the Star Chamber. Under these
changed circumstances, John Cotton's tenure became increasingly
precarious.

As if all this were not enough to make Anne look to Separatism as
her personal solution, the outer world came intruding on life in
Alford with a vengeance. At the time of the new King's coronation,
England was laid low by plague as well as by severe drought alter-
nating with flooding storms. Local crops were ruined, animals were
killed—the result was frightening famine and economic problems.
And the threnody went on: England was further mired in financial
chaos brought on by the Thirty Years War that had broken out on
the Continent in 1618 and slowly but surely had cut off North European customers. So far none of this was the fault of King Charles.
However, there was no source of glory or national pride to fall back
on in times of trouble, as there had been under Elizabeth. And for
this, the new King was to blame completely. He was turning out to
be an even worse ruler than his father James I, who during his
twenty-two years on the throne had seemed abysmally inept and
selfishly despotic.

An early warning of the disaster that would soon engulf England
occurred just one year after the twenty-five-year-old King ascended
the throne. Almost his first act was to assign foreign policy to his
spectacularly handsome but totally incompetent chief advisor and
administrator, thirty-five-year-old George Villiers, duke of Buck-
ingham. The duke's initial foreign venture was an attempt to cap-
ture the Spanish fleet at Cadiz, in 1626. But for his campaign he
used rickety old ships, manned by forcibly impressed crews.

Disorganized and demoralized, the sailors went on a drinking binge at the first Spanish village they reached, so that they were easily routed by the Spanish. To say the least, this was a humiliating contrast to the glorious defeat of the Spanish Armada in British waters under Queen Elizabeth back in 1588.

Women let the country know that they were as concerned about and as adversely affected by all this as were the men. England's best-known prophet, the aristocratic Lady Eleanor Davis, daughter of the earl of Castlehaven, reported that she "heard early in the morning a Voice from Heaven, speaking as through a trumpet these words: 'There is nineteen years and a half to the Judgment Day.'" Another woman who similarly attracted the attention of all England was Jane Hawkins of St. Ives, Huntingdonshire—soon to become one of Anne Hutchinson's closest friends. Mrs. Hawkins prophesied in 1629 the downfall of the Anglican church and its bishops. (Revealing God's word through prophecy via a "Voice from Heaven" was, of course, the only way for women to make themselves heard.)

These women reflected a strong feeling among the opponents of King Charles that his Establishment was tottering on the brink of extinction. If and when that happened, Puritanism would then take over. Thus, John Cotton, who, like Anne Hutchinson, had been vacillating over joining the Separatists, decided to remain in England. In 1629, he wrote a tract taking a public stand against Separatism. He would embrace Puritanism wholeheartedly, he decided, and remain in England working to purify the Church and reform the government.

For the moment, Anne and William Hutchinson made the same decision.

But the next year was 1630, the start of a decade of infamy for England, turmoil for the Hutchinsons.

5

"TO NEW ENGLAND...
I MUST GO"

 Repeatedly, Anne's detractors translated her marriage and the decision to go to New England into an Eve and Adam parable. Leading the pack was Gov. John Winthrop, who smugly described Anne's husband William as "a man of very mild temper and weak parts and wholly guided by his wife."

But in no way could Anne ever see herself in the role of siren, consorting with the devil-snake to lure the innocent man from paradise, and to ensure disaster in their new abode. Brains and stubborn independence she certainly had in abundance. Beauty, or the body of a temptress, never.* As for forcing William to do something against his will, the very thought was ridiculous. Neither she nor William ever made a major decision unless both agreed.

And agree they certainly could that England in the early 1630s was no paradise. Thus, side by side, they agonized over the exciting but frightening idea of abandoning long-settled England for the

---

*None of Anne's denunciators ever mentioned a word about her physical appearance, not even John Winthrop who at the height of lurid criticism about Anne's good friend, Mary Dyer, referred to Mistress Dyer as "a very proper and comely young woman."

wilds of Massachusetts. Together they pored over all the promotion propaganda, including the widely circulated pamphlet with the title that told all: *Reasons to be Considered in Justifying the Undertakers of the Intended Plantation in New England and for Encouraging Such Whose Hearts God Shall Move to Join with Them in It*. This was the work of John Winthrop who in the winter of 1630 had been elected governor of the company of a thousand preparing to depart for America.

Anne was intrigued by the special appeals made to women to emigrate, strongly implying that a World advertising itself as New would have no use for woman-trammeling tradition. One member of the Winthrop company wrote of "the kind usage of the English [in Massachusetts Bay] to their wives," and of "the English houses where *pares cum paribus congregatae* [equals gather with equals]."

Besides, as a mother, she could not help but be impressed by paeans to the purity of New England air. From New England one promoter wrote that his formerly ill child "since he came hither is very well as ever he was, and there is hope of perfect recovery shortly, even by the very wholesomeness of the air; . . . for a sup of New England's air is better than a whole draught of old England's ale." And in stark contrast to the ever-present threat of national famine in old England, reports from New England described food in the area as a readily available feast: blueberries, plums, raspberries, and strawberries—all free for the picking. And the surrounding sea provided cod, mussels, oysters, and lobsters weighing up to twenty-five pounds.

As for William whose business was staggering under royal restrictions and national stagnation, he looked to America, with its limitless land and location three thousand miles from royal supervision as the pluperfect place for him and his family. Along these very lines, John Cotton, in a sermon delivered to the departing Winthrop company, had pointed to emigration as the best possible solution for economic distress: "Nature teaches bees . . . when the hive is too full, they seek abroad for new dwellings; so when the hive of the Commonwealth is so full that the tradesmen cannot live one by another, but eat up one another, in this case it is lawful to remove."

But for the time being at least, Anne and William had to conclude reluctantly that departure would have to be postponed. She had just given birth to their twelfth child, Katherine, at the beginning of February 1630; and he had no wish to leave behind forever his father, Edward, who, at the age of sixty-six, made clear his intention to live out his life at home in Alford.

In the course of all this painful evaluation, Anne had only to look beyond her sheltered home in tiny Alford to discover for herself a whole new world of people and practices out there. Her marriage was different from that of most couples; she was a full partner. If she were the wife of just about anyone else in England, she would be unceremoniously reduced to silent, subordinate helpmate. Proving this point was none other than John Winthrop himself, who, in a public letter to a private friend, explained why even his wife had to take second place to his God-given calling. Referring to himself in the third person, the governor wrote: "If he should refuse this opportunity [to lead the Massachusetts Bay Company to New England], that talent which God hath bestowed upon him for public service were like to be buried." And so Margaret Winthrop, who was pregnant at the time of John's departure, remained behind, gave birth to the couple's child in solitude, and finally joined her husband in New England after eighteen months of separation. (Not privy to the Winthrops' personal correspondence, Anne would never learn that John signed all his letters to Margaret, "Thy Faithful Husband.")

Meanwhile, Anne and William, having decided to stay put for the time being, received an unexpected piece of good news. Their idol, John Cotton, announced his intention to remain at the pulpit of St. Botolph's in nearby Boston. His parishioner and good friend William Coddington had invited him to deliver the farewell sermon to the Winthrop company, he explained. However, he promised his congregation, he would be gone only long enough to travel to and from the port of Southampton at the other end of England.

Eventually, the Hutchinsons got word that the fleet of five ships had set sail on April 8, 1630. But more than a month went by, with no word of Cotton's return—till a day in May shattered Anne and William with the news that their beloved minister was near death, a victim of the dreaded tertiary ague, a debilitating malarialike fever that struck with monstrous regularity every other day. Elizabeth, his wife of eighteen years, who was stricken at the same time, never recovered consciousness, and died. Over the next two years the word from Boston was discouraging: The Reverend Mr. Cotton was still alive, but too weak and too overcome with grief to resume his preaching. He would continue indefinitely to recuperate at Tattershall, the estate owned by Theophilus Fiennes-Clinton, a devout Puritan and the fourth earl of Lincoln.

Without John Cotton to lean on, the Hutchinsons had nowhere to turn for inspiration and support. And at this worst of all times, double tragedy struck in the bosom of their own family. Two times in less than four weeks they were forced to watch two of their daughters writhe in pain, victims of some strange, nameless illness that refused to respond to prayer, or to any of the herbs or medical techniques Anne had used so effectively on others in her long nursing career. In desperation they followed every suggestion, no matter how wild or improbable it sounded. To cleanse the air in the sickroom, they dipped a red-hot brick in a basin of vinegar. And when that proved no help, they combined dried rosemary, juniper, and bay leaves, burned them in a chafing dish, and carried the fiery mixture from room to room. Next, they tried a remedy guaranteed to attract away all infection: They left three or four peeled onions on the floor inside the house; and immediately outside, another three or four on the ground.

But folk medicine was not good enough. And fate showed no mercy. On September 8, 1630, Anne and William buried their eldest daughter, Susanna, the very week that she turned sixteen. And before they could recover from the throes of their sorrow, eight-year-old Elizabeth died, on October 4.

Quite possibly, they were victims of a plaguelike illness that was attacking Alford with a vengeance around this time. Every night and every morning, the death cart could be heard rattling along its sorrowful rounds, picking up bodies to be dumped into jam-packed pits filled with lime and reeking with the stench of disease and death. The epidemic began on July 22, 1630 ("incipit pestis" reads the official record for this date), and by July 31 there were twenty burials. Then, forty-seven for the month of August; twenty-six in September; nine in October; six for November; three for December; twelve for January, seven for February; and after that the disease subsided, with eight recorded to the end of 1631. In all, there were 138 epidemic-related deaths recorded for Alford during this outbreak, at a time when the town's population is estimated to have been considerably under one thousand.

The townspeople were amazingly resourceful. Alford was cut off from the rest of England during this siege, so that there was justifiable fear that starvation would cause as many deaths as the disease itself. When outsiders refused to enter the town with needed supplies, the town came up with a makeshift solution. A large hollowed-out stone was set up on Mills Cross Hill overlooking all of Alford. Alfordians would place money into the hollow, which had been filled with vinegar for purposes of decontamination. Then they would hasten away to their homes. Residents of surrounding areas would bring supplies in exchange for the sanitized money.

Amid these circumstances, Anne and William Hutchinson, struggling to rise from their private abyss of grief, were dealt an even crueler blow—society's repeated insistence that child death was the parents' punishment for failure to do their God-given duty. They were required to display a sign on their house consisting of a conspicuously bright red cross inscribed with the words, "Lord have mercy upon us." This would warn all passersby to stay clear of the contamination of both the disease and the sin. At this point, the Hutchinsons desperately needed John Cotton whose direct line to God was neither encrusted with superstition nor encumbered with guilt.

Fortunately, within the next year they found themselves a new ally, forty-one-year-old John Wheelwright who since 1623 had been vicar of Bilby, just a mile from Alford. This fearlessly outspoken minister was a kindred spirit to take the place of John Cotton, who, though reportedly feeling better, still gave no indication of when, or even whether, he would return to St. Botolph's. And best of all, the Reverend Mr. Wheelwright had married into the Hutchinson family, choosing as his second wife (he was a widower) William's youngest sister, twenty-six-year-old Mary.

Even so, by 1632 Anne and William were again actively discussing the idea of moving to New England. The previous fall their lives had taken a radical change in direction, when death and birth came to their family in quick succession. On September 14, 1631, William's father Edward died; and exactly two weeks later, Anne and William brought their thirteenth child, William Jr., to church for baptism. Almost as though the law sought to comfort William in his grief, an inheritance of a goodly sum of money came to him as his father's oldest son. He would have no financial worries for the foreseeable future, if he could keep the Royal Treasury at a distance.

But this was not to be. Instead, all through 1632 word spread everywhere in England that Charles I, emulating his late father in setting himself up as God on earth, needed funds to support this exaltation, and so had ordered his treasury agents to resort to out-and-out financial extortion, disguised in the form of innovative taxation. Unhappily, these agents were striking closer and closer all the time. As a matter of fact, they forced their way into the Hutchinson family circle, slapping into prison Anne's wealthy uncle, seventy-year-old Sir Erasmus Dryden, brother of her mother, Bridget, and owner of Canons Ashby, one of England's grandest estates. His crime was refusal to pay a forced loan levied on orders of the King.*

If this could happen to Sir Erasmus who had once hobnobbed with Queen Elizabeth and King James, receiving all sorts of royal favors and honors, William saw little hope for himself as a lowly businessman with no far-flung network of supporters among the landed gentry. Once again William looked to the New World as the only salvation.

Getting Anne to concur was no problem. She was feeling personally affronted by still another group of the King's men, who came blustering into her life. William Laud, the King's favorite and chief religious advisor, was sending surrogates up and down the country, imprisoning, exiling, or—at the very least—silencing all Puritan

---

*This was a flimsy device concocted by Charles I in order to raise money without having to resort to Parliament for approval.

The King, after angrily dissolving Parliament back in 1629, now ignored England's vaunted "ancient rights and privileges," as he relentlessly persecuted all opponents and kept his ramshackle chaotic government in operation by wild money-raising schemes. In the process, he made England a second-rate nation. For example, Holland had now overtaken Britain as leader in world trade.

ministers. To her horror and dismay, Anne learned that the bishop's tentacles had closed around her brother-in-law, John Wheelwright, making him one of the first to be ensnared. And still in a state of shock, she heard that the bishop's men were in hot pursuit of John Cotton.

By the spring of 1633, Anne and William began making definite plans to join the Winthrop company in New England, targeting that summer as their departure date—only to be stopped cold once again on learning that Anne was pregnant, expecting in November. So for the moment they took the next best step, subsidizing two close relatives to prepare the way for thirteen Hutchinsons (Anne, William, and eleven children, assuming that the new baby would be born alive and remain healthy). At least, they could console themselves, their decision to emigrate had taken on reality and finality.

Meanwhile, they were relieved to hear that John Cotton had succeeded in eluding the authorities, though he was still—in his own words—feeling the effects of "a long and sore sickness, the dregs whereof still hang about me." Warned in advance by an underground network of Puritans, the Reverend Mr. Cotton had discarded his ministerial robes for ordinary layman's clothes, taken an assumed name, and remained hidden in the homes of various London friends and sympathizers. Then, wearing an even more elaborate disguise, he had somehow managed to make his way to the Kentish coast of southern England, where he boarded the *Griffin* in July 1633 for the voyage to New England. (Before Cotton decided to flee, a highly placed sympathizer, the earl of Dorset, sent word that had he been guilty of a lesser crime—such as drunkenness—the earl could have obtained a pardon for him. But since his crimes were Nonconformity and Puritanism, a pardon was out of the question. "You must fly for your safety," he advised.)

Until forced to change their plans, the Hutchinsons had hoped to sail on the *Griffin* also, though they had not the faintest notion that their minister would be aboard. Instead—still by complete coincidence—John Cotton's fellow travelers included the Hutchinsons' twenty-one-year-old son Edward, their oldest child, as well as another Edward Hutchinson, William's youngest brother, who, at age twenty-six, made the ocean crossing accompanied by his wife, Sarah.

Also aboard, Anne and William later learned, was Sarah Hawkridge Story Cotton, the widow the recently recuperated Reverend Mr. Cotton had married some time during the previous year. The new Mrs. Cotton was in the late stages of pregnancy at the time of departure, and in the course of the voyage presented the previously childless minister with a son, prosaically named Seaborn.

Awaiting the birth of her fourteenth child, Anne was more certain than ever before that the New World was the only answer. "The Lord carrying Mr. Cotton to New England, . . . I must go thither also," she later recalled, elaborating: "When our teacher [John Cotton] came to New England, it was a great trouble with me, my brother Wheelwright being put by also [i.e., silenced by William Laud], I was then much troubled concerning the ministry under which I lived."

The ministry to which Anne referred was completely dominated by William Laud, who in August 1633 was made archbishop of Canterbury, second in power only to the King himself. Once again there emerged that old similarity in official attitudes toward Puritans and women. The archbishop, a self-declared scourge of Puritans, was a fussy, short-tempered bachelor of sixty who lost no love or sympathy for women. One time when a pregnant woman named Goody Taylor balked at approaching the communion table because it had been placed, altarlike, at the top of three steps, the archbishop refused to excuse her. Nor would he yield when twenty-five mothers present at the church that day complained that the archbishop did not understand the discomforts of pregnancy. They promised that all childbearing women would make a special prayer for him if he would relieve them of climbing these "lofty and bleak stairs." The archbishop ignored their plea (another reason why women over the years had gathered in the bosom of Anne's makeshift living-room church).

Stories like this made the decision easy and irrevocable for Anne Hutchinson.

Determined to stay out of the King's way, Anne and William

faded almost into invisibility over the next year. William handed over the family business to his brother John, his junior by nine years, who had decided to remain in Alford, come what might. (Almost everyone else in William's family—his brothers, sisters, and widowed mother—were actively considering a move to the New World.) And Anne silenced herself, holding no more women's meetings for the duration, though she worked hard, and successfully, to convince her twenty-four-year-old sister Katherine (born shortly before their father Francis's death and Anne's very earliest disciple) to join the Hutchinsons, along with Katherine's husband of two years, Richard Scott.*

Shortly after the birth of their newest daughter, Susanna—who arrived in mid-November and was named in memory of their deceased oldest daughter—Anne and William began dismantling more than two decades of marriage. Painfully, they had to give away even their most treasured possessions. They barely could carry the absolute essentials needed for the voyage and for their new home as they went from Alford to the dock at the other end of England by horse and wagon.

Abandoning their lifelong homeland, they were exchanging an unbearable present for an unknown future. John Cotton captured the emotions of similar leave-taking in deceptively simple doggerel:

> When I think of the sweet and gracious company
>   That at BOSTON once I had,
> And of the long peace of a fruitful ministry,
>   For twenty years enjoy'd;

*Eventually, there were three Hutchinson brothers and two sisters, plus their mother, in New England—compared with only two Marbury sisters. The reason may well have been that the Marburys were all members of the lesser gentry who, unlike the business-oriented Hutchinsons, depended for their income on inherited land. Thus, they would have chosen to remain in England to protect their nonportable fortunes.

Surely, these observable, recorded statistics should further refute the contention that Anne was the instigator and William her weak follower, carting all his children to New England only because of her insistent nagging. All indications point to a mutually agreed upon decision to migrate.

The joy that I found in all that happiness
Doth still so much refresh me,
That the grief to be cast out into a wilderness
Doth not so much distress me.

The great adventure began for Anne and William, but with very bad omens. The King's men were patrolling back roads, halting all caravans without warning, insisting that no one had permission to leave the country, for the time being at least. For the Hutchinsons this meant that they had to either return to Alford or go on to London where they could wait while the King decided whether to allow departures. Too many were leaving for New England and taking too much money with them, the King contended—till various shipmasters convinced him of New England's profit-making potential for old England. In the end, the King allowed the Hutchinsons, who had decided to take their chances in London, to obtain the necessary papers (the equivalent of the modern passport, but issued in the seventeenth century only after certifying that the head of the family owed no taxes to the King).

But still the Hutchinsons had to remain in London, this time waiting for a definite announcement of the departure date. They would be leaving on the *Griffin*, the same vessel that had carried two Hutchinsons and the Cottons the previous summer. In constant use to and from the New World, this ship required complete overhauling to ensure seaworthiness. Also, to make the voyage profitable, Captain Thomas Babb needed to secure a sufficient complement of passengers and cargo. (Almost a year later, in the spring of 1635, Richard Mather wrote in his journal of leaving home April 16, arriving at port in Bristol a week later. He and his family finally boarded the ship a month later only to find "things very unready, . . . many goods being not stowed, but lying on disordered heaps here and there in the ship." They had to stay on the ship twelve days before sailing, due to a combination of lack of wind, goods slowly stored, and the shipmaster and sailors repeatedly going onshore for one last fling before sailing. Finally on June 4 they set sail.)

Luckily, Anne and William found lodgings for themselves and ten of their children at the home of William Bartholomew and his wife,

Mary, Puritans also planning to sail on the *Griffin*. Thinking herself finally in friendly territory among Puritans who were all as enlightened as John Cotton or John Wheelwright, Anne had the uncanny feeling of being at her long-dreamed destination already. Gone from her life forever, she was sure, was the onerous dictum that women should be seen but never heard.

Accordingly, strolling through St. Paul's churchyard with William Bartholomew one day, she exulted that she constantly received revelations directly from God. She told the astonished Bartholomew—who listened without comment while recording her every word in his diarylike mind—"that she had never had any great thing done about her but it was revealed to her beforehand. . . . And also that she was to come to New England but for Mr. Cotton's sake."

To assure that her host understood the lofty and exclusive status of those who communicated directly with God through revelations, she cited the words of the eminent Puritan preacher, Thomas Hooker, who had said in the course of a sermon: "*It was revealed to me* yesterday that England should be destroyed." (Emphasis added.) Listening to Anne, his indignation rising that an ordinary woman would dare claim for herself a competence reserved for only a few Puritan dignitaries, Bartholomew filed for future disclosure this biting recollection: "She took notice of that passage and it was very acceptable with her."

But Anne, seeing no reason to rein in her tongue, blithely proceeded to talk to all New England-bound Puritans—male as well as female—on a one-to-one basis. Meeting the straitlaced Reverend Zechariah Symmes just before the voyage, she immediately antagonized him, making him certain that "she did slight the ministers of the word of God" (meaning himself, of course). He was an Oxford graduate, but eight years younger than Anne who let him know in no uncertain terms that intelligence would finally take precedence over gender in the Utopia to which they were all heading.

The dislike between the Reverend Mr. Symmes and Anne was quite mutual—and, not long after the *Griffin* finally set sail in July 1634, was exacerbated into shouting matches by the miseries and terrors of the voyage. For eight to ten weeks, some one hundred passengers—who had lived a lifetime on *terra firma*—plus a crew of about fifty officers and men were somehow crammed into the three-hundred-ton ship, along with their household pots and utensils unavailable in New England, their few most treasured possessions, and family supplies of food. Keeping their balance, mental as well as physical, was no easy matter when each day brought new threats: roving pirates, enemy ships, severe storms, torrid sun, lack of wind. Like caged animals in a zoo, they had to live amid the stench of their own excrement, which no amount of washing down the decks with vinegar could eliminate or sweeten. And as if all this were not enough, they also had to contend with the cattle dung from the herd of one hundred that Governor Winthrop had ordered.

Anne, tired of the Reverend Mr. Symmes's long-winded preaching—he frequently went on for five hours, nonstop—and disgusted by his constant denigration of women, exploded that as soon as she arrived in Boston she would publicly expose his opinions as riddled with errors. For the rest of the voyage she would ignore him, she announced, urging the other women aboard to follow her lead. To fill the resultant void, she resumed her old Alford practice of holding women's meetings, with herself in the role of lecturer. Much to her surprise, some of the husbands labeled her activities a dark conspiracy against men. They threw the Bible at her, citing I Corinthians 14:35: "And if they [women] will learn anything, let them ask their husbands at home."

"Corrupt" and "narrow" were the epithets the Reverend Mr. Symmes used against Anne to describe her activities. He would report her unseemly behavior to the authorities the minute they landed, he threatened, hoping to silence her. Instead, Anne grew bolder and bolder. She announced another revelation, the kind everyone aboard thirsted to believe in the midst of the painfully interminable voyage. "What would you say if we should be at New England within these three weeks," she baited him in front of the whole ship. Her forecast proved accurate, and so thoroughly unhinged the Reverend Mr. Symmes that on arrival he immediately reported the story to the authorities.

At the same time, Anne's London host, William Bartholomew, long since alerted to what he privately termed her sinister proclivities, now concluded that, like a witch, she had endowed her own daughter with forbidden powers. Horrified, this man never forgot that Anne's eldest daughter—seventeen-year-old Faith— "had a revelation that a young man on the ship should be saved, but he must walk in the ways of her mother." To Bartholomew and his friends this proved beyond a doubt that Anne, left to her own devices, would defy the Scriptural command laid down by the Apostle Paul: "For the man is not of the woman, but the woman of the man." [I Corinthians 11:8.] (This, of course, was difficult for a woman who had given birth to fourteen children, including eight sons, to accept.)

Just in case more was needed to convince everyone in listening range of the menace posed by this would-be settler, a woman, Bartholomew later reported that as the *Griffin* had approached Boston harbor, Anne expressed trepidation about her new home:

> I would remember one word of Mrs. Hutchinson among many others. She, knowing that I did know her opinions, being she was at my house at London, she was afraid, I conceive, or loath to impart herself unto me, but when she came within sight of Boston, and looking upon the meanness of the place, I conceive, she uttered these words, if she had not a sure word that England should be destroyed her heart would shake. Now it seemed to me at that time very strange that she should say so.

Anne, when confronted with this statement, denied it vehemently: "I do not remember that I looked upon the meanness of the place, nor did it discourage me, because I knew the bounds of my habitation were determined."

And from the ship, Boston did indeed look exactly the way Anne had expected—based on her reading of the colonization propaganda that had long been flooding old England. The town she saw was the business and political center of the new colony, but looked more like her native backwater village of Alford than bustling, overcrowded London, England's capital city. As far as her eye could see, Boston was flat pasture and swamp, edged with three hills, and resting on a bay whose Charles River all but separated it from the mainland.

Fittingly, the first building to strike Anne's eye, when the *Griffin* finally docked on September 18, 1634, was the church-meeting house—a good-sized, though barnlike, square-shaped building, one story high, its boards sealed together with mud.

This was the main building in town—very soon to be the focal point of Anne's life.

And vice versa.

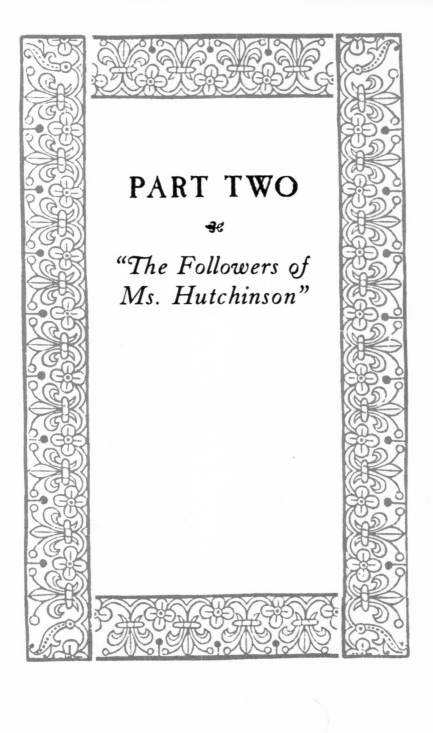

PART TWO

❦

"The Followers of Ms. Hutchinson"

6

"THE THIRD THIRD DAY
OF THE THIRD MONTH"

The old settlers began looking at Anne with hostility and suspicion even before she settled into her new home. Her tale-bearing fellow voyagers, William Bartholomew and Rev. Zechariah Symmes, had reported her shipboard activities to the authorities the moment the *Griffin* docked at Boston, exactly as they had threatened.

As a direct result, Anne flunked her first official test, and found her acceptance into the hundred-member church at Boston delayed for a full week after her husband had been duly judged one of God's elect—in Puritan parlance, a "Visible Saint." The records of the First Church of Boston, listing admissions to membership, rebuked her publicly in two pithy sentences: "26th of 8th month, 1634, William Hutchinson, merchant; . . . 2d of 9th month, Anne Hutchinson, wife of our brother William Hutchinson."*

---

*The dots represent omission of other names, husbands and wives admitted together on both these dates, as was the usual procedure when the couple had arrived together.

The "8th month" was October, and the "9th month" November. Puritans preferred to number their months rather than revert to the ancient designa-

During that week-long delay, Anne's unorthodox views were made a test case for the colony's powers of discipline. Unluckily for her, she had arrived at a time of near-fatal turmoil for Massachusetts. During this very month of October 1634, the colonial fathers had barely managed to avoid royal reprisal when one of the Bay Colony's first settlers—impetuous old John Endecott of Salem, after listening to the rousing sermons of his hotheaded young minister, Roger Williams—was galvanized into cutting the red cross of St. George the dragon-slayer from the King's official ensign. It was an outrageous specimen of Catholicism, he claimed. But the General Court (legislature and judiciary of the Massachusetts Bay Colony), worrying that old England might construe this action of one of the nine assistants of the colony as official policy, quickly and ostentatiously censured Endecott and forbade him to hold office for a year.

The timing of Endecott's action could hardly have been worse. The same ship that had carried Anne and her family across the Atlantic had also brought a demand from the King for return of the Bay Colony's precious charter of independence. Off and on, the King had made this particular demand before, but informally and never in writing. So far, the colony had been saved from the King's claws by the threat of civil war in England itself. Charles I was too busy fending off his enemies at home to pay more than lip service to the idea of instituting his own government in a land three thousand miles away.

Under these circumstances, the colonial fathers elevated continued assurance of the King's benign neglect to the realm of high public policy. Thus, they devoted considerable attention to taming their outlandishly boat-rocking newcomer—Anne—from the very beginning. They called a special hearing to force her to apologize

---

tions they considered vestiges of paganism. They continued to regard March as the first month of the year, however.

To avoid confusion, I will follow accepted modern practice among historians, referring to months by name, as they appear in today's calendar, and treating January and February as the first two months of the new year.

meekly and recant submissively, an example to all others who might be tempted to think or behave similarly. Presiding was Thomas Dudley, who at fifty-eight was senior in age to just about everyone in the Bay Colony and who prided himself on his inflexibility. As a matter of fact, just six months before, at the annual May election, he had finally defeated John Winthrop—after five tries—on a platform of no tolerance for dissenters and no leniency for troublemakers.

Not knowing what to expect, Anne arrived at the austere but awesome church-meeting house where, among her four simply-attired, steely-eyed interrogators, she came face to face with her old friend and idol, Rev. John Cotton. In the space of one year, this ruddy-cheeked, forty-nine-year-old scholar had come to exercise so much influence on all problems of religion and politics that no important answers were ever reached without him. The new governor, whose forte was literature, not theology, had invited him to question Anne, along with hidebound John Wilson who had served as pastor of Boston's church since the first days of settlement. The forty-six-year-old Reverend Mr. Wilson had the reputation of being so strict and so devout that at Sunday meals he instructed all at his table to remain silent or to speak only of God. Her chief accuser, thirty-five-year-old Zechariah Symmes, recently installed as minister of neighboring Charlestown, also participated.

The hearing dragged on until Governor Dudley finally pronounced himself "satisfied that she held nothing different from us." And the Reverend Mr. Wilson, noting that he spoke for the other ministers as well, ruled that "in her answers she gave full satisfaction."

But it was John Winthrop who, intending to damn Anne, inadvertently demonstrated why she had every reason to burst with newly acquired self-confidence. The forty-six-year-old former governor—he was not quite three years older than Anne—had organized and governed the colony from the beginning, but had been demoted to assistant (member of the governor's council) in the May election. Consequently, he had taken no part in the hearing, but was given a full report, apparently as a courtesy. On this basis, he felt qualified to contend that she "cunningly dissembled and coloured her opinions . . . and was admitted into the Church."

Anne could be pardoned for feeling that in the future there would be no stopping her. She had been outnumbered (four men to one woman), and outranked (leaders of the Colonial Establishment versus a woman who, by reason of being born female, was not even a member of the Establishment). Yet she had outreasoned her inquisitors (three Cambridge-educated ministers and one classical scholar), discussing minute points of contention so authoritatively and so articulately that she won official—and public—vindication.

As a matter of fact, the next few months were very probably the best time of her life. Everything was beginning to go her way. Immediately following the hearing, John Wilson returned to England temporarily (to persuade his reluctant wife to emigrate), so that her adored John Cotton was in complete charge of the Boston church.* For a change, she was not pregnant, though more than a year had passed since the birth of her fourteenth child, Susanna. As an urban housewife, she was relieved of complete dependence on the family farm. Food was easily purchased and inexpensive: A penny bought a quart of milk or four eggs; by the pound, butter cost six pence, Chesire Cheese five pence, and potatoes two pence. And at last she and her family could move into their new home, finally united under one roof after being forced to stay with various friends and relatives since their arrival.

Even the weather had been on her side, warm and without any rain for six weeks all through October and well into November, a paradisiacal introduction to the New World, and perfect for William, working with hired labor, to build their house. Since William was considered a good catch for the colony—he had

---

*John Cotton had been named "teacher" of the Boston church on October 10, 1633, shortly after his arrival in Massachusetts. The "pastor" was John Wilson, one of the original colonists who had sailed with John Winthrop in 1630.

Theoretically, there was a difference between the teacher and the pastor. The teacher was responsible for supervising the doctrine of the congregation and for delivering sermons. The pastor would supervise the practice of the congregation, preside over services, and administer sacraments. But the two offices overlapped, so that the pastor frequently delivered the sermon and the teacher took over administering the sacraments.

brought with him a tremendous sum of money, close to one thousand guineas in gold, and was always addressed as "Mr.," a title of great respect, rather than "Goodman"—the Hutchinsons were granted a half-acre lot in the best section of town, on the corner of Sentry Lane and High Street. Just a few steps down the already deeply rutted main road were the church-meeting house and the site of the regular Thursday market, as well as the precious spring that provided the luxury of pure, easily accessible water. Directly across the way was the home of Margaret and John Winthrop, the man called the Father of New England, and a little farther on was the house of John and Sarah Cotton, surrounded by the homes of other luminaries Anne had known, at least by name, at St. Botolph's in Boston, England: Hannah and Thomas Leverett, now elder of the new Boston church,* and Elizabeth and Atherton Hough, "a gentleman of good estate" once accused of smashing the stained-glass windows of St. Botolph's Church under the spell of John Cotton's preaching there. Also nearby neighbors and good friends in new Boston were Mary and John Coggeshall, a prosperous merchant, and Mary Coddington and her husband, William, who, besides being a wealthy businessman and treasurer of the colony, had another claim to fame: He had built Boston's only house to be constructed of locally manufactured brick.

All of the other large dwellings clustered here in the center of town looked to the simple yet commodious Winthrop residence as the model home, the exterior constructed of wood with a mud chimney and thatched roof, with a good-sized garden patch in the rear. Inside there were two stories containing lofts, garrets, and six main rooms. On the ground floor were the hall or living room, a parlor filled with beds and chests for storage, and the kitchen with a fireplace. Upstairs were two additional bedchambers and a study.

"The toil of a new plantation [is] like the labors of Hercules never

---

*Thomas Hutchinson, Anne's great-great-grandson, writing the informative *History of the Colony and Province of Massachusetts-Bay* in 1764, defined elders as "men of advice and counsel in religious matters; they visited the sick, and had a general inspection and oversight of the conduct of their brethren."

at an end," marveled a contemporary. And indeed, all colonists, no matter their station or degree of prosperity, were expected to do manual labor whenever necessary. Thus, "Mr." William Hutchinson would both supervise and himself pitch in on the building of his family's house. Among other things, taking precautions against the New England winter that old-timers had warned him about, he would prevent drafts by filling chinks on inside walls with clay and brick; and balancing the desire for some light with the need for insulation, he would carefully install small windows made with the glass the Hutchinsons had brought along with them from England, as the Winthrop company instructed all English emigrants to do. To provide room for a shop where he could display and sell his textiles, he would attach a lean-to to the ground floor. Furthermore, being a shrewd businessman, he would undoubtedly see to it that the parlor windows were curtained, excellent advertisement for his wares.

Similarly, "Mistress" or "Mrs." or "Ms."—not "Goodwife"—Anne Hutchinson in the beginning would have responsibility for setting up housekeeping, which meant mainly unpacking the belongings the family had carried with them: mattresses, placed directly on the floor and filling every room, except maybe the kitchen, where the Hutchinson women would cook with their old English pots, kettles, and utensils, and all would eat from plain wooden trenchers, using spoons, knives, and a liberal assist from fingers (forks were not yet in general use). Like other wealthy colonists, they were bound to have some truly luxurious items: a table for the parlor, one or two chairs, a desk, a cupboard, and long benches for the children.

Once settled in, Anne could begin looking around at her new homeland. Almost the only resemblance to the life she had lived back in England for forty-three years was the language. But even that was beginning to change as it accommodated names of food she had never seen, heard of, or tasted: for example, samp (cornmeal mush), succotash, and squash. Such words were derived from names bestowed on indigenous food by native Americans.

As a matter of fact, the food and living conditions struck one anonymous balladeer as so strange and unfamiliar that he or she went around singing about them in detail, beginning in 1630—in words ringing so traumatic yet true that the song passed orally from generation to generation till finally transcribed in 1785 "from the lips of an old lady at the advanced age of ninety-six":

> New England's annoyances you that would know
>   them,
> Pray ponder these verses which briefly doth show
>   them.
> The place where we live is a wilderness wood,
> Where grass is much wanting that's fruitful and
>   good:
> Our mountains and hills and our valleys below,
> Being commonly covered with ice and with snow;
> And when the north-west wind with violence blows,
> Then every man pulls his cap over his nose:
> But if any's so hardy and will it withstand,
> He forfeits a finger, a foot, or a hand.
>
> But when the Spring opens we then take the hoe,
> And make the ground ready to plant and to sow;
> Our corn being planted and seed being sown,
> The worms destroy much before it is grown;
> And when it is growing, some spoil there is made
> By birds and by squirrels that pluck up the blade;
> And when it is come to full corn in the ear,
> It is often destroyed by raccoon and by deer.
>
> And now our garments begin to grow thin,
> And wool is much wanted to card and to spin;
> And if we can get a garment to cover without,
> Our other in-garments are clout upon clout:
> Our clothes we brought with us are apt to be torn,
> They need to be clouted soon after they're worn,
> But clouting our garments they hinder us nothing,
> Clouts double are warmer than single whole
>   clothing.

If fresh meat be wanting to fill up our dish,
We have carrots and turnips as much as we wish:
And if there's a mind for a delicate dish
We repair to the clam-banks, and there we catch
  fish.
Instead of pottage and puddings and custards and
  pies,
Our pumpkins and parsnips are common supplies;
We have pumpkins at morning and pumpkins at
  noon,
If it was not for pumpkins we should be undone!

If barley were wanting to make into malt,
We must be contented, and think it no fault;
For we can make liquor to sweeten our lips,
Of pumpkins and parsnips and walnut-tree
  chips . . .

In this setting, the Bay Colony was forced to discard the past precipitously, bending and molding the present almost beyond recognition in order to survive for the future. At least two times a day, at meals, Anne had sharp reminders that tradition was out, innovation was in. The first problem was to stay alive, learning to make palatable almost anything that grew locally, or that could be obtained easily. For example, there was no beer, so New Englanders drank water, "even the most honored as well as others, contentedly rejoicing in a cup of cold water, blessing the Lord that had given them the taste of that living water, and that they had not the water that slakes the thirst of their natural bodies, given them by measure, but might drink to the full." And when they had no bread, they feasted on fish: alewives, a young herring; oysters, "some a foot long . . . in form of a shoehorn"; mussels, "which if they were in England would be more esteemed of the poorer sort"; and clams, "a shellfish not much unlike a cockle." They also, when necessary, ate lobsters, even though "their plenty makes them little esteemed and seldom eaten," and they were used by "Indians . . . to bait their hooks . . . and to eat when they can get no bass."

Native Americans, coming in from outlying areas, introduced corn, unfamiliar in the diet of old England, but soon the main staple of New England. In fact, two of the Bay Colony's most abundant and important foods were beans and corn, both of which when dried would keep indefinitely. When these two vegetables were stewed together, sometimes with other food, sometimes simply sweetened with maple syrup, the all-purpose sweetener and seasoner that replaced hard-to-obtain salt during the first decade of settlement, the result was succotash. Since the sugar maple did not grow in Europe, the Puritans had never seen or heard of it at home.

Special treats included Indian pudding (made with cornmeal as the main ingredient); and milk toast, this made from Indian bannock, which was cornmeal combined with water, spread an inch thick on a board, and propped into a slanting position before the fire to bake.

Also, before too long, cornmeal was used to bake bread, substituting for the barley, millet, oats, rice, rye, and wheat of Europe.

Equally indispensable were squash and pumpkin. Typically, they were baked whole over embers in a dying fire, after which they were moistened with animal fat, maple syrup, or honey. Both were also used in making a soup. For variety, pumpkins were sometimes filled with hot milk.

During these early years, "it would have been a strange thing to see a piece of roast beef, mutton, or veal, though it was not long before there was roast goat," commented Roger Clap who had arrived in 1630. Most settlers ate game, similar but not identical to what they had known back home. The turkey, for instance, was at least a distant cousin to the cranelike bustard or the grouselike capercaillie.

In the Hutchinson household, Anne was chief cook, in charge of feeding fifteen: William, herself, their eleven living children (Edward, twenty-two; Richard, nineteen; Faith, seventeen; Bridget, fifteen; Francis, fourteen; Samuel, ten; young Anne, eight; Mary, six; Katherine, four; little William, three; and Susanna, one), as well as two of William's unmarried, fortyish cousins, Anne and Frances Freiston. Servants were not needed. As a matter of course, and moral obligation on both sides, the two adult female relatives lived and ate with the Hutchinsons, and in return contributed free domestic service, perceptibly lessening the burden on Anne.

Looking beyond pots, kettles, and the dining table, Anne was never for a moment allowed to forget that this evil old world had found a second chance in the establishment of New England. Here, the colonial fathers could carry out God's original intent and establish paradise on earth. Even nature cooperated, providing a novel backdrop of distinctly unfamiliar time and weather. An hour might still be sixty minutes, but in summer the days were two hours shorter than in England and in winter two hours longer. Also, summer was much hotter and winter much colder than back home in the old country.

Staring Anne in the face each time she opened her front door was the home of her nearest neighbor, John Winthrop, who wielded the greatest political power in New England. Yet he was not a remote, never-seen king, a ten-day journey away. In fact, he was nothing like a king—as his recent defeat for governor had so vividly demonstrated. In theory, "where there was so much of equality in the circumstances of the inhabitants, and once a year every office expired, it is not strange that every order of men should be fond of acquiring and retaining their full share of power and authority."

What Anne could see of the practice and philosophy of local politics she found highly encouraging. Even the concept that participation involved "every order of *men*" presented no obstacle in the seventeenth century that defined *man* as "human being, male as well as female" (deriving the word and its definition from the Anglo-Saxon *mann*).

If John Winthrop was a symbol of the new society, so was the church just a little farther up the road. Here the symbolism was innate in the very construction of the church, its mud walls and grass-thatched roof exuding earthiness, exalting the land. No spire or ivy covering adorned the steeply sloping roof, partly because the building was thrown up in a hurry, but mostly because the Bay colonists looked on spires as too suggestive of Catholicism. In contrast, back home Anne had known the huge cathedrals and churches of London, Lincoln, Boston, and Alford, all solidly constructed of stone, their inner sanctuaries ranging from imposing to magnificent.

The plain building of Boston, Massachusetts, expressed Puritan rebellion against the ostentation of the Church of England, and at the same time was an instant indication of the difference between the recently planted wilderness of New England and long-settled old England—where the completion of religious edifices took one, two, or three centuries, or sometimes forever.

Total rejection of the Church of England became a way of life. Sunday was called the Lord's Day or the Sabbath, and was the only day of the week to receive an appellation. All the other days of the week, and the months, too, were distinguished by numbering them, so that the third Tuesday in May was "the third third day of the third month" (the first month of the year continued to be counted from the month called March in old England). In addition, the word "saint" was discarded from the language, "apostle" used instead. Even place names came under this proscription, so that the Island of Saint Christophers was known simply as Christophers.

Despite all this, Puritans saw no contradiction in allowing their own carefully re-formed church to permeate their lives—much as the old Church of England dominated the lives of its congregants. Thus, Christmas holidays that had been the occasion for great celebration in England among the well-to-do were abolished in New England, denounced synonymously as pagan-popish-Anglican. And as though pouring life into a new mold to create a new form, Puritans conspicuously revised the marriage ceremony, inviting a magistrate or specially appointed officials to perform the rites, never a minister. Gov. John Winthrop himself explained: "We were not willing to bring in the English custom of ministers performing the solemnity of marriage."*

So far, so good, as far as Anne was concerned, though she could easily find areas requiring further improvement. No one had yet

---

*Some 150 years later, Anne Hutchinson's direct descendant, the historian Thomas Hutchinson, wrote: "It is difficult to assign a reason for so sudden a change." A possible explanation is that marriage was considered not a religious sacrament but an agreement between two individuals, a contract setting terms of ownership, residence, and inheritance. This, too, raised the status of women in New England.

gotten around to throwing out the old custom of segregating the sexes in the church, women on one side of the pastor, men on the other, both seated according to social standing in the community. Nor had anyone yet given a second thought to the fact that women entered the church by one door, men by another. Still, so much had changed in such a short time that Anne had every reason to believe that innovation was an ongoing process. For example, in the rush toward permanence and stability, the self-appointed founders of each new town gathered their own church by subscribing publicly to a covenant they themselves had formulated. They saw no need to wait for word from on high from the hierarchy of the Established Church of England. Furthermore, church members were chosen by each congregation, admitted by vote of fellow colonists—nothing like English custom whereby people received lifelong membership by virtue of being born into the church of their parents. Even scrutiny of individual behavior was left to each local church, not to a remote and therefore unknown hierarchy. All these new practices were part and parcel of New England "Congregationalism," the term devised by Anne's hero John Cotton, revered in New England as he had been in old England as a leading expert and practitioner of nonconformity.

But a little nonconformity can be a dangerous thing. Anne, for instance, spurred on by the avalanche of revolutionary changes already put into effect, assumed that she had free rein to choose her own direction and run her own life. Yet, just the day before her arrival, the authorities had enacted into law a new dress code:

The Court taking into consideration the great, superfluous and unnecessary expenses occasioned by reason of some new and immodest fashions, as also the ordinary wearing of silver, gold, and silk laces, girdles, hatbands etc., has therefore ordered that no person, either man or woman, shall hereafter make or buy any apparel, either woolen, silk or linen, with any lace on it, silver, gold, silk or thread, under the penalty of forfeiture of such clothes.

Also, that no person, either man or woman, shall make or buy any slashed clothes, other than one slash in each sleeve, and another in the back; also, all cutworks, embroidered or needlework caps, bands and rails [neckerchiefs], are forbidden hereafter to be made and worn, under the aforesaid penalty; also, all gold or silver girdles, hatbands, belts, rugs, beaver hats, are prohibited to be bought and worn hereafter, under the aforesaid penalty.

Moreover, it is agreed, if any man shall judge the wearing of any of the forenamed particulars, new fashions, or long hair, or anything of the like nature, to be uncomely, or prejudicial to the common good, and the party offending reform not upon notice given him, that then the next Assistant, being informed thereof, shall have power to bind the party so offending to answer it at the next court, if the case so requires; provided and it is the meaning of the Court that men and women shall have liberty to wear out such apparel as they are now provided of (except the immoderate great rails, long wings [appendages], etc.) . . .

This was the first throwback to old English ways to come to Anne's attention. King James and Queen Elizabeth, too, had considered it a prime royal obligation to supervise every detail of their subjects' personal behavior, and so had promulgated sumptuary laws and dress codes.

But side by side with this demonstrable lack of imagination, the Puritan fathers outdid themselves pampering female colonists. Exactly as William Wood had promised in his promotional tract, *New England's Prospect*, the women of New England had already taken several steep steps upward. For example, in Europe where women vastly outnumbered men so that supply outran demand, wifebeating was a commonly used technique to keep women in their place. In New England, however, where the sex ratio was distinctly favorable to women—only two women for every three men—wifebeating was not allowed, nor were men permitted to treat their wives as servants; and both proscriptions were enforced on pain of jail or heavy fine. From the beginning, Massachusetts Bay had gone out of its way to indulge its women, to make sure that they were happy, and that they would write glowing letters to England enticing their sisters there to come too.

It is likely that Anne felt more justified than ever in her adulation for John Cotton when she learned that shortly before her arrival he had led a successful fight against forcing women to wear veils. The suggestion had come from old John Endecott no less, an early leader of the colony who had arrived in Salem a full year before Winthrop and company. He had proposed reviving this ancient Biblical custom, long considered an excellent way to prevent women from flaunting their beauty to lead men to lust. The suggestion was too much even for the usually straitlaced John Winthrop who was governor at the time and who hastily called a halt to the debate when John Endecott refused to give in.

Abruptly, on March 4, 1635, just four months after her victory concerning admission to the church, Anne was consigned to oblivion simply because she was female.

Once again the royal threat to rescind the colony's charter affected Anne personally. To strengthen the colony for any showdown with King Charles, the General Court made drastic changes in the Freeman's Oath. They lowered to sixteen the age for freemen (those entitled to vote and to hold office). The aim was to increase substantially the numbers of those who would swear allegiance to the colony, and, by so doing, conspicuously snub the royal government. Grudgingly, Anne could force herself to accept her husband William's taking the oath, while she was ignored. She knew the painful pattern all too well. All during her forty-three years in old England—as an adolescent, a young married matron, and a middle-aged housewife—women were nonpersons and politically invisible (with the great and glorious exception of Queen Elizabeth). But here in New England, where she had come with great expectations, she must have felt completely demoralized when her young sons were also invited to take the oath, solely on the basis of gender, not knowledge or experience.

Worse still, the authorities felt themselves able to bend the age requirement of sixteen years in their frantic quest for signatures—but not the sex requirement. Thus two of Anne's sons took the oath: Richard who had just turned nineteen, as well as Francis who had inhabited this earth for a total time of fourteen years and three months.

Anne was not alone in harking back to England's most successful monarch, Elizabeth, a female who positively shone in comparison with her male successors. Writing at her desk long after the family had gone to sleep, Governor Dudley's young married daughter, Anne Bradstreet, celebrated politics, female division:

> She hath wiped away the aspersion of her sex,
> That women wisdom lack to play the Rex.
> . . . .
>
> Now, say, have women worth, or have they none?
> Or had they some, but with our queen is't gone?
> Nay, masculines, you have thus taxed us long,
> But, she, though dead, will vindicate our wrong.
> Let such as say our sex is void of reason,
> Know 'tis a slander now, but once was treason.

7

"FIFTY, SIXTY, OR EIGHTY AT ONCE"

Within months of Anne's arrival, she had split Boston in two: her eager devoted followers on one side, fearful angry opponents on the other. Stripped of high-toned bombast, polite euphemism, and nasty name-calling, the issue boiled down to individual responsibility versus tyrannic supervision as one side contended, or chaos versus stability as the other side put it. Each faction was sure it had the sublime solution for the success of this colony all settlers looked to as a City upon a Hill, the Utopia of the New World, New Canaan.

The struggle began innocently, almost unnoticed even by Anne's closest neighbor, the elegantly bearded, primly aristocratic John Winthrop, whose dedication to the colony he had founded almost single-handedly would one day earn for him the sobriquet of Moses the Lawgiver. Her early activities did nothing to raise his already permanently arched eyebrows even when she began holding assemblies for women on a more or less regular basis at her own home.

She later recalled that she took up the practice slowly, informally, meeting at most once a week with only five or six women at first.

These sessions for women alone were simply the logical extension of the church's own practice of segregation—seating females on one side of the aisle, and maintaining a separate door for women. Her sole purpose was to discuss the latest sermon of John Cotton, she let it be known, explaining that she had called such meetings after being warned by a friend that she was courting trouble for her nonattendance at other meetings scheduled for a similar purpose:

> The ground of my taking it up was, when I first came to this land because I did not go to such meetings . . . , it was presently reported that I did not allow of such meetings but held them unlawful and therefore in that regard they said I was proud and did despise all ordinances. Upon that a friend came unto me and told me of it and I to prevent such aspersions took it up.

If she had stopped to think about it, she might have added another reason for her meetings: her distinct disappointment at the unavailability of John Cotton for philosophical disputation. Having followed him all the way to New England, she discovered—as had all other intruders on his routine of study—that "if any came to visit him, he would be very civil to them, having learned it as his duty . . . and yet he would often say with some regret after the departure of a visitant, 'I had rather have given this man an handful of money than have been kept thus long out of my study.' " His guiding rules were that "the time not spent in study, for the most part, swirled away; . . . that more benefit was obtained . . . by conversing with the dead (in books) than with the living (in talks); and that needless visits do commonly unframe our spirits, and perhaps disturb our comforts." In addition to studying for twelve hours each day, John Cotton preached more than once a week and spent time on doctrinal matters and controversies involving church and government.

In any case, Anne's impressive self-confidence and hypnotic speaking ability eventually made the ever-watchful John Winthrop describe her, with compliments descending into sneering insult, as "a woman of a haughty and fierce carriage, of a nimble wit and active spirit, and a very voluble tongue, more bold than a man, though in understanding and judgment inferior to many women."

Luckily for Anne, "the godly magistrates and elders of the church . . . winked at . . . her practice" for several months, even though her audiences grew larger and larger till she was seen accommodating in her cramped living room almost every woman in Boston, and some from neighboring towns, too. Uncomplainingly, these women stood for an hour or more, squeezed tightly against one another as Anne led discussions, encouraged mutual support for the problems of adjustment to colonial life, and invariably sent everyone home ready to face the next few days.

Anne's devoted listeners were mostly women in their late thirties or forties, afflicted by painful loneliness and terrified at the prospect of permanent separation from sisters and friends to whom in the past they had turned for advice and comfort on pregnancy and frighteningly unexplainable bodily changes and ills. Raised amid the civilization and culture of the Old World, they had been plunked down in the cold barren wilderness of the New World—and many of them reacted violently. A Mrs. Hett of Boston, for example, half crazed, seized her small infant and threw it into the well, reconsidered almost immediately, and pulled the child out just before it drowned. Another woman, Dorothy Talbye, after several attempts to kill her husband, her children, and herself, finally succeeded in murdering her three-year-old daughter, for which she was hanged in Boston. Her husband was censured by the court for "much pride and unnaturalness to his wife." Other women, frustrated by the intellectual stagnation that was their lot as outsiders, were similarly driven to insanity. Interestingly, John Winthrop, later describing one such case in the privacy of his own diary, argues the male point of view:

[Anne Hopkins], a godly young woman and of special parts, was fallen into a sad infirmity, the loss of her understanding and reason, which had been growing upon her divers years, by occasion of her giving herself wholly to reading and writing, and had written many books. Her husband, being very loving and tender of her was loath to grieve her; but he saw his error,

when it was too late. For if she had attended her household affairs, and such things as belong to women, and not gone out of
her way and calling to meddle in such things as are proper for
men, whose minds are stronger, etc. she had kept her wits, and
might have improved them usefully and honorably in the place
God had set her.

And an anonymous letter writer, identified only as "a
gentlewoman," sent a bitter note back home to England, struggling
to reconcile the wide and unexpected gap between promise and
reality:

When I remember the high commendations some have given of
the place, and find it inferior to the reports, I have thought the
reason thereof to be this, that they wrote surely in strawberry
time. . . . I have fancied the eyes of the writers were so fixed on
their old English chimney tops that the smoke put them out. The
air of the country is sharp, the rocks many, the trees in-
numerable, the grass little, the winter cold, the summer hot, the
gnats in summer biting, the wolves at midnight howling, etc.

John Winthrop—highly sensitive as always to the mere suggestion of a threat to the colony he loved like his own flesh and
blood—put the number in attendance at Anne's house at
"threescore or fourscore persons." His ministerial alter ego, the
Reverend Thomas Weld of neighboring Roxbury, agreed (they later
co-authored a blow-by-blow account of Anne's trials and the colony's tribulations), but modernized the former governor's estimate
to read "fixty, sixty, or eighty at once."

"As soon as she was admitted into the church," John Winthrop
came to realize later, "she began to go to work, and being a woman
very helpful in times of childbirth and other occasions of bodily infirmities, and well furnished for means of those purposes, she easily insinuated herself into the affections of many."

John Cotton, who wanted only to be left alone in his study, far
from the glare of controversy, issued a statement to which friends,
enemies, and neutrals could all subscribe: "She did much good in

our town, in woman's meeting and at childbirth travails, wherein she was not only skilful and helpful, but readily fell into good discourse with the women."

Calling on all their resources of insight and perception, Massachusetts's two giants, John Winthrop in politics and John Cotton in religion, had cut directly to the core and there each found seeds for evil: Anne's conspicuous abilities as nurse and midwife. She was so skilled in her ministrations—after all, her experience went back almost three decades to her teenaged days in London— that her sick patients generally felt better, and mothers and newborn infants under her care almost always came through in good condition. At one point John Winthrop himself felt impelled to bestow the sneering compliment that "this woman had learned her skill in England."

In eternal gratitude, women worshipped her as a near-goddess and began flocking to her living-room meetings in such numbers that she sometimes had to resort to additional meetings. At the same time, and for the same reasons, many husbands began looking on her as the Devil's agent, and labeled her meetings sinister in their secrecy and blasphemous in their exclusion of men. John Winthrop, witnessing the stepped-up pace of all these goings and comings from his window across the road, denounced Anne's gatherings, noting that "the pretense was to repeat sermons, but when that was done, she would comment . . . and she would be sure to make it serve her turn." His equally public-spirited friend and co-author, Rev. Thomas Weld, concurred, adding sarcastically that "the custom was for her scholars to propound questions and she (gravely sitting in the chair) did make answers thereunto."*

None of Anne's critics ever attended any of her meetings. And her

---

*Chairs were still so rare at this date that usually each family had only one, reserved for the head of the household who used it at the dining table or board, whereas everyone else present sat on long benches. Hence the expression, "chairman of the board." Unconventional as always, the Hutchinson household either had two chairs, one for Anne and another for William, or shared the one chair equally between husband and wife.

In any case, the Reverend Mr. Weld here, by placing Anne "in the chair," purposely adds to her authority.

loyal female followers maintained strict silence. Fearing the worst, the authorities convinced John Cotton that for the great good of all—including himself—he ought to send spies to her meetings. But, as he recalled long after the event, Anne was too clever for them: "I sent some sisters of the Church on purpose to her repetitions so that I might know the truth. But when she discerned any such present, no speech fell from her that could be excepted against."

At a loss to come up with a satisfactory reason for this remarkable display of loyalty to Anne, one observer bellowed and blustered and finally fell back on the Devil theory: "Midwives . . . not only have familiarity with the Devil, but also in that service commit devilish malefices."

But the explanation was far from supernatural. The cures Anne repeatedly achieved at the bedside of the sick, or for women in pregnancy, derived from tried and true experience as well as expert use of herbal medicine. Anne was way ahead of her time in the pregynecological, highly superstitious seventeenth century that understood nothing about conception, pregnancy, or birth—or the vast catalogue of serious illnesses and puzzling discomforts, ranging from breast cancer to menses and menopause.*

The truth was that as a knowledgeable nurse and midwife Anne had no competition. The old recommended treatments were positively sadistic. For example: "For a person that is distracted if it be a woman: Take the milk of a nurse that gives suck to a male child and also take a he-cat and cut off one of his ears or a piece of it and let it bleed into the milk and then let the sick woman drink it."

---

*The words *obstetrics*—the science or art of ministering to women before, during, and after pregnancy—and *gynaecology*—the branch of medicine treating women and their diseases—were introduced into the English language only in the nineteenth century, following the establishment of professional schools to which, in the beginning, only men were admitted.

Of course, it has to be recognized that even in the highly scientific, superstition-scoffing twentieth century there is a great deal that is not yet understood about pregnancy: for example, the exact moment of conception, the cause of the onset of labor, and, in most cases, the sex of the unborn child. And little research has been done on what are euphemistically and deprecatingly known as "female troubles."

Or another equally highly touted nostrum:

For sharp and difficult travail in women with child: Take a lock of virgin's hair on any part of the head, of half the age of the woman in travail. Cut it very small to fine powder. Then take twelve ants' eggs dried in an oven after the bread is drawn or otherwise make them dry and make them to powder with the hair. Give this with a quarter of a pint of red cows milk or for want of it give it in strong ale wort.

Anne's preference was to use locally grown herbs similar to the ones she had used for so many years in England. Native Americans had long relied on basil and mint-flavored dittany to speed childbirth, dill and fennel to increase the mother's milk, the yellow-flowered groundsel to ease swollen or painful breasts, and penny-royal for pain in the back due to pregnancy. Horehound and mugwort were two herbs highly effective in expelling the afterbirth.

But Anne found herself up against old England's superstitions about midwifery and attitudes about the proper place of women in the running of society—all the heavy baggage the authorities had transported to New England, despite their constantly reiterated intention to reject the worst of English practices and procedures. Long before New England was even a gleam in their eyes, the colonial fathers had all grown to middle age convinced of the absolute necessity of imposing strict controls on the practice of midwifery. As a matter of fact, just about the time the colonists were embarking for America, a catalogue was published listing the widespread evils attributed to midwives. Among the abuses to be outlawed, a midwife must never (1) cause or allow a woman to name the wrong father of her child; or (2) claim another woman's child as her own; or (3) murder or maim an infant; or (4) use witchcraft, charms, or sorcery; or (5) administer any herbs or potions that would cause abortion; or (6) allow a woman to deliver her baby in secret.

The colonial authorities who had spent their formative years hating King James found themselves in complete agreement with his strong feelings on the subject of baptism by midwives. At the Hampton Court Conference of 1604 (the King's unsuccessful attempt to reconcile Puritanism and the Church of England), the official reporter had carefully recorded an incidental royal observation: "That any but a lawful minister might baptize anywhere, [King James] utterly disliked: and in this point his highness grew somewhat earnest against the baptizing by women."

Actually, in an emergency, when it seemed likely that the baby would die, instant baptism was necessary—but somehow this innocent practice was blown all out of proportion until it assumed sinister ramifications. Governments invariably worried that the midwife would purposely exceed her authority whenever she could. And from this could flow all kinds of evils: She might baptize the infant into the Catholic or Anglican churches; she might claim the infant and the mother as members of her own private religious cult; and she might contend that allowing her the privilege of baptism conferred on her an office in the church.

Or, stretching her devilish powers to the outer limits, she might, as John Winthrop accused Anne Hutchinson, establish "the community of women . . . their abominable wickedness." In other words, by the subterfuge of midwifery, Anne might succeed in gathering a large enough female following to subjugate men—the New England version of fears expressed in previous millennia in tales of the all-conquering women warriors, the Amazons, who, in their contempt for all males, killed their own infant sons at birth; or in another myth, the Eleusinian mysteries of the Greek mother goddess Demeter and her daughter Persephone who, excluding men from their elaborate ceremonies, passed on dark secrets.

The Reverend Thomas Weld found evidence of an imminent female takeover when Anne began attracting adherents beyond Boston. "Some being tainted conveyed the infection to others," he remarked. Flabbergasted, he conceded that the latest list of Anne's followers included men highly respected throughout the colony: "some of the magistrates, some gentlemen, some scholars and men of learning, some burgesses of our General Court, some of our captains and soldiers, some chief men in towns, and some eminent for religion, parts, and wit."

In his horror at this development, he then proceeded to give an excellent demonstration of why Anne was so exercised. The Reverend Mr. Weld, of course, was quite accustomed to relying on

Original Sin to keep men in subjection to authority and women in subordination to their husbands—all in the higher interest of making the Bay Colony the Garden of Eden in the New World. Thus, with no difficulty at all, he correlated Eve's primary role in the Fall with Anne's activities, which "began to raise sedition amongst us, to the endangering of the commonwealth . . . Mistress Hutchinson's opinions . . . commonly labored to work first upon women, being . . . the weaker to resist: the more flexible, tender, and ready to yield: and if once they could wind in them they [might] by them, as by an Eve, catch their husbands also, which often proved too true amongst us."

It was exactly this kind of reliance on the Bible to keep women in their place that made Anne insist on her ability to communicate directly with God, and thereby come up with her own interpretations of the Scriptures. Horrified that this was the path that would lead straight to ruin, John Winthrop protested: "She would comment upon the doctrines and interpret all passages at her pleasure, and expound dark places of Scripture, so as whatsoever the letter held forth . . . she would be sure to make it serve her turn."

Ignoring her critics, Anne went right on finding further fault with the church and state of Puritan Massachusetts. As an intelligent midwife and sensitive woman, she could not for a minute accept the Establishment's insistence that only the manifestation of outer piety could assure human salvation. A chief component of this outer piety was strict observance of the Sabbath, which Anne publicly rejected; neither birth labor nor family emergencies were respecters of Sabbath hours. Anne chose to behave in accord with a pithy poem written by Hendrik Niclaes of Munster, the sixteenth-century advocate of Familism, the radical philosophy that had been whirling around London during Anne's teenaged years there, and around Ely, not far from Alford, during her years as a young married matron:

> To be obedient unto God, that is my manifestation:
> Which God doth work in me, to his praise and
>   glorification.
> I seek not also mine own honor to procure:
> But I am obedient unto God's doctrine pure.

I never shrink from him, through any bad
    intention.
I seek neither subtlety, nor any new invention.
I cannot any way God's holy law transgress.
Therefore lives plain and just, with me in justness.

The same exaltation of individual worth and responsibility that made women—history's eternal outsiders—flock to Anne's leadership, caused businessmen to join her movement, too. Glumly reporting this latest ominous development, John Winthrop, himself a self-sufficient member of the landed gentry and therefore far removed from the world of profit and loss (he even refused a salary as governor), commented:

> It was a wonder upon what a sudden the whole Church of Boston (some few excepted) were become her new converts and infected with her opinions, and many also out of the church and of other churches also, yea, many profane persons became of her opinion, for it was a very easy and acceptable way to heaven to see nothing, to have nothing, but wait for Christ to do all.

As a matter of fact, businessmen gravitated to Anne Hutchinson because they had purposely wrenched themselves from an England dominated by the Crown, bishops, and aristocracy—which had shown little inclination to allow them to share the reins of power. The men who settled in Boston, where the rocky soil and excellent port dictated the establishment of trade and commerce, rebelled against the authoritarianism of the newly established Puritan church and political magistracy. Inexorably, there soon developed constant conflict between the immovable and the irresistible: the colony's need to establish political and economic stability, versus the individual merchant's goal to make a profit sufficient to reward his labors amid the unprecedented difficulties and requirements of a frontier society. For example, the magistrates, with the enthusiastic support of the clergy, had imposed a series of wage and price controls from the very beginning. At first the merchants of Boston objected strenuously, insisting that supply and demand alone should control prices. However, by 1635, sensing that they would have to conciliate or perish, Boston businessmen took matters into their own hands, setting up their own committee in an effort to satisfy both their own need for profit and the magistrates' demand for regulation. Members were three prominent merchants: William Brenton, William Colburn—and William Hutchinson.

Soon Anne began holding two meetings a week to make room for her new followers, the usual one on Thursday, plus another on Monday.

After several months of Anne's meetings, the political archrivals Thomas Dudley and John Winthrop behaved as though convinced that evil had broken loose in the colony. Neither was returned to top office in the annual election of May 1635. This time, both of them— stalwart founders of the colony—were demoted to assistants. Flailing about to explain the inexplicable, they reverted to the medieval reasoning they had known so well in the England of King James: Where there is evil, there must be woman. From this, they arrived at a syllogism: (1) Before the arrival of Anne Hutchinson, there had been virtual unity. (2) Then New England had been cursed with her presence. (3) Ergo, goaded by her activities, factionalism became a clear and present danger. (Since the arrival of the Winthrop company in 1630, some individual troublemakers had been banished. But none had attracted any followers.)

Undoubtedly insulting to the egos of these two elder statesmen were the men chosen by the voters to replace them. John Haynes, the new governor, had arrived only in 1633. Extraordinarily wealthy, he had conducted some highly effective grandstanding, telling his constituents he would not accept any money for his services as governor, "partly in respect of their love showed towards him [i.e., they had elected him], and partly for that he observed how much the people had been pressed lately with public charges, which the poorer sort did much groan under."*

---

*There had been near-rebellion over staggeringly heavy taxes. More than anything, this had made the voters look for new men in the government.

To the two former governors, the voters' choice of Richard Bellingham as deputy governor also reeked with blatant—and inexplicable—ingratitude. A long-winded and temperamental lawyer,
he had arrived just the year before.

However, not quite knowing how to proceed, since they were out
of power, the two ex-governors did nothing for the moment. And
miraculously, from their point of view, Anne quieted down. In fact,
she seemed to retire from the public scene completely.

Actually, by the fall of 1635, Anne, suffering a series of private
defeats, saw her life go downhill to utter discouragement. First, at
the same May election that brought loss of office for the two old colony founders, her husband William had been elected a Boston
representative to the General Court. She loved and admired her
husband, and shared his pleasure when he was honored. But she
could hardly be blamed for feeling more than a twinge of envy at his
election to the legislature. And she could find further evidence of
William's meteoric rise—in business, politics, and God's special
favor—when he joined that special committee of three Boston
businessmen to propose wage and price controls (especially on
essential items that were in heavy demand but short supply:
clothing, kitchen and dining equipment, ironware, textiles, dairy
and work animals). William joined the committee in September,
exactly one year after their arrival.

That same month of September, Anne had a sharp reminder of
her own God-given calling: At the age of forty-four, she was un-
mistakably two or three months pregnant, for the fifteenth time.
The contrast between her own destiny and that of her husband was
never more clear, and, unhappily, fit in all too well with the nearly
universal Puritan conviction that women must be excluded from the
sources of power.

Eventually, Anne's mental and physical energy gave her emotional resilience. Her new house was in good order and comfortably
furnished; as always during her pregnancies, she expected to be in
excellent health and bursting with newfound vitality; and she had
sufficient help from children and live-in relatives to allow her plenty
of free time. Awaiting the new birth, she planned to study around
the clock, this time to formalize and strengthen her religious

philosophy, and expand her thinking about long-dominant religious-political theory that made Eve, evil, and woman synonymous. In so doing she would develop additional "strange opinions" (Thomas Dudley's words, widely shared by the Establishment in Massachusetts) that would make her a charismatic leader to one faction, a subversive traitor to the other.

At the moment it was difficult for Anne to find any difference between the Puritanism of New England and the policies of old England. Both made society miserable for man and a living hell for woman. Discouragingly, in her new homeland, she saw Puritans treating woman as nothing more than a necessary evil—necessary only because she supplied the children to ensure the future, evil because she was the incarnation of Eve. Consequently, every time a woman went beyond the calling of wife, mother, and family mainstay, which the Puritans' God had staked out for her, men in power mumbled under their breath, shouted aloud, or wrote diatribes equating her with Evelike evil.

Under these circumstances, Anne began nudging Puritanism toward a theory that would emphasize and embrace the talents of women as well as those of men. In the future, after the birth of the new baby, she planned to work and reason to convince a society on the verge of chaos to call on its women for help.

In the process she would bring Massachusetts almost to its knees. Exactly as John Winthrop had foreseen.

8

"GRAND MISTRESS OF THEM ALL"

 By the time Anne reemerged from her temporary retirement, there would be drastic changes in the cast of characters on center stage.

The fast-paced drama began in the early days of October 1635. Almost simultaneously, the *Defence* and the *Abigail* arrived at Bendall's Dock, about a fifteen-minute walk down the road from the houses of the Hutchinsons, the Winthrops, and the Cottons. The passenger everyone knew best was Boston's original pastor, old gravel-voiced John Wilson, the sour look of unhappiness permanently frozen on his face—perhaps because of the hard times his wellborn wife Elizabeth (daughter of Lady Mansfield, widow of Sir John Mansfield, master of the Royal Armory) had given him over the past five years. Since at least 1630, she had adamantly refused to accompany him to New England, her initial hesitation compounded by reports of many deaths among women colonists during the first year of settlement. The Reverend Mr. Wilson had made his first torturous trip back home to collect her at the end of March 1631, less than ten months after his arrival in Massachusetts. But she stood her ground, so conspicuously in fact, that Margaret Winthrop, impatiently awaiting her own embarkation to join her governor-husband in New England, had commented in a letter to her stepson, John Jr.: "Mr. Wilson cannot yet persuade his wife to go, for all that he hath taken pains to come and fetch her. I marvel what mettle she is made of. Sure she will yield at last."

Once again, at the end of October 1634, Mr. Wilson had made the miserable trip back to England. Returning now, almost a full year later, he finally had Mrs. Wilson at his side. How much patience or sympathy he would have in the future for willful women was a good question; though maybe, with John Cotton firmly entrenched in the pastorate at the Boston church and high in the echelons of the Colonial Establishment, John Wilson would have to spend most of his time recultivating the support of powerful men, paying little attention to the women who had no influence anyway.

Another notable passenger debarking at the same time was the thirty-six-year-old Rev. Hugh Peter who had fled for his life from the authorities in England, settling for a time in Rotterdam—where, interestingly, the word was that he had allowed women to vote in his congregation.

But the newcomer who excited the colony's top leader, John Winthrop, into thinking all his past ordeals in founding Massachusetts were about to pay off was twenty-two-year-old Henry Vane. Admittedly, this highborn aristocrat was a generation younger than John Winthrop, appeared hedonistically un-Puritan with his long flowing locks and elegant clothes, and had been preceded to Boston by his reputation as a troublemaking rebel. But none of this mattered. He was also, exulted John Winthrop, "the son and heir of [Sir] Henry Vane, comptroller of the King's house, who being a young gentleman of excellent parts and had been employed by his father, when he was ambassador, in foreign affairs; yet being called to the obedience of the gospel, forsook the honors and preferments of the court." The former governor added that Sir Henry Vane, the father, had strongly opposed this remove, but had been ordered by the King to send the youth to America. The King considered this a doubly brilliant stroke: The troublemaking young Henry would be removed from the English scene; and in the New World, viewing Puritanism firsthand, he was bound to see the light—and return home chastened.

John Winthrop had every reason to expect that the mere presence of young Vane in Massachusetts would give the colony direct access to the royal court, invaluable at a time when the King was threatening to rescind the original charter. Equally excited, the usually asocial John Cotton invited the newcomer to stay with him temporarily, till his own house could be built on the adjoining lot. (Like all the well-to-do influential Bostonians living in the center of town, the Cottons had a small mansion set in a large garden.)

At the moment, neither Anne Hutchinson nor John Winthrop had any reason to suspect that it was Anne who should have been gloating in triumph over young Henry Vane's arrival while John Winthrop trembled in apprehension. But even before events turned Winthrop's initial gratification into the dregs of bitter disappointment, his attention was diverted from the colony's prize catch to the man who had so far exceeded Anne Hutchinson as prime troublemaker.

This was the thirty-two-year-old brilliant hothead, Reverend Roger Williams, who had been associated with the former governor in the establishment of the Bay Colony from the beginning— although, foreshadowing the doubts about New England that sporadically troubled him, he had held off sailing to the New World with the original colonizers in 1630, arriving instead eight months later, in February 1631. He was a Cambridge-educated minister whose ideas on native Americans (the land belonged to them, he claimed; the King's granting a charter to the Bay Colony was "a solemn public lie") and separation of church and state ran centuries ahead of most of his contemporaries.

Over the years, the General Court repeatedly summoned him to explain his statements and to receive reprimands—after which the authorities invariably gave him still another chance to make peace and join the Establishment. At the same time, the court also applied special pressure on his Salem congregation by refusing to grant the town additional land and denying Salem's deputies the right to attend sessions of the General Court. Probably because of his demonstrable lack of political sophistication, Roger Williams never seemed to attract much of a following in Massachusetts, however: only about twenty colonists, who were all from his Salem church. Hard-pressed settlers who had painfully uprooted themselves from their homeland, usually in their middle years, were hardly overjoyed to hear him charge that they had no right to reside on land that he correctly claimed belonged to native Americans. And the women who had at first been among his most devout followers did not much like his insistence that they veil their heads and faces. Gossip credited John Cotton, traveling to Salem to deliver a sermon soon after Williams had put this requirement into effect, with convincing his listeners that the veiled women in the Bible had nothing in common with female colonists. His exact words, released much later, included these: "The married women had no pretense to wear veils as virgins, neither married nor unmarried would choose to do it from the example of Tamar the harlot, nor need they do it for such purposes as Ruth in her widowhood."

Nor could it have helped the Reverend Mr. Williams's standing with women when he singled out his own wife of six years, twenty-six-year-old Mary Barnard Williams, for extra chastisement. He refused to pray with her, as indeed he refused to pray with all parishioners who would not go along with his declaration that Salem must separate from the hopelessly corrupt churches in the other towns of the colony, all slavishly intertwined with the ineffectual civil government and with the tyrannical Church of England, he claimed. (A ministerial refusal to pray with a parishioner was a very serious punishment, depriving sinners of a vital intermediary between themselves and God.) The additional insulting punishment reserved for Mrs. Williams was her husband's unwillingness to say grace at mealtimes when she was present at the table.

On October 9, 1636, three days after the arrival of Henry Vane, the General Court finally ordered Roger Williams banished. Along with a long list of miscellaneous problems—the prison at Boston, the fishing trade, purchasing lead for construction of the fort at Castle Island, licensing a ferryman—Roger Williams was called to stand as defendant at the lower end of a long table, and hear the pointedly brief verdict in his case:

Whereas Mr. Roger Williams, one of the elders of the church of Salem, hath broached and divulged diverse new and dangerous opinions, against the authority of magistrates, as also wrote letters of defamation, both of the magistrates and churches here, and that before any conviction, and yet maintaineth the same without retraction, it is therefore ordered, that the said Mr. Williams shall depart out of this jurisdiction within six weeks now next ensuing, which if he neglect to perform, it shall be lawful for the Governor and two of the magistrates to send him to some place out of the jurisdiction, not to return any more without license from the Court.

Exhibiting an uncharacteristically ambivalent attitude, John Winthrop (demoted five months before to mere assistant on the governor's council) warned Roger Williams to flee when he faced imminent arrest and forceful deportation to England because, in addition to paying no attention to the order to leave the colony, the young minister had continued to speak in words as inflammatory as ever. (On January 8, 1636, Williams finally went to Rhode Island, beyond the jurisdiction of Massachusetts.)

The court displayed extreme patience and forbearance in the case of Roger Williams. Even after finally issuing the order for banishment, the magistrates made no move to keep him under house arrest or close supervision. The actions and nonactions of the court, plus the role played by John Winthrop, would all return to haunt the future—and the life of Anne Hutchinson.

Meanwhile, during all this time, young Henry Vane was making his way into the Establishment. Less than a month after his landing, he was admitted to the Boston church, on November 1, 1635. And from that point on, his rise to preeminence and power in the colony was meteoric. The leaders knew a good man when they saw him, and young Henry's father, besides being the chief adviser of Charles I, was a special favorite of his influential queen, Henrietta Maria. Thus, at the end of that same month of November, the town of Boston recorded the first official appointment for their prize young catch: "At a general meeting, agreed that none of the members of this congregation or inhabitants among us, shall sue one another at the law before Mr. H. Vane, and the two elders, Mr. Thos. Oliver and Thos. Leverett, have had the hearing and the deciding of the cause if they can."

Thomas Oliver, a surgeon who came with John Winthrop in

1630, was, at the age of sixty-nine, old enough to be his colleague's grandfather, and Thomas Leverett, John Cotton's loyal and influential parishioner back in old Boston, was approaching fifty, about a year or two younger than Henry Vane's father.

Additional recognition was bestowed on young Henry in January. Resident in Boston for only three months, he was called to preside over a meeting that in effect put on public trial the differing approaches to government taken by the colony's founding fathers, the venerable John Winthrop and his chief rival Thomas Dudley. The two men had previously fought the issue out in the election of May 1634 when Dudley defeated Winthrop, and again in May 1635 when both lost out to newcomers John Haynes, who was elected governor, and Richard Bellingham, chosen deputy governor. Convinced, in the early years, of the overriding need to attract and keep new settlers in the still incompletely organized infant colony, Winthrop had favored enlightened leniency over blind discipline. For example, back in 1632, the second year of the colony's existence, when two men had been convicted of "foul, scandalous invectives against our churches and government," Winthrop, in the governor's chair at the time, had postponed executing the sentence of banishment on the ground that to force the offenders to depart in the middle of a bitter winter was like imposing a death sentence. Dudley took the exact opposite point of view.

Totally unfazed at the prospect of passing judgment on his highly respected elders, Henry Vane—who had by now cut his hair to shoulder length but still dressed like a young dandy—opened the proceedings, on January 18, 1636, declaring that the purpose of the meeting was "a more firm and friendly uniting of minds, especially of the said Mr. Dudley and Mr. Winthrop." Serving with—perhaps under—Vane on the panel were six of the colony's leading lights: four ministers—John Cotton and John Wilson of Boston; Hugh Peter of Salem, who had been particularly vociferous in urging such a meeting; and the renowned Puritan preacher Thomas Hooker from Newtown, across the Charles River from Boston—plus John Haynes and Richard Bellingham.

Recessing overnight, the panel announced its decision the next morning: "that strict discipline . . . was more needful in plantations than in a settled state, as tending to the honor and safety of the gospel." John Winthrop, determined above all to preserve the colony and ensure its success, "acknowledged that he was convinced that he had failed in over much leniency and remissness, and would endeavor (by God's assistance) to take a more strict course hereafter." This was a lesson John Winthrop would never forget—and a terrible blow to his pride, administered as it was by a group whose chairman was a totally inexperienced newcomer young enough to be his son.

Just about two months later, Anne Hutchinson returned to society, following the baptism of her son Zuriel on March 13, 1636, her twelfth living child. In short order, she came to feel seething contempt for the preaching of the recently returned Rev. John Wilson. She had had almost no contact with him before this, because he had been in England during her first year in Massachusetts, and after his return, she had temporarily retired from society.* Unlike John Cotton, whose intellectually provocative words had in the past set her mind spinning, John Wilson invariably delivered set pieces wherein rank superstition was dressed up as a lesson in morality. For example, there was his famous interpretation of "a great combat between a mouse and a snake" at nearby Watertown, in which "after a long fight, the mouse prevailed and killed the snake: The snake was the devil; the mouse was a poor contemptible people, which God had brought hither, which should overcome Satan here, and dispossess him of his kingdom."

Discouraged and disgusted, Anne at one point led her female followers en masse out of the church-meeting house, in the middle of one of John Wilson's sermons. Resuming her former practice of lecture-discussions in her own living room, she in effect set up a rival church in Boston. Before too long, young Henry Vane became her

---

*On the basis of Anne's relatively advanced age of over forty-four, her later obstetrical history (see chapters 11, 13, and 14), and the fact that Zuriel apparently died young, it seems fair to assume that this particular pregnancy was more difficult than usual, toward the end, forcing her into an unfamiliar state of inactivity.

latest convert—her stress on individual choice and responsibility fitting in completely with his defiance of tradition, expressed in his refusal to dress or behave according to the dictates of convention.

Under the circumstances, Anne was elated and John Winthrop dismayed when the choice of the freemen of the colony for governor turned out to be none other than Henry Vane, on May 25, 1636, just one day after his twenty-third birthday and a little more than seven months since he had first set foot in Boston. Pouring his heart out to his journal, John Winthrop minced no words in accounting for the results of the election (in which Winthrop, himself a candidate, was defeated for the third time in a row, but given the consolation prize of election as deputy governor): "Henry Vane, Esq., . . . was chosen governor . . . because he was son and heir to a privy counsellor in England."

A great believer in pomp and ceremony, Vane, brought up in the royal court of England and an impressionable observer of kingly magnificence during his continental tour of duty, instituted the decidedly un-Puritan practice of an honor guard for the governor, four colorfully uniformed sergeants, complete with halberds and stiff military bearing. And on the day of his election, he ordered all fifteen ships then docked in Boston, "to congratulate his election with a volley of great shot." This, of course, further widened the rift between Vane and Winthrop, who was incensed at the new governor's failure to take into consideration the expense involved, especially since the colony was strapped for funds for defense and otherwise.

Fate, seemingly intent on keeping John Winthrop off balance, followed up on the election of young Vane by bringing into the colony the very next day—May 26—John Wheelwright and his wife, Mary, William Hutchinson's youngest sister. John Wheelwright was the highly sympathetic minister of Bilby, one mile from the Hutchinsons' former home in Alford. When John Cotton was unavailable, they had depended on the Reverend Mr. Wheelwright for solace and sermons back in old England. Along with William's widowed mother, Susanna, who had accompanied them, the Wheelwrights moved in with the Hutchinsons temporarily. Welcomed enthusiastically, the Wheelwrights were admitted to the Boston church on June 12, just seventeen days after their arrival.

Anne now had her very own minister, and her very own governor.

Further, her husband William was extremely active politically. Already elected a deputy to the General Court in 1635 (representing the approximately one hundred freemen of Boston whose attendance at all meetings of the legislature would have been too cumbersome), he was additionally honored by his Boston neighbors who chose him as Boston selectman, responsible for local problems such as maintenance of roads, prevention of fire, allotment of land (a post to which he would be elected three more times, serving four consecutive six-month terms). At the same time, the court appointed him appraiser to settle small cases in the so-called particular courts.*

Anne, smiled on from every official direction, went on all that spring and summer, attracting larger and larger gatherings at her home. In fact, when Edward Johnson, New England's ebullient eyewitness chronicler, arrived in Boston in that summer of 1636, he was greeted by an enthusiastic follower of Anne Hutchinson, a man:

> Come along with me, . . . I'll bring you to a woman that preaches better than any of your black-coats that have been at the ninneversity, a woman of another kind of spirit, who hath had many revelations of things to come, and for my part, sayeth he, I had rather hear such a one that speaks from the mere motion of the spirit, without any study at all, than any of your learned scholars, although they may be fuller of Scripture. . . .

In addition, Johnson told the story of "a little nimble-tongued woman" among Anne's followers:

> who said she could bring me acquainted with one of her own sex that would show me a way, if I could attain it, even revelations, full of such ravishing joy that I should never have cause

---

*Writing during the following generation, historian William Hubbard explained: "Besides the quarter courts, when all the magistrates were wont to meet, other particular courts were ordered to be kept at Boston, Newtown, Salem, and Ipswich, consisting of one magistrate at least, and three or four associates, chosen by the court out of the persons nominated by the freemen of their several jurisdictions, with liberty of appeal to the quarter courts. . . ."

to be sorry for sin, so long as I live, and as for her part she had attained it already: a company of legal professors, quoth she, lie, pouring on the law which Christ hath abolished, and when you break it, then you break your joy, and now no way will serve your turn, but a deep sorrow.

Repeatedly, Johnson called attention to Anne's leadership, describing her, for example, as "the grand mistress of all the rest"; "their chief mistress"; "grand mistress of them all"; "this woman, who had the chief rule of all the roost."

Everyone who picked up Edward Johnson's writings recognized immediately that his quote about "legal professors" referred not to members of a "ninneversity," but rather to ministers who insisted on accepting every word in the Bible as literal truth, eternal law. Ridiculing such ministers, Anne told her followers that they might "all sit till doomsday under their legal sermons and never see light." Anne much preferred her own method, the one she was sure she had learned from her father, John Cotton, and John Wheelwright. Thus, when the "legal professors" criticized her for holding women's meetings that had no Biblical sanction, she fired back in response that Titus of the New Testament clearly permitted that "the elder women should instruct the younger." (Demonstrating her carefully honed technique here, she had picked, chosen, and ultimately truncated the quote that best suited her needs. The original words, taken from Titus 2:3–5, actually read: "The aged women . . . may teach the young women to be sober, to love their husbands, to love their children.")

Explaining why the businessmen of Boston also looked to Anne for leadership, her brother-in-law John Wheelwright observed: "We must look at them as men who had left their estates, friends, pleasures of their native soil; spiritual chemists, extracting the sweetness of all into freedom of conscience, doubting not but they might find all in that elixir; but as no chemist yet got it, so they were many of them deceived."

Anne's religious philosophy emphasizing individual initiative, worth, and responsibility, plus more than twenty years as marriage partner of an ambitious and conscientious businessman, enabled her to talk to the men of Boston, as well as to their wives, in language they understood. The special problems of Boston, a teeming port and commercial oasis in an otherwise agricultural colony, had been consistently ignored by all governors before the election of Henry Vane, as well as by the General Court, where the twenty-eight deputies representing the other thirteen towns of the colony continually ganged up on Boston's three representatives. All legislation regulating the economy seemed aimed at Boston alone. Consequently, the town's traders, businessmen, and craftsmen felt themselves cast as outsiders in their own colony, even though they provided indispensable goods and services, and paid a disproportionate share of taxes.

Therefore, to the Hutchinson living room every Monday and Thursday now paraded the highest concentration of wealth in the colony, as well as politically active Bostonians (one governor, twelve who at various times served as town selectmen, and eight who represented Boston during different years as deputies to the General Court, and lesser officeholders, such as fenceviewers (charged with policing lot boundaries), and their wives. Among Anne's newest disciples were members of her own family: her husband, William, and Edward Hutchinson, her brother-in-law, and his wife, Sarah. Then in an ever-widening circle came her close Boston neighbors, the Coggeshalls, the Houghs, and the Coddingtons. Farther down High Street were additional supporters, hot-tongued William Aspinwall and his wife, Elizabeth, longtime settlers who had sailed with the Winthrop fleet back in 1630, as well as Anne and Thomas Oliver, the old surgeon who served on the arbitration committee with Henry Vane. Somewhat farther away from the Hutchinson house were Margery and William Colburn, town assessor, and Mary and William Dyer, a milliner. Other prosperous merchants and their wives who counted themselves among her followers were Anne and Samuel Cole, Dorothy and William Brenton, and Phillipa and Robert Harding. Boston's all-important innkeeper, William Baulston, who dispensed hospitality at a good price and exchanged the latest news, information, and gossip for free, and Edward Bendall, the prominent dockman, were also adherents, along with their wives, Elizabeth Baulston and Anne Bendall. And present on a more or less regular basis were craftsman John Compton and servant Matthew Jyans, plus some who had been denied admission to the church, for example, Richard Hawkins and his wife, Jane (who had prophesied the downfall of the King and his church in 1629 when she lived in Huntington, and who in Boston rapidly became one of Anne's closest friends), and Samuel Sherman who had never even applied.

By the summer and fall of 1636, Anne and her followers had grown into a noticeably strong constituency, actively supported by Gov. Henry Vane in politics and Rev. John Wheelwright in religion. In addition, the movement was helped immeasurably by the removal from high office of Richard Bellingham, the deputy governor who had been defeated in the recent annual election; the conspicuous demotion of John Winthrop to second-in-command to Gov. Henry Vane; and the virtual immobilization of Rev. John Wilson, preoccupied by his struggle to make himself heard at least occasionally in the Boston church that was dominated by John Cotton, now his archrival. Together with Reverend John Cotton, who was making a heroic attempt to maintain neutrality—balancing aid to John Winthrop with comfort to Anne Hutchinson—these four men may well have been the "some few excepted," mentioned but not named by John Winthrop as being set apart in Boston from everyone else in the town who flocked to Anne as their leader.

John Winthrop decided that he, for one, could no longer sit back quietly. Never again could the Bay Colony afford to treat dissenters with the gentleness it had shown Roger Williams. That treatment had almost proved fatal, the ex-governor was reminded by a recent letter from England, congratulating him for "disclaiming Mr. Williams's opinions," telling him that the court's action (in banishing Roger Williams forever) "took off much prejudice from you with us." The correspondent added that letters arriving from New England and reporting schismatic activities had so far been kept out of the hands of the authorities, otherwise they might cause "your undoing."

But for the moment, the only step possible for the relatively powerless deputy governor to take was to report the new crisis to his own journal. Thus, included in the entry for October 21, 1636, was his denunciation of the "dangerous errors" brought to New England by "Mrs. Hutchinson, a member of the church of Boston." He added: "There joined with her in these opinions a brother of hers, one Mr. Wheelwright, a silenced minister sometime in England." No matter how hard he tried, John Winthrop could never bring himself to understand John Wheelwright's throwing in his lot with Anne Hutchinson. The forty-four-year-old, Cambridge-educated minister had come to New England with the highest of credentials: He had been hounded out of England by King Charles's favorite, William Laud, recently promoted to archbishop of Canterbury. The Puritans took special delight in mocking this man, second only to the King in the hierarchy of the Anglican church, as "that little meddling hocus-pocus."

As for John Winthrop's own superior, Governor Vane, the ex-governor apparently decided the less said the better—this time at least. Even in the privacy of his own journal, he refrained from attacking young Henry, although the powerful support of Henry Vane as the new chief executive drastically changed the whole complexion of Anne's movement.

9

"GUILTY OF SEDITION
AND ALSO OF
CONTEMPT"

Anne was well on her way to banishing Original Sin from Massachusetts—the shibboleth the founding fathers held indispensable to the success of the colony. She had had to take direct aim against the literal, "legalist" reading of Genesis, promoted by the former governor, John Winthrop, acting in concert with all Bay Colony ministers, except for her brother-in-law, John Wheelwright—and possibly her old teacher, John Cotton. Her opponents, all using almost identical language, maintained that long ago and far away, God had given the earth to man (Adam) on strict conditions. But Adam, seduced by woman (Eve), had violated the terms. Therefore, the original contract between God and man, the Covenant of Works, had been abrogated. All was not lost, however: The virgin society being set up in New England gave man a rare second chance to carry out the contract with God, and thus attain salvation on earth and eternal afterlife in heaven. In time, Massachusetts would be the new Garden of Eden—provided, of course, that man never again let woman lead him astray.

Anne disagreed wholeheartedly. Out with the Covenant of Works, she insisted, based as it was on Original Sin, and used to keep all but a few colonists in medieval-like subjection. For a substitute, she offered her own version of the Renaissance-inspired Covenant of Grace: each person's actions to be guided by his or her own conscience and inner morality; each person to communicate directly with God, without need of outside supervision; life in the here-and-now to be stressed, afterlife de-emphasized. In this scheme of things, church and state would be relieved of any role as intermediary, and would instead provide a solid superstructure designed to ensure law and order for society, peace and safety for the individual. Massachusetts would then be building for the future, not attempting to reconstruct the Middle Ages, when the model establishment consisted of an all-powerful ruler, aided and counseled by an exclusive nobility and a select church hierarchy. Accordingly, women, liberated from the curse on Eve, would be invited to lend their talents to the running of society; and the rising class of businessmen, no longer suffering from the curse on Adam, would be free to pursue their newly evolving vocation, relieved of eternal subjugation to unbending authority.

John Winthrop, taking upon himself the mantle of chief spokesman for opposition to Anne's radical ideas, denounced "such a course as this to be greatly prejudicial to the state." Addressing her directly, he elaborated: "Your opinions being known to be different from the word of God may seduce many simple souls that resort unto you, besides that . . . such as have frequented your meetings . . . are flown off from magistrates and ministers, and this since they have come to you."

As a matter of fact, Anne, after two years in Massachusetts, had the strongest constituency of any leader in the whole colony, and her Boston disciples were beginning to spread the word to the other thirteen towns. Furthermore, with Gov. Henry Vane in her corner, she had entrée into the inner sanctum of Massachusetts politics.

So far, however, she had no official ministerial support in the Boston church. The utter contempt she repeatedly displayed for Boston preacher John Wilson, he unfailingly returned in kind. And John Cotton, who wanted only to be left in isolation to pursue Utopia through scholarship, had little taste either for public confrontation or for choosing one side over the other. Therefore, Anne reverted to the Familism she had learned about back in old

England. This philosophy, besides denouncing Original Sin and showing itself highly receptive to female participation in society, taught that all institutions are open to review by individual reason and popular consent—and, most important, considering the problem at hand, asserted that each congregation be empowered to name its own minister (in striking contrast to Establishment practice of having the hierarchy impose the man of its choice, from on high, and at a distance).

By the end of October 1636, the Boston congregation, unable to cast out John Wilson, the sour-faced preacher they considered totally inflexible and uninspiring, decided to act on their own. With Anne in the lead, they proposed making John Wheelwright assistant teacher, thereby reinforcing the teachings of John Cotton, the man they found generally acceptable but usually unapproachable. John Wheelwright, the powerfully built minister with the carefully upturned mustache, Vandyke beard, and ever-ready sense of humor, they welcomed as one of their own in both spirit and substance. The ultimate goal was to ease out John Wilson gradually, raise John Cotton to the number one position of preacher, and make John Wheelwright teacher—thus removing the rumbling rivalry between preacher Wilson and teacher Cotton that was getting on everyone's nerves and restricting the church's growth and progress. (All through the summer and into the fall, no new members joined the Boston church.) Emphasizing that Anne, a woman, had assumed leadership, John Winthrop confided to his journal for October 30, 1636: "Some of the church of Boston, being of the opinion of Mrs. Hutchinson, had labored to have Mr. Wheelwright to be called a teacher there."

Similarly viewing the Reverend Mr. Wheelwright as nothing more than a simple surrogate for promoting Anne's ideas from the pulpit, William Bartholomew, Anne's tale-bearing London host and shipmate, hid behind his wife's skirts to destroy both in one simultaneous swoop: "My wife hath said that Mr. Wheelwright was not acquainted with this way until that she imparted it unto him."

Sunday, October 30, 1636, was the date set for debating the new appointment. As usual, early that morning the beating of a drum—there were no bells yet—had summoned some 150 members of the

Boston church to worship. The sabbath service consisted of extemporaneous prayers, singing psalms without musical accompaniment, and a sermon preached without notes "while the glass was turned up twice" (two hours measured by the hourglass). Afterward, in the unheated church-meeting house, the women seated on one side on long hard benches, men on the other, the disputation began.

Even relegated to deputy governor, John Winthrop, founding father par excellence, was still a man whose every word demanded attention. A minority of one—or perhaps one and a half, counting John Wilson, the virtually silenced, direct object of the dispute—the ex-governor led a successful attack against installing John Wheelwright as assistant teacher. The Boston church, he contended, already had "able ministers" (i.e., John Wilson and John Cotton) whom they already knew. They should not chance a minister "whose spirit they knew not and one who seemed to dissent in judgment."

At this point, John Cotton, in an attempt to be conciliatory, stood strongly on both sides of the issue, simultaneously. First, he conceded that he agreed with John Wheelwright on doctrine, "so as he could be content to live under such a ministry." But then gliding to Winthrop's side of the argument, he added that "seeing [Wheelwright] was apt to raise doubtful disputations, he could not consent to choose him to that place."

Toward the end of the day, several of the church "brethren" (the word John Winthrop used, ignoring Anne Hutchinson and all of her woman friends who were members of the church) voiced displeasure at the deputy governor's stand against Wheelwright. In response, Winthrop apologized for reacting so emotionally, but refused to back away from his strong position. Silence followed his apology, and he commented to his journal with a hint of hurt disappointment: "How this was taken by the congregation did not appear, for no man spake to it."

For the moment, the dispute was papered over with a compromise: The beleaguered Mr. Wilson remained Boston preacher, theoretically superior to the brilliant John Cotton, renowned teacher of the church; and Mr. Wheelwright was given a special appointment to a newly gathered church at Mount Wollaston, a tiny farming community about ten miles from the Boston meetinghouse (and thus a hard day's travel for the families living in that area and yet wishing to attend sabbath services). Among his occasional congregants would be William Coddington and William Hutchinson and their wives, since both families maintained farms there to supplement their food supply at their Boston homes.*

The foreboding cold and early darkness of December provided the backdrop a few weeks later for the raging confrontations that began spilling out into public view one after another in quick succession. The first occurred between Governor Henry Vane and John Winthrop, who was currently serving as deputy governor. Disturbed that young Vane was lending Anne Hutchinson the considerable prestige of the office that he, Winthrop, had so carefully and devotedly molded into a position of high respect, Winthrop quietly debated doctrine with the new governor "in writing for the peace sake of the church, which all were tender of." The young governor's response was to bring the disagreement into the open. At a meeting of the governor's council he indicated that he had had

---

*William Wood, who had lived in the Bay Colony from 1629 to 1633, described this arrangement in his book *New England's Prospect*, published in London in 1634: "Those that live [in Boston] upon their cattle must be constrained to take farms in the country or else they cannot subsist, the place being too small to contain many, and fittest for such as can trade into England for such commodities as the country lacks, being the chief place for shipping and merchandise."

Consequently, John Winthrop had the 600-acre Ten Hill Farm in Medford to the north of Boston and another 1200 acres "about six miles from Concord Northwards," as the Boston Records phrased it. Thomas Dudley had a total of 1700 acres in Cambridge and north of Concord. When, in May 1634, the General Court ordered Boston extended by annexing Mount Wollaston, the first two lots were assigned to William Coddington and Edmund Quincy (for whom the town was named Quincy 150 years later) on December 14, 1634. On January 4, 1636, and January 9, 1637, William Hutchinson was allotted a total of 600 acres "betwixt Dorchester bounds and Mount Wollaston river," and early in 1637, John Wheelwright was alloted 250 acres south of Mount Wollaston and "extended into the country."

quite enough of Massachusetts politics and intended to return home. This may have been only a trial balloon, but with insulting alacrity the council compliantly set the following week as the date for a special election to choose both a new governor and deputy governor. Immediately, the Boston church convened in a special session, following which almost every member sent requests to both Vane and to the council to reconsider—"whereupon," in the resigned words of John Winthrop, "the governor expressed himself to be an obedient child to the church, and therefore, notwithstanding the license of the court, yet, without the leave of the church, he durst not go away." Further, to John Winthrop's astonishment, "a great part of the [General] Court and country" decided that, for the moment anyway, they preferred to have Henry Vane remain in office, and consequently, instead of holding a special election would hold off until the regular annual election in May.

So far, Anne Hutchinson and John Winthrop had each won one and lost one: she successfully promoting retention of Henry Vane as governor, he dispatching John Wheelwright to Mount Wollaston. But the contest went on. In the days when Vane had threatened to resign, the magistrates and ministers had arranged to hold a conference without having first consulted him. Thirty-seven-year-old Hugh Peter, who in New England had apparently abandoned all sympathy for outspoken women or their sympathizers—which he had shown by permitting women to vote during his Rotterdam exile—now scolded the young governor for rash behavior, urging him "humbly to consider his youth and short experience in the things of God." Furthermore, added the Reverend Mr. Peter who had sailed to the Bay Colony on the same ship with Henry Vane and who had succeeded Roger Williams as minister of Salem: "Before [Henry Vane] came, within less than two years since, the churches were in peace."

Next, at this same conference, "Mr. Wilson made a very sad speech on the condition of our churches, and . . . laid the blame upon these new opinions [expressed by Anne Hutchinson] risen up amongst us, which all the magistrates except the governor [Vane] and two others, did confirm, and all the ministers but two [Cotton and Wheelwright]." The sum of Wilson's speech proved so nasty and harsh that Cotton and several others of the Boston church moved to censure him formally—a threat eventually dropped in the interests of harmony, but one that obviously made the deeply wounded Wilson vow never to forgive or forget Anne's role in this attempt to disgrace him publicly.

After dealing with Henry Vane and John Wilson, the ministers called Anne Hutchinson for questioning at a meeting held at John Cotton's house. Facing the panel of seven ministers she could reflect that she had made perceptible progress since the first inquisitorial proceedings held just after her arrival in the fall of 1634 to determine whether she should be admitted to the Boston church. Then, all her interrogators had been initially hostile. This time she had three potential supporters: the Reverends John Cotton and John Wheelwright, as well as her old Lincolnshire acquaintance, Elder Thomas Leverett, all connected with the Boston church. Opposed were John Wilson, Hugh Peter, Thomas Weld, and George Phillips, minister of Watertown who had sailed with John Winthrop on the *Arbella* in 1630. Over and over she was asked why she insisted that only John Cotton and John Wheelwright were able ministers. Again and again she explained that they were the only two ministers in the colony preaching the acceptable Covenant of Grace. The others, she pointed out, were all guilty of teaching the hated Covenant of Works. In the end the confrontation proved inconclusive—although it further widened the breach between the two sides until Anne Hutchinson and John Wheelwright both remarked that the difference was "as great as between heaven and hell." John Cotton, uncomfortable at being positioned against his ministerial colleagues, hastily adjourned the meeting.

As it turned out, he had acted none too soon. Deputy Governor Winthrop began writing to him privately in an unsuccessful attempt to win him away from supporting the Covenant of Grace and Anne Hutchinson. Similarly, the ministers from other towns conferred with Cotton singly and together, and when these efforts failed to change his preaching, ministers began using their pulpits to promote enthusiastic reinstatement of the now battered and bruised concept of Original Sin as incorporated in the Covenant of Works.

The campaign failed miserably. Strife, not harmony, resulted. A general fast day was kept in all churches, January 20, 1637, in hopes of finding an answer.

But of all preachers, it was Anne's brother-in-law John Wheelwright who seized the moment to speak out. In Boston on the fast day, after Cotton had given his sermon, Wheelwright, who was present, was invited "to exercise as a private brother." His subject was the Covenant of Works versus the Covenant of Grace, and John Wilson—despised by his congregation and by no means welcomed back after the failed attempt to censure him—was forced to listen to what amounted to an indictment of his own preaching and his own party. Essentially, the sermon was thoroughly conventional, interminable, and dull. But certain phrases and paragraphs, lifted out of context and reinterpreted, could be made to sound a call for civil war. For example: "We must all of us prepare for battle and come out against the enemies of the Lord, and if we do not strive, those under a Covenant of Works will prevail." Or another, "The Lord hath given true believers power over the nations. . . . If we will prevail, if we be called, we must be willing to lay down our lives, and shall be overcome by so doing."

Most significantly, Wheelwright addressed his sermon to both "brethren and sisters." Looking to the Bible for some examples of "valiant men" (i.e., "humans" in seventeenth-century parlance), he cited two males, David and Barak, and two females, Deborah and Jael.

It would be almost two months before the General Court took action against this sermon, however. The deputies were otherwise preoccupied. The political front was exploding in crisis, too. That same gloomy month of December that had produced confrontations between Vane and Winthrop, and Wilson and Cotton—with Anne Hutchinson always in the middle, supported by John Wheelwright—saw the businessmen of Boston further alienated from the other towns of the colony. Strongly protesting was Anne's best friend in all the world, her husband William Hutchinson, who resigned as one of Boston's three deputies to the General Court and at the same time left his post as appraiser for the particular courts. The General Court, tilting as always toward the rural interests at the expense of commercial Boston, passed, on December 13, 1636, harsh legislation imposing inordinately heavy fines on businessmen accused of overcharging for imported goods. One lone man, chosen by the governor and the governor's council, was authorized to search all incoming vessels and warehouses, and "the said officer, for his pains, shall have a third part of all such benefit as shall come to the commonwealth by his service therein." Two things were radically wrong with this legislation: First, the authorization for search without warrant was exactly the kind of activity pursued by King Charles and his government that had led to the flight of so many businessmen from England; second, the fact that the appointed officer would receive a "third part of all such benefit" could all too easily degenerate into an incentive for imposing high fines.

As always, politics and religion proceeded in tandem in Massachusetts. Not surprisingly, therefore, when the General Court, early in March 1637, decided to look into Wheelwright's sermon, the businessmen of Boston all signed a petition requesting public proceedings—having perhaps been organized for the purpose by Anne Hutchinson who, as a woman, was not allowed to petition the court. "Groundless and presumptuous," the court responded to the petitioners as it withdrew into a private session frighteningly reminiscent of Star Chamber proceedings back in England. After a day of private deliberations, with all ministers present for consultation, the court—Governor Vane protesting vociferously—found John Wheelwright "guilty of sedition and also of contempt" but postponed his actual sentencing till after the May election, when John Winthrop and his followers were certain they would have a more sympathetic governor. The final action taken by this meeting of the court was to move the annual election out of Boston to Newtown, full of John Winthrop's supporters and well beyond the reach of Anne's influence. The single concession to Anne and her sublieutenants, Henry Vane and John Wheelwright, was to defer to the Boston church the question of whether or not Wheelwright should be silenced in the interim.

Responding to the verdict of the court, fifty-eight men of Boston plus seventeen from Charlestown, Ipswich, Roxbury, Newbury, and Salem signed a "remonstrance" protesting the conviction. Emulating John Winthrop and the "legalist professors," the petitioners (Anne certainly aiding, if not actually dictating) cited pertinent passages in the Bible to point out that "Paul was counted a pestilent fellow, or mover of sedition, and a ring-leader of a sect, Acts 24:5, and Christ himself, as well as Paul, was charged to be a teacher of new doctrine, Mark 1:27, Acts 17:19." Once again, Anne could not sign the petition—a document eventually considered so inflammatory it would be used as evidence of sedition on the part of all signatories. Her family was very well represented, however: husband William, son Richard, brother-in-law Edward, and sons-in-law Thomas Savage and John Sanford.

Interestingly, John Cotton, who had so far been a pillar of salt as far as Anne was concerned, now behaved in a way that gave her great hope of his future support. On April 6, he joined with Governor Vane and John Wheelwright in boycotting a meeting of the Concord church that had recently chosen as teacher and pastor the Reverends Peter Bulkley and John Jones, men whom the Bostonians "accounted as legal preachers and therefore would not give approbation to their ordination."

This was light years removed from Cotton's behavior toward Anne earlier that same year when, smarting from her public approval of his preaching a Covenant of Grace, he had, by his own account, "dealt with Mrs. Hutchinson of the erroneousness of those tenets and the injury done to myself in fathering them upon me."

Around one o'clock on May 17, 1637, two angry factions, having gathered for the annual election, glared at each other on an idyllic New England day, the sun brighter, the sky bluer, the grass on Newtown's common greener than even the most enthusiastic promotion propaganda had led colonists to expect. Henry Vane, still serving as governor, prepared to open the meeting by reading the petition that the Bostonians present were clamoring to resubmit on behalf of convicted John Wheelwright (the same petition the court had initially rejected at its March meeting). Instantly, John Winthrop protested such a move as out of order at a Court of Elections. "Fierce speeches followed, some laid hands on others," but in the end Boston's man, Henry Vane, was defeated. John Winthrop once again would serve as governor and Thomas Dudley as deputy governor, the same team that had organized and governed the Bay Colony during its first three years of existence, 1630–33.

Unquestionably, it was a bleak day in Massachusetts' history, each side pressing for petty recriminations against the other. For example, the honor guard that faithfully attended Henry Vane during his incumbency threw their halberds to the ground, ostentatiously turned on their heels, and went home, forcing Governor-elect Winthrop to use his own servants as attendants. And the court tried every way possible to exclude Boston's elected deputies until "not finding how they might reject them, they were admitted."

Even so, this election produced a fascinating and durable by-product, America's first genuinely indigenous tall tale—an attempt to promote John Winthrop to divinity by parroting the Biblical story of climbing up into a sycamore tree to see Jesus (Luke 19:4). Hero, in an outstanding performance, was gravel-voiced, forty-nine-year-old John Wilson, who, amid all the confusion and tumult, succeeded in turning the mob back to right reason:

> Mr. Wilson, the minister, in his zeal gat upon the bough of a tree . . . and there made a speech, advising the people to look to their charter and to consider the present work of the day, which was designed for the choosing of the governor, deputy governor, and the rest of the assistants for the government of the commonwealth. His speech was well received by the people, who presently called out, "Election, election," which turned the scale.

In any case, the same court that elected John Winthrop governor also passed an alien exclusion act, the purpose of which, Winthrop explained, was "to keep out all such persons as might be dangerous to the commonwealth, by imposing a penalty upon all such as should retain any, above three weeks, which should not be allowed by some of the magistrates; for it was very probable that they expected many of their opinion to come out of England from Mr. Brierly his church etc." (Roger Brierly, curate at Grindleton in northwest England, was a staunch advocate of Familism, the philosophy Anne Hutchinson found so congenial to her thinking.

Among other doctrines, he preached the superiority of the spirit over the letter of the Bible, denounced Original Sin, and contended that "a man [human being] having the spirit may read, pray, or preach without any other calling whatsoever.")

For nine whole days, John Winthrop was allowed to savor his success in putting Paradise back on track. Then the Pequot War erupted, a short, decisive encounter (May 26–July 28, 1637), shifting hegemony to the colonists who were better organized and more fully armed than the more numerous native Americans. "Divine slaughter," the Reverend Thomas Shepard of Newtown characterized the killing of every Pequot in sight.

Absolutely unforgivable from the governor's point of view, therefore, was the refusal of Anne Hutchinson and her followers to support the war. The Boston church rejected all pleas for money, supplies, or soldiers. Winthrop was certain that this was a misplaced attempt to take revenge for the recent election and alien exclusion act, or for the appointment of the Reverend Mr. Wilson as military chaplain, "not one man [from the Boston church] accompanying their pastor, when he was sent by the joint consent of the Court and all the elders upon that expedition, not so much as bidding him farewell."

But the war was described by one observer as a "quarrel being as ancient as Adam's time, propagated from that old enmity between the seed of the woman and the seed of the serpent who was the grand signor of this war." And another colonist commented: "God permitted Satan to stir up the Pequot Indians to kill divers English Men." In the eyes of the Colonial Establishment, native Americans were inferiors and outsiders—just as were women and businessmen.

Nevertheless, when all was said and done, despite profound disagreements over specific details and directions, there was one point on which all New Englanders concurred: the overriding necessity to fend off King Charles's repeated attempts to rescind the original charter of independence and impose royal control over Massachusetts. Strong supporters of unanimity on this matter included Anne Hutchinson and those colonists who, like John Cotton during the past few months, refused to conform unquestioningly to New England Puritanism. Twice in the month of June 1637, ships

arrived bearing orders from the King, substituting his own appointed commissioners for the locally elected government in the colony, insisting that in Massachusetts as presently constituted "there
was no lawful authority in force." Discouragingly, this was the
response to the message sent to England the previous February by
Boston's preacher, John Wilson, and its teacher, John Cotton,
archrivals who disagreed on virtually everything. Boston was so
awash with harmony, the two ministers had asserted, that "no man
could tell . . . where any difference was."

Under the circumstances, John Cotton agreed to preach a sermon
of reconciliation following the recent raucous election and the
outspoken opposition of the Hutchinsonian party* to the Pequot
War. And from the governor's seat, John Winthrop declared that
the two sides were not fatally far apart, that dissension was by no
means making the Bay Colony a likely prospect for royal subjugation: "Such as knew the bottom of the tenets of those of the other
party, few could see where the difference was."

To give substance to his declaration, the governor proposed the
calling of a religious synod at Newtown, beginning on August 30, to
iron out all differences. This was the first religious synod ever called
in New England.

Along with magistrates and ministers, the public also was invited.
Details were relayed to all villages and towns by the official
trumpeter who, in those pre-town crier and pre-newspaper days,
went on horseback from market square to market square, where he
would loudly blow his horn, alerting all residents to his presence.

The synod, which lasted for nine days, was the beginning of the
end for Anne. Everything was going wrong. Henry Vane, unwanted
and unloved except in Boston, had returned to England on August
3. The weather, so hot all summer that, as John Winthrop noted,
the only time to travel was at night, made everyone edgy. John

---

*The first author to refer to Anne Hutchinson and her followers as "the
Hutchinsonian party" was John Winthrop's direct descendant, Robert
Winthrop, in his two-volume *Life and Letters of John Winthrop*, published
well over two centuries later, 1864–67. The reference can be found on page
207 of vol. 2.

Cotton and John Wilson were making conspicuous attempts at reconciliation. And John Wheelwright who might have been Anne's last best hope was waiting final disposition of his sentence.

The mood of the synod was overwhelmingly conservative. Early in the proceedings it found eighty-two of the opinions held by Anne and her disciples to be erroneous or blasphemous. And at the last session on September 7, it aimed directly at Anne, resolving:

> That though women might meet (some few together) to pray and edify one another; yet such a set assembly (as was then in practice at Boston), where sixty or more did meet every week, and one woman (in a prophetical way, by resolving questions of doctrine, and expounding scripture) took upon her the whole exercise, was agreed to be disorderly, and without rule.

The synod took care of religious differences. But there still remained the problem of political differences—and the problem of somehow silencing Anne Hutchinson who, though a woman, was a strong leader challenging the stewardship of John Winthrop himself. Her doctrine of individual reason unencumbered by the reins of Original Sin encouraged turmoil in place of stability, her opposition contended. The Hutchinsonians, in addition to refusing to support the Pequot War, were denouncing tax rates and land allotments (some less affluent members of the Boston church were demanding assurance that large parcels of land not go exclusively to the wealthy)—and in general showing brazen disrespect for the authorities at every turn.

Anne would have to be called to account at the November meeting of the General Court. To make sure that the correct verdict was returned, the court so painfully elected at the recent May election was abruptly dissolved and a new one elected in its place.

As in old England, the court hearing would be held not to ensure justice, but to frighten other would-be offenders into submission. John Winthrop would now put into effect a resolution passed almost two years before, on January 18, 1636. That was his own day of public humiliation, when he had been forced to defend himself against Deputy Governor Thomas Dudley's charge of over-lenient behavior, at a meeting called at the urging of twenty-three-year-old Henry Vane, Anne's disciple and powerful ally. The resolution passed as a result of this meeting was that "the magistrates should (as far as might be) ripen their consultations beforehand, that their vote in public might bear (as the voice of God)."

Anne's fate was decided. Now all that was necessary was the public trial. As governor, John Winthrop would preside, of course.

IO

"THE APPLE OF THEIR OWN EYE"

Grudgingly, Governor Winthrop had to postpone Anne's public silencing for two months. First he would have to put together a General Court sufficiently compliant to guarantee ratification and enforcement of the resolutions adopted by the Newtown synod: No hostile questioners wanted, no organized opposition admitted. On September 26, 1637, the court so recently and raucously elected "was dissolved until a new be called and to be kept at Newtown." All due haste was necessary. The court would have to be scheduled for the beginning of November at the latest since, as John Winthrop himself explained, "by reason of the great snows and frosts, we used not to keep courts in the three winter months."

Meanwhile, Anne refused to abandon her regular routine. Right under the nose of John Winthrop across the street, she defiantly held "her wonted meetings and exercises," just to show her contempt for the recent synod, he supposed. And during these same weeks, she made countless house calls to the sick and pregnant, somehow managing to keep the details secret from her all-seeing neighbor—for the time being at least.

On October 17, 1637, she answered an emergency summons from

135

the other end of town. Young Mary Dyer, the milliner's wife, her body worn and torn from three pregnancies in four years, was suffering abnormally excruciating labor pains, two months before term. Anne rushed to the little house on Mylne Road to find her good friend, midwife Jane Hawkins, in worried attendance. The fetus was positioned upside down—breeched hip-wise, the buttocks, not the head, appearing first—and the mother was so far unable to expel it even with help. The two women pulled and pushed feverishly, even after all signs of infant life ceased and the mother lapsed into unconsciousness. No anesthesia was available.

The tiny, deformed stillborn girl, when finally delivered, was too grotesque to present to the mother, herself teetering on the verge of death, the two midwives agreed. Should she recover, she would still be too weak physically to withstand the emotional shock. Therefore, while Mary Dyer lay unconscious, Anne raced to the home of John Cotton for advice. Conceal it, he recommended, so as not to discourage other pregnant women. If this had happened to his own wife, he added, "he would have desired to have had it concealed." Then with a flash of the nonconformity Anne had admired back in England, he dismissed the ancient folk wisdom that held that infant death was conspicuous punishment for the parents' sins. "He had known other monstrous births, which had been concealed," he later told John Winthrop, who then recorded in his journal that Cotton "thought God might intend only the instruction of the parents, and such other to whom it was known."

Acting on this special dispensation by John Cotton, Jane Hawkins and Anne buried the stillborn child—exactly as they had always done in old England where custom-imbedded law dictated to the midwife: "If any child be dead born, you yourself shall see it buried in such secret place as neither hog nor dog, nor any other beast may come unto it, and in such sort done, as it may not be found or perceived, as much as you may."

John Cotton's sympathetic reaction encouraged Anne to feel that at this late date they continued to share a common philosophy—and this despite the recent synod at which John Winthrop let it be known to the rebellious Boston church that "Mr. Cotton had in public view consented with the rest." In fact, if she stopped to think about it, Anne could justifiably conclude that her skilled practice of midwifery, which had brought her the undying adoration of women, from time to time induced their husbands to treat her with gratitude bordering on awe. John Cotton was a perfect example. Periodically he showed himself as capable as the next man of viewing midwives as Devil's agents. But Mary Dyer's stillbirth had obviously reawakened old sorrows, based on his own family experience. He had had to wait until age forty-eight to become a father for the first time with the birth of his son Seaborn, delivered on the high seas in the summer of 1633, as he and his second wife, Sarah Story Cotton, had made their way from old to New England. And in the fall of 1635, at the age of fifty, he was the proud father of a baby girl, Sarah, baptized September 20. Doubtless, the childlessness of his first wife, Elizabeth, to whom he had been married for eighteen years, made the entire birth process a miracle in his eyes, and stillbirth an inexplicable torture requiring understanding not recrimination (Cotton's sympathetic advice about Mary Dyer strongly implies that Elizabeth Cotton had also suffered the tragedy of stillbirth). The attending midwife at the birth of his baby daughter must have been Anne who lived only steps away, since years later John Cotton remarked that "almost in every family, some" had looked to Anne "as the apple of their own eye." (Though Anne herself had been in early pregnancy at the time, she remained active at least through that month of September.)

Almost incredibly, the same situation prevailed in the family of Anne's most powerful opponent, John Winthrop. His devoted wife, Margaret, sent him—while he was in Newtown on official business—a gently affecting letter in which she loyally tried to overcome the feeling of being drawn into Anne's sphere of influence. Datelining her letter, "Sad Boston, 1637," she confided:

> Dear in my thoughts,—I blush to think how much I have neglected the opportunity of presenting my love to you. Sad thoughts possess my spirits, and I cannot repulse them; which makes me unfit for anything, wondering what the Lord means by all these troubles among us. Sure I am, that all shall work to the best to them that love God, or rather are loved of him. I know he will bring light out of obscurity, and make his righteousness shine forth as clear as the noon day. Yet I find in

myself an adverse spirit, and a trembling heart, not so willing to submit to the will of God as I desire. There is a time to plant, and a time to pull up that which is planted, which I could desire might not be yet. But the Lord knoweth what is best, and his will be done . . .

Your loving wife,
Margaret Winthrop

At the moment, John Winthrop's answer was to apologize for not writing every day: "Business would not permit me." He continued: "I suppose thou hearest much news from hence. It may be grievous to thee, but be not troubled. I assure thee things go well, and they must needs do so, for God is with us and thou shalt see a happy issue."

Of course, Anne was right there on the spot to help and console Margaret Winthrop whenever she needed her—as had apparently been the case ever since the Hutchinsons moved across the street from the Winthrops. Margaret Winthrop was the same age as Anne Hutchinson—forty-six—but in comparison to Anne had a discouraging obstetrical history. She had married John Winthrop on April 29, 1618, when she was twenty-seven and he thirty (his previous two wives had died). Of nine children to whom she had given birth, only four sons survived, all born during her years in England. In addition to the two infants she had lost in England, her last three babies died: Anne, just over a year old, died at sea on the voyage to New England; and in Boston, William, baptized August 26, 1632, and Sarah, baptized June 29, 1634, both died early. Probably suffering through the frightening mysteries of menopause, Margaret Winthrop was never again pregnant and died ten years later on June 14, 1647, aged fifty-six.* Very likely John Winthrop spoke from firsthand knowledge when he remarked that Anne Hutchinson was

---

*In the seventeenth century, women, worn out by frequent pregnancy and pregnancy-related illness, regularly predeceased their husbands. Thus, six months after Margaret Winthrop died at age fifty-six, her still sprightly fifty-nine-year-old husband remarried and fathered a son born in October 1648. John Winthrop died on March 26, 1649, at the age of sixty-one. Today the situation is reversed. Women tend to outlive men by five to seven years.

very helpful to women in childbirth—and also "on other occasions of bodily infirmities."

With Sarah Cotton and Margaret Winthrop in her corner, Anne could find reason to count on the support of John Cotton at her upcoming General Court hearing, and to hope for gentle treatment by John Winthrop. And happily, she had at least one very good omen. Just as she was about to set off for Newtown early in November, she was called as midwife for her first grandchild, Elishua Hutchinson, born to her son Edward and his wife, the former Katherine Hamby. Edward, the first of her immediate family in New England, had returned to old England where on October 13, 1636, he married, and apparently sailed at once for Boston where Elishua was baptized on Sunday, November 5, 1637.

It was difficult for Anne to attend the baptism. The General Court had finally convened on November 2, and although her case was not the first order of business, she was expected to present herself for the hearing as soon as possible.

The distance from her home in Boston to the meeting house in Newtown was almost five miles, about a half day of treacherous travel. Luckily, she had company. The court had summoned, among many others, her thirty-year-old brother-in-law Edward Hutchinson, to explain his signature on the Wheelwright petition.

Unfortunately, an unseasonably severe ice and snowstorm during the first week of November made every step of the way life-threatening. Usually, the first half of November was a time of crisp, cool weather when the only hints of the winter to come were bare trees and early darkness. But this year, on November 1, both Newtown and Boston were ablaze with the report that "a young man, coming alone in a skiff from Newtown, in a New England storm of wind and snow was found dead in his boat."*

---

*According to the calendar used in America and England today, November 1, 1637, would be November 12. From 1582 to 1752, the anti-Catholic British Empire stubbornly clung to the 45 B.C. calendar of Julius Caesar, preferring traditional confusion to the adoption of the modern Gregorian calendar, the inspiration of Roman Catholic Pope Gregory XIII as the sensible way to catch up with the true vernal equinox. Under the Gregorian calendar, ten days were immediately added to Julian calendar dates, and an eleventh day was added in the eighteenth century.

Under these conditions, travel by cart or horse was impossible.* Anne and Edward would have to go on foot about a mile to the northern tip of the Boston peninsula where they would board the oar-propelled ferryboat to carry them the one-quarter mile over the Charles River to Charlestown. Amid the rough wind and waves, they were happy to be in the friendly hands of the spirited ferryman Thomas Marshall, himself a confirmed Hutchinsonian.

Once they arrived on the Charlestown side of the river, they would then walk over well-trod Indian paths taking them through the forest to "a spacious plain, more like a bowling green than a wilderness." En route they would pass goats, swine, and cattle grazing and eating the young shoots of trees on the still wooded common land. And looking to the left and right as they walked along the aptly named Wood Street, they could see clusters of houses roofed with shingles or slate, not thatched with marsh grass. Here, in "one of the neatest and best compacted towns in New England," the houses were set six feet back from the road and the streets were laid out straight and symmetrically except for Crooked Lane, which was allowed to wander in order to avoid the brook used for watering cattle.

They had to be on constant lookout for wolves or hostile strangers, though they would be unlikely to meet any native Americans. A plaguelike disease, attacking along the shores of New England in 1617, had killed off almost all coastal natives (leaving behind for the colonists, who began arriving in Plymouth in the 1620s and in Massachusetts Bay in the 1630s, a legacy of forest areas already cleared for the planting of corn—and of recipes for using that corn when harvested). Nevertheless, always on guard against the unexpected, the General Court passed an ordinance in 1636 requiring all travelers to carry guns:

Whereas many complaints have been made to this Court . . . of the great neglect of all sorts of people, of using the lawful and necessary means of their safety, especially in this

---

*Sleighs, with wooden runners, would come into use only around the turn of the eighteenth century.

time of so great danger from the Indians, it is therefore ordered that . . . no person shall travel above one mile from his dwelling-house, except in places where other houses are near together, without some arms; upon pain of twelvepence for every default.

There was no move to repeal this order even after the massive slaughter of interior-dwelling natives in the recent two-month Pequot War.

When Anne finally reached her destination, the meetinghouse at the corner of Spring and Water Streets (present-day Mt. Auburn and Dunster Streets), her ears were assaulted with reports of the court's treatment of her putative supporters. William Aspinwall, a member of the original Winthrop company of 1630, known for his fiery temper, was accused of "seditious libel" for helping to draft and then signing the Wheelwright petition. He was dismissed as Boston deputy, disfranchised, sentenced to banishment—and given till the last of March to settle his business affairs and depart. Next, forty-six-year-old John Coggeshall, wealthy silk merchant, variously elected church deacon, town selectman, and deputy to the General Court, similarly was refused permission to take his seat, though he had not actually signed the petition. Accused of strong support for the Wheelwright petition, he retorted that he knew "not one example in Scripture that a man was banished for his judgment." The court, wanting nothing to do with the promotion of freedom of speech, replied: "If he had kept his judgment to himself so as the public peace had not been troubled or endangered by it, we should have left him to himself, for we do not challenge power over men's consciences, but when seditious speeches and practices discover such a corrupt conscience, it is our duty to use authority to reform both." He was disfranchised "with admonition no more to occasion any disturbance of the public peace, either by speech or otherwise, upon pain of banishment and further censure."

Boston's third deputy, thirty-nine-year-old William Coddington, was allowed to take his seat. He had not signed the petition, but at this meeting of the court he made two unsuccessful motions to rescind the censure against Wheelwright and to revoke the alien exclusion law. Maybe his strong credentials saved him: He had served as assistant and colony treasurer as well as deputy from Boston, had been a founder of the colony with John Winthrop in 1630, and was the wealthiest man in the colony and so a fountain of finance.

In place of Aspinwall and Coggeshall, William Colburn, Boston assessor and selectman, and John Oliver were chosen as Boston's deputies. But on further examination, the name of twenty-two-year-old Oliver, a surveyor who had arrived in 1630 and been admitted as freeman in 1634, was found on the petition and so he too was rejected. Boston's representation was effectively reduced from three deputies to two, with no further attempt to find a replacement.

An even stormier session followed the next day. John Wheelwright, Anne's brother-in-law and focus of all the strife over the petition, was sentenced to disfranchisement and banishment. His threat to appeal to the King for commutation of his sentence was turned back, the court maintaining that under the Massachusetts charter, still in effect, the colony had the right to hear and determine all cases locally. Finally, Wheelwright yielded, agreeing to depart within fourteen days. Though it was wintry, he went north to New Hampshire, rather than subject himself to house arrest till spring.

Now in the court meetinghouse waiting for her own fate to be sealed, Anne watched as John Winthrop relentlessly proceeded to close in on her. Like a king of old, stripping offenders of their knighthood, he disfranchised several of her best friends and supporters. Heading this particular segment was Edward Hutchinson, Sr., Anne's brother-in-law, who had aroused the enmity of John Winthrop by insulting him personally and threatening his beloved colony. At the time of the May election, Edward Hutchinson was one of the sergeants refusing to attend John Winthrop, the newly elected governor, though with great pomp and ceremony he had attended defeated governor Henry Vane at all public occasions. Henry Vane, of course, had been the most powerful Hutchinsonian in the select inner circle of Massachusetts government. Likewise, another man whom John Winthrop pointedly labeled as "one of the sergeants of Boston" was called to defend himself. He was William Baulston, Boston's innkeeper, also a town selectman and assessor.

Neither man accepted the accusation of disloyalty meekly. Hutchinson exploded scornfully that if they took away his estate, they must keep his wife and children. Immediately, he was slapped into prison to spend the night reconsidering. And Baulston protested that if the Wheelwright petition had been presented "in any other place in the world there would have been no fault found with it." With feelings sinking into foreboding, Anne saw for herself the extra punishment meted out to these two men. Of all those brought before the court, only her brother-in-law was jailed. And only he and Baulston were fined in addition to being stripped of office and disfranchised. Worse still, Edward Hutchinson was fined twice as much as William Baulston, forty pounds as opposed to twenty. After one night without sleep in the unlighted, freezing cold local jail, Edward Hutchinson decided to apologize to the court for his outburst and so was released.

Four others were dismissed peremptorily by John Winthrop in his aristocrat manqué fashion as "very apt to meddle in public affairs beyond [their] calling and skill." They were Thomas Marshall, about forty, the Boston-Charlestown ferryman and fence overseer; William Dynely, around thirty, a barber-surgeon, about whom a member of the opposition quipped bitterly that "so soon as any were set down in his chair, he would commonly be cutting of their hair and the truth together"; William Dyer, the milliner and husband of Mary whose recent grotesque stillbirth and near-death still haunted Anne; and Richard Gridley, thirty-six, brickmaker and fence overseer, for whom John Winthrop reserved his greatest scorn, calling him "an honest poor man . . . of mean condition and weak parts." All were disfranchised.

Ironically, the court could not accuse Anne of signing the Wheelwright petition. Nor could they disfranchise her.

But the colonial fathers found other ways to deal with Anne, whom John Winthrop labeled "the head of all this faction (Dux Foemina Facti)* a woman who had been the breeder and nourisher of all these distempers." Determined to isolate her by removing her supporters from church and government, the authorities, with John

---

*Derisively, John Winthrop here quoted the Latin poet Virgil's first-century B.C. phrase meaning "a woman as leader of the action." This was the same phrase used exultantly to describe Queen Elizabeth back in 1588, when her navy defeated the Spanish Armada.

Winthrop in the lead, had executed a series of extreme measures over the past six months: Two separate elections—instead of the designated single annual election—were called, in order that not one of the nine magistrates (governor, deputy governor, and seven assistants acting as a governor's council) would be sympathetic to her ideas or willing to follow her leadership; Boston's deputies in the General Court (the colonial legislature) were reduced from three to two (in fact, just before Anne Hutchinson was scheduled to appear as defendant, John Oliver of Boston had been denied permission to take his place as elected deputy); and twenty-one of the thirty-one deputies representing the fourteen towns of the colony were newly elected and put on notice to follow the governor's lead if they wished to retain their seats. And the alien exclusion law, enacted to bar entry of all immigrants even suspected of sympathy with Anne, took effect just about the time of the November General Court and resulted in the banishment of Anne's brother-in-law Samuel Hutchinson and others whom "the governor thought not fit to allow . . . to sit down among us." (The law had provided that unwanted immigrants must leave the colony within three weeks of their landing. However, the Hutchinsonian immigrants, against whom the law was specifically aimed, were given four months from their arrival in mid-July, on grounds that they could not have known about the law before their departure from England.)

The Reverend Thomas Weld, Governor Winthrop's like-minded colleague, reflected the frantic fear felt about Anne Hutchinson and her followers: "What an height they were grown into in a short time; and what a spirit of pride, insolency, contempt of authority, division, sedition they were acted by. It was a wonder of mercy that they had not set our commonwealth and churches on a fire and consumed us all therein."

As for Anne, their leader, she was "audaciously insolent, and high-flown in spirit and speech," the Reverend Mr. Weld concluded. At the civil court hearing, he would be one of her specially invited ministerial inquisitors.

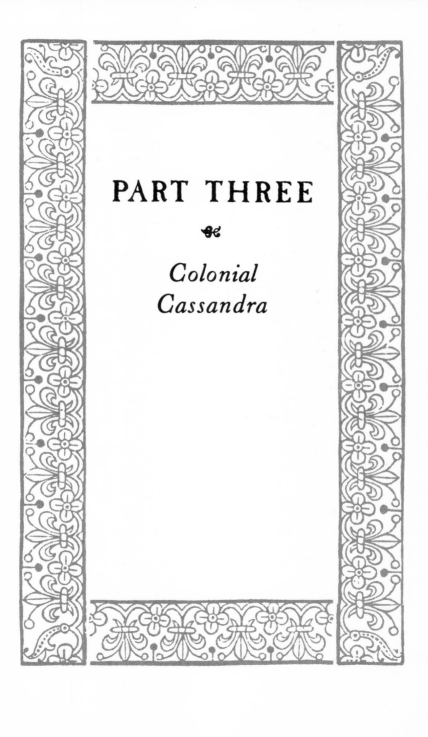

PART THREE

❦

*Colonial
Cassandra*

II

"NOR FITTING FOR
YOUR SEX"

Unexpectedly, the frenzied activities of John Winthrop and his allies boomeranged. Alone Anne certainly was—but in the limelight. On center stage, every eye and ear riveted on her, she confronted her forty-nine inquisitors, possessing among themselves the highest concentration of wealth, power, and brains in the entire colony. Altogether there were nine magistrates and thirty-one deputies—in effect exercising the executive, legislative, and judicial functions of government—as well as eight ministers and one church elder. In addition, large numbers of the public had squeezed themselves into every bit of empty space in the barn-like, square-shaped meeting house (each side measuring just under forty feet).

Forced to remain standing, Anne faced her inquisitors seated in long rows of backless wooden benches—except for John Winthrop who, as governor, chief judge, and prosecutor, was accorded a separate desk, his own chair complete with cushion, and some extra breathing space. The longer Anne stood, always in strong focus, the more her judges seemed to dissolve into a blur of black hats perched on layer after layer of heavy clothing, topped by a greatcoat and thick gloves. The additional clothes were worn in a largely vain attempt to ward off the frigid winds blowing through the cracks in the mud-plaster walls of the flimsily constructed building. Wood-burning stoves and fireplaces for public buildings were a luxury for the distant future, and so there was absolutely no heat and very little light in the cavernous church-meetinghouse.

Even wearing heavy, asexual outer clothing, the lonely defendant was instantly recognizable as a woman. Whereas her inquisitors all had beards, ranging from scrubby to elegant, and shoulder-length hair falling beneath their hats, Anne's long hair was completely hidden under her bonnet, an occasional strand escaping onto her forehead in moments of head-shaking excitement. ("If a woman have long hair, it is a glory to her . . . ," the Bible decreed, I Corinthians 11:15. So be it, Western society agreed, but commanded that woman's hair, so seductive to man, so tempting to the Devil, be covered completely at all times, day, evening, and night.)*

Whenever the court finally decided to call the hearing to an end, Anne faced the loss of personal freedom through prison and banishment. But these proceedings were set up as a legislative hearing, with the ministers sitting in to act as advisors and chief witnesses for the prosecution. Therefore, she was allowed no lawyer to help in her defense. Nor would her husband of twenty-five years, William Hutchinson, to whom she was devoted—and vice versa—be allowed to testify in her behalf.†

Quite inadvertently, the colonial fathers, aiming to silence Anne then and there, instead promoted her to immortality by letting her address posterity in her own words. Governor Winthrop recorded his personal account of the hearing, as did a mysteriously anonymous scribe who, moderately sympathetic to Anne, narrated everything as she herself might have set it down.

Without greeting or smile—they were, after all, neighbors who

---

*Jewelry, which might have helped set Anne apart as a woman, was frowned upon by Puritans, who forbade even the wearing of a wedding ring.

†For elaboration of seventeenth-century refusal to allow testimony by husband or wife, whether in favor of or in opposition to a spouse, see the classic *Law of Evidence* by John H. Wigmore, Sec. 103.

had lived across the street from each other for almost three years—Governor Winthrop opened the hearing, letting loose against Anne all his pent-up grievances, accusations, and emotions:

Mrs. Hutchinson, you are called here as one of those that have troubled the peace of the commonwealth and the churches here; you are known to be a woman that hath had a great share in the promoting and divulging of those opinions that are causes of this trouble, and to be nearly joined not only in affinity and affections with some of those the court had taken notice of and passed censure upon, but you have spoken divers things as we have been informed very prejudicial to the honour of the churches and ministers thereof, and you have maintained a meeting and an assembly in your house that hath been condemned by the general assembly as a thing not tolerable nor comely in the sight of God nor fitting for your sex, and notwithstanding that was cried down you have continued the same. Therefore, we have thought good to send for you to understand how things are, that if you be in an erroneous way we may reduce you so you may become a profitable member here among us; otherwise if you be obstinate in your course that then the court may take such course that you may trouble us no further.

Hardly pausing to catch his breath, the governor—fully aware that as a woman Anne was not allowed to sign the Wheelwright petition—interjected a hypothesis he hoped would serve to prove her criminal involvement: "I would entreat you to express whether you do not assent and hold in practice to those opinions and factions that have been handled in court already, that is to say, whether you do not justify Mr. Wheelwright's sermon and the petition."

Anne was incensed by the governor's denunciation of her behavior as "nor fitting for your sex" and his threat that "we may reduce you so that you may become a profitable member among us." If ever she agreed to abide by the governor's highly favored Covenant of Works, she was certain that, as a woman, she would—in the governor's own discouragingly apt phrase—be "reduced" to consummate outsider, completely subject to an all-male church and state, which would constantly interfere with the private dialogue between her conscience and God. Only under the Covenant of Grace could she expect to function as a worthy, individual, human being.

Refusing to dignify the governor's charges with any show of respect, she retorted defiantly: "I am called here to answer before you, but I hear no things laid to my charge."

For the next few minutes, spectators were treated to an angry exchange between the highest officer of their colony and the woman he had hauled into court:

GOV.   I have told you some already and more I can tell you.

MRS. H.   Name one, sir.

GOV.   Have I not named some already?

MRS. H.   What have I said or done?

GOV.   Why for your doings, this you did harbour and countenance those that are parties to this faction that you have heard of.

MRS. H.   That's matter of conscience, sir.

The governor dropped this argument; Anne Hutchinson had fought him to a draw.

Still, he felt himself under political obligation and personal pressure to vanquish this woman. Certainly, she was the single worst threat to the continued existence of the colony to which he had single-mindedly devoted his life, family, and fortune for the better part of a decade.

The problem was that their points of view and aims were diametrically opposed and neither saw any way of making these compatible. As far as the governor was concerned, he agreed absolutely with the legendary Aesop who more than two thousand years before had made the pronouncement that in unity there is strength. In direct contrast, Anne was inspired by the still-uncompleted Renaissance to insist that in individualism lies the only hope for progress—and she emphasized her belief that individualism was androgynous. Unfortunately for Anne, the governor was in total charge and backed by the power of the entire Colonial Establishment. Anne, forced to be on the defensive, had recourse only to the power of her own words and intellect.

Under the circumstances, and with the colony sinking into chaos and endangered on all sides—by the King, native Americans, and the French and Spanish, all of whom were threatening imminent takeover—the governor was thoroughly convinced that this was the worst possible time for testing the feasibility of a middle ground. Besides, he had his own private reasons for displaying intense hostility toward Anne. The three elections he had lost for governor, in 1634, 1635, and 1636, were to opponents who had called him too lenient and wrongheaded. Returned to the highest office only in 1637, with the indispensable support of the clergy, he had an excellent opportunity to use the case before him to display his new-found toughness and superior leadership.

Consequently, the governor decided to bring forth another accusation. Anne Hutchinson had broken a pivotal law, he charged. This was the Fifth Commandment, "Honor thy father and mother," which the Puritans had deftly translated into a command to obey the rulers (fathers only) of the colony—"fathers of the commonwealth," John Winthrop called them. (In this era of no separation between church and state, on all questions of public concern, the Bible was the colonial code of laws. Religion was used to mold public opinion and the church enforced political decisions.)

But Anne defused the governor's arguments one after another until he brought this part of the dialogue to an end, snapping scornfully: "We do not mean to discourse with those of your sex but only this; you do endeavor to set forward this faction and so you do dishonor us."

Next, the governor reverted to the sensitive subject of Anne's twice-weekly meetings, insisting that she had no right to preach, even in the confines of her own home.

Here Anne decided to respond in kind. As far as she was concerned, the governor and his fellow Puritans had bent the Fifth Commandment for their own purposes. Very well, she would do the same. She returned to her perennially reconstructed paraphrase from the Bible: "I conceive there lies a clear rule in Titus, that the elder women should instruct the younger, and then I must have a time wherein I must do it."

Unmoved, the governor responded: "Suppose a man should come and say, 'Mrs. Hutchinson, I hear that you are a woman that God hath given his grace unto and you have knowledge in the word of God. I pray, instruct me a little.' Ought you not to instruct this man?"

Triumphantly, Anne taunted the governor: "I think I may. Do you think it not lawful for me to teach men and why do you call me to teach the court?"

The governor retorted: "We do not call you to teach the court but to lay open yourself."

Certain that female participation of the kind proposed by Anne would destroy social and political stability, the governor elaborated, "You have a plain rule against it: I permit not a woman to teach." For his cohorts, all thoroughly schooled in the Bible, the governor's New Testament paraphrase proved his point completely, casting Anne as a spoiler, sacrilegiously defying the Scriptures. From Anne's point of view, however, the full passage was a painful example of why she rejected strict, "legalist" reading of the Bible:

> But I suffer not a woman to teach, nor to usurp authority over the man, but to be in silence.
> For Adam was first formed, then Eve.
> And Adam was not deceived, but the woman being deceived was in the transgression.

> [I Timothy 2:12-14]

So far, not one of the other forty-eight inquisitors had spoken a single word. Not the two Anne counted on for support, Boston deputies William Coddington and William Colburn, her husband William's business colleagues and her own good friends. Not her old hero, the Reverend John Cotton, who over the past few months had sometimes come to her aid, and had sometimes sided with her opposition. And certainly not any of the members of the governor's huge clique of magistrates, deputies, and ministers. Anne and the governor continued their deadly duel, each aiming for public burial of the other's ideas:

MRS. H. I desire that you would then set me down a rule by which I may put them away that come unto me and so have peace in so doing.

GOV. You must show your rule to receive them.

MRS. H. I have done it.

GOV. I deny it because I have brought more arguments than you have.

(This childlike reliance on quantity on the part of the governor is omitted from his own written record of the proceedings, but included in the account by Anne's anonymous sympathizer.)

Now, for the first time in several hours, another voice was heard. Realizing that the governor had backed himself into a corner, Assistant John Endecott of Salem—the forty-eight-year-old hothead best remembered for mutilating the King's flag and for carrying his crusade for veiled women to Boston, back in 1634—tried coming to John Winthrop's aid, hurling this challenge at Anne Hutchinson: "You say there are some rules unto you. I think there is a contradiction in your own words. What rule for your practice do you bring, only a custom in Boston."

Firmly, Anne reiterated her reliance on Titus.

Once again, the governor took over, launching into a long speech attacking Anne for fomenting religious disharmony and breeding political dissension. Toward the end, apparently worrying that he was getting nowhere, he unleashed a new accusation—to demonstrate that Anne had tempted women to go far beyond their God-given calling of wife, mother, and family mainstay: "Your ministry is public. . . . It is your exercise which draws [so many to your meetings], and by occasion thereof, many families are neglected, and much time lost, and a great damage come to the commonwealth which we that are betrusted with, as the Fathers of the Commonwealth, are not to suffer."

Anne denied the accusation totally, the governor reaffirmed it categorically, thundering: "We are your judges, and not you ours, and we must compel you to it."

Obviously, however, logic, obloquy, and threat—whether used singly or in combination—had not yet succeeded in subduing or silencing Anne. So the governor resorted to a new tactic, using praise to cajole her into returning to her proper place in society: "Yes, you are the woman of most note, and of best abilities, and if some others take upon them the like, it is by your teaching and example, but you show not in all this by what authority you take upon you to be such a public instructor."

Anne's reaction stunned the governor. Suddenly, she looked ill, on the verge of collapse. For the first time, John Winthrop came close to extending sympathy; he had seen his own wife, Margaret, suffer, without warning, the mysterious discomforts of women in their mid-forties (Anne Hutchinson and Margaret Winthrop were both now forty-six). "After she had stood a short time [sic]," he noted in his private record of the proceedings, "the Court gave her leave to sit down for her countenance discovered some bodily infirmity."*

After a chair was brought for Anne, thirty-four-year-old Simon Bradstreet of Andover, who had served as secretary and assistant of the colony ever since his arrival with John Winthrop in 1630, entered the colloquy. Seated prominently on the front bench with the other six assistants, he gave Anne the first hint of support and encouragement she had had all day: "I am not against all women's meetings but do think them to be lawful."

Simon Bradstreet, of course, was none other than the husband of Anne Dudley Bradstreet, America's first poet, who in the preface to her work, which was finally published in 1650, showed herself in perfect agreement with—perhaps even influenced by—Anne's promotion of female talent:

> I am obnoxious to each carping tongue
> Who says my hand a needle better fits,
> A poet's pen all scorn I should thus wrong,

---

*In the inhumanly cold courtroom, Anne was forced to stand for hours while her inquisitors remained seated. Even so, the respected historian of the Hutchinsonian controversy, Charles F. Adams, wrote in 1903 that the colonial authorities "loved controversy; but this was no case for controversy. God's kingdom was threatened from within. . . . So they sternly girded themselves for the fray: and opposed to them was one woman only; but her tongue was as a sword, *and she had her sex for a shield*." (Italics added.)

For such despite they cast on female wits:
If what I do prove well, it won't advance,
They'll say it's stol'n, or else it was by chance.

However, from Anne Bradstreet's father, Deputy Governor
Thomas Dudley—at sixty-one he was the oldest of the judges—
Anne Hutchinson got little sympathy and no support. Like John
Winthrop, he had never had much use for Anne's preaching, though
on almost every other issue he had disagreed publicly and
vehemently with the governor, and the two had been consummate
public rivals. Now, further mellowed by the fact that he and the
governor shared grandchildren (their children Mary Winthrop and
Samuel Dudley had married in 1633), he tried coming to
Winthrop's aid, initiating some murky theological disputation. In
this, he was joined by three others: the always outspoken John
Endecott; thirty-eight-year-old Rev. Hugh Peter of Salem, first to
take advantage of the General Court's invitation to ministers to sit
in on the hearing and to question Anne whenever the spirit moved
them; and John Wilson, pastor of Boston, determined to avenge
himself for Anne's long series of insults and the unsuccessful attempt
to censure him.

Five more ministers plunged in, all graduates of Cambridge
University and highly respected members of the colonial elite. One
was forty-four-year-old George Phillips of Watertown, who set a
record of sorts, reading the Bible from beginning to end six times
every year, sometimes in the original Hebrew, sometimes in Greek.
In fact, his daily routine epitomized the role of the Bible in the intellectual life of the colony. Excitedly, he told his family "that every
time he read the Bible he observed or collected something which he
never did before." Another minister was forty-two-year-old Thomas
Weld of Roxbury, the governor's trusted friend and staunch supporter. Also from Roxbury was thirty-three-year-old John Eliot,
studious, vigorous, portly, and loved by both the Roxbury congregation and the Natick Indians with and for whom he worked
closely. Still another member of this particular grouping was thirty-
eight-year-old Zechariah Symmes, Anne's hostile fellow voyager
and minister of Charlestown. And finally, there was the thirty-two-

year-old Rev. Thomas Shepard of Newtown, who found himself in a painful position. He was by no means unsympathetic to Anne Hutchinson; in his memoirs, he recalled that hearing of Familism as a twenty-year-old student, he had questioned "whether that glorious estate of perfection might not be the truth." But now he was a member of the Colonial Establishment—and, more uncomfortably still, as pastor of the very meetinghouse in which the court had convened, he was duty bound to produce harmony in Newtown, contrasting conspicuously with the fractiousness displayed in Boston. So he tried his hand at peacemaking: "I am loathe to speak in this assembly concerning the gentlewoman in question," he said, adding, "for what concerns the gentlewoman I do not well remember every particular." Then, referring to Anne's castigating all colonial ministers except John Cotton and John Wheelwright as preachers of the outmoded Covenant of Works, he proposed a face-saving way out for both sides: "I desire to speak this word. It may be but a slip of her tongue, and I hope she will be sorry for it, and then we shall be glad of it."

Thomas Shepard got the glimmerings of support from his fellow minister, the similarly youthful John Eliot who tried giving the court a lesson in cutting short the proceedings: "I am loathe to spend time. Therefore, I shall consent to what hath been said."

But the other ministers present refused to take notice. They were determined to restore the prestige of their ministry, so badly battered by this woman. Hunted and persecuted by the government in England, and forced to flee pleasant homes and good livings there, they intended to be in full charge of their flocks in the pristine though primitive New England wilderness. Allowing a parishioner—a woman—to talk back to any one of them was the last thing they intended to allow.

Consequently, back and forth they went, the Covenant of Works versus the Covenant of Grace; ministers as well as colonial officials versus one woman, Anne Hutchinson. But even bringing in so much heavy ministerial artillery did little to change the debate results. Anne had so far defended her position very clearly, leading the governor to announce: "Mrs. Hutchinson, the court you see hath labored to bring you to acknowledge the error of your way so that you might be reduced. The time now grows late. We shall therefore give you a little more time to consider of it, and therefore desire that you attend the court again in the morning."

Anne had less than twelve hours to pore over her notes on everything she had said and done over the past three years, review the proceedings of this day,* prepare for the next day's questions— and get some sleep.

---

*It is more than likely that Anne's anonymous sympathizer, having taken notes, lent them to her for overnight study.

12

"SAY NO MORE"

The following morning, Governor Winthrop resumed proceedings, opening with the summary pronouncement that at the hearing the day before, "here was sufficient proof made of that of which [Mrs. Hutchinson] was accused."

Unimpressed, Anne responded by lashing out at the governor's chief Boston ally, pastor John Wilson. Overnight, she had studied the notes that "Mr. Wilson did then write" at the time of her conference with the ministers at John Cotton's home the previous December, "and," she charged, "I find things not to be as hath been alleged. Therefore," she demanded, "if [the ministers] accuse me, I desire it may be upon oath."

Manfully, John Winthrop retorted that only the court could make a decision about requiring oaths before testimony, and furthermore, this was not a case before a jury. Then he laid down a challenge: "Let those that are not satisfied in the court speak." To his surprise, several in the crowd of spectators shouted out, "We are not satisfied." Also, John Coggeshall—Anne's good friend and neighbor, stripped of office as deputy for Boston, but allowed to remain at the hearing as witness for her—stood up to urge that the ministers be put under oath.

Once again, impetuous old John Endecott, assistant from Salem, tried coming to the governor's aid, frenziedly accusing Coggeshall of "further casting dirt upon the faces of the judges." To restore calm, and to put the hearing back on track, the governor bypassed the oath-taking issue for the moment. That seemed the best way to achieve his stated goal: to "reduce" Anne Hutchinson to a "profitable member" of the colony.

Anne Hutchinson "walked by such a rule as cannot stand with the peace of any state," the governor charged, convinced that she was an anarchist in the employ of Satan. Somehow she must be made to recant humbly, and publicly, her arrogant pronouncement—at that private December conference with the ministers—that only John Cotton and John Wheelwright preached the Covenant of Grace, which God had revealed to her directly as the only true covenant. Her revelations, the governor contended, "if they be allowed in one thing must be admitted a rule in all things, for they being above reason and Scripture, they are not subject to control."

So far, Anne had been an unyielding, unexpectedly effective adversary. Deciding that conciliation might be the best tactic, the governor allowed her to call her own witnesses. First came John Coggeshall, already rebuffed once, but willing to try again. "I dare say she did not say all that which they lay against her," he asserted.

"How dare you look into the court to say such a word," exclaimed Rev. Hugh Peter of Salem, taking it on himself to put the witness in his place.

"Mr. Peter takes upon him to forbid me, I shall be silent," Anne's first witness murmured, losing courage.

John Coggeshall was not heard from again at this fateful hearing.

Another witness, Thomas Leverett, a ruling elder of the church in new Boston and John Cotton's protector and disciple in the church at old Boston, said almost nothing, but said it wordily. No one reacted either way.

At this point, in a show of symbolic, though silent, support, the third defense witness, John Cotton himself, "came and sat down by Mrs. Hutchinson." When John Winthrop asked him to recall everything he could remember about the December conference between the ministers and Anne Hutchinson, he first blurted out a disclaimer: "I did not think I should be called to bear witness in this cause and therefore did not labor to call to remembrance what was done." Then he stammered out a long answer, expressing regret that rumor had spread throughout the colony "that she had spoken some condemning words of the ministry, and . . . sorry I was that any comparison should be between me and my brethren, and uncomfortable it was." He concluded: "If you put me in mind of anything I shall speak it."

Gently, John Winthrop prodded: "You say you do not remember, but can you say she did not speak so." Before the minister could respond, Rev. Hugh Peter jumped in, trying to draw an admission that Anne Hutchinson had indeed said that all ministers except John Cotton preached a Covenant of Works. But Cotton refused to nudge his memory.

Getting nowhere, John Winthrop, "weary of the clamor and so that all mouths be stopped," partially consented to Anne's demand and allowed three, who volunteered, to take an oath. Two ministers from Roxbury, Thomas Weld and John Eliot, volunteered to be officially sworn, as did Dorchester Assistant Israel Stoughton, leader of the 160 men Massachusetts had sent to fight the recent Pequot War.

Anne now made a long speech, riveting the courtroom with her story of the time "the Lord did reveal himself to me, sitting upon a throne of justice, and all the world appearing before him, and though I must come to New England, yet I must not fear nor be dismayed." Buttressing her words with a quote from Isaiah, she elaborated these divine directions: "The Lord spake this to me with a strong hand, and instructed me that I should not walk in the way of this people."

Desperate to subdue this woman who claimed leadership on the basis of direct communication with God, John Winthrop "demanded how she did know it was God that did reveal these things to her, and not Satan."

Her answer: "How did Abraham know that it was the voice of God when he commanded him to sacrifice his son, being a breach of the Sixth Commandment." ("Thou shalt not kill.") Anne here drew on personal feelings as mother of twelve living children, including six sons.

Clumsily, Deputy Governor Thomas Dudley, trying to come to the governor's aid, played into Anne's hands, responding that Abraham knew "by an immediate voice" that he was being commanded by God to sacrifice Isaac.

Triumphantly, Anne echoed: "So to me by an immediate revelation."

Then, furious that her judges continually took it upon themselves to behave in ways out of bounds to her because she was a woman—for example, throughout his political career in New England, John Winthrop reminded his constituents that his power in office was authorized directly by God—Anne felt called on to warn the court:

> You have no power over my body, neither can you do me any harm. . . . No further do I esteem of any mortal man. . . . I fear none but the great Jehovah, which hath foretold me of these things, and I do verily believe that he will deliver me out of your hands. . . . Therefore, take heed how you proceed against me; for I know that for this you go about to do to me, God will ruin you and your posterity, and this whole state.

Needing intellectual reinforcement, John Winthrop appealed to John Cotton "to deliver his judgment about Mistress Hutchinson, her revelations."

John Cotton was on the spot. But still he remained on Anne's side—and by his words in public court gave a good inkling as to how he must have acted and spoken to Anne in both old and New England:

> Though the word revelation be rare in common speech and we make it uncouth in our ordinary expressions, yet notwithstanding, being understood in the scripture sense I think they are not only lawful but such as Christians may receive and God bear witness to it in his word. . . .
> *That she may have some special providence of God to help her is a thing that I cannot bear witness against.* (Emphasis added.)

New Englanders revered John Cotton. For a long time there was even a rumor that they had named their leading town Boston in order to entice him to immigrate, and once here, to feel completely at home. But they feared Anne Hutchinson even more than they adored their most eminent minister. The strong majority here at the meetinghouse were certain, beyond any doubt, that they had to condemn Anne—but first they had somehow to bring John Cotton into line. Deputy Governor Dudley began badgering John Cotton, relentlessly asking the same question over and over again in different words: "I desire Mr. Cotton to tell us whether you do approve of Mrs. Hutchinson's revelations as she hath laid them down." And again: "Do you believe that her revelations are true?" And again: "Good Sir, I do ask whether this revelation be of God or not."

Unperturbed, and with more sympathy and understanding than anyone had shown Anne Hutchinson up to this point, Cotton at length responded with a question of his own: "I should desire to know whether the sentence of the court will bring her to any calamity, and then I would know of her whether she expects to be delivered from that calamity by a miracle or a providence of God."

Anne answered directly: "By a providence of God, I say I expect to be delivered from some calamity that shall come to me."

For the court, John Winthrop's response was to rely on this same "providence of God"—and at the same time, to proclaim victory: "The case is altered and will not stand with us now, but I see a marvellous providence of God to bring things to this pass that they are. . . . Now the mercy of God by a providence hath answered our desires and made her to lay open herself and the ground of all these disturbances to be by revelations."

Amid the chorus of agreement from the judges, and silence from Anne and her supporters, the unrelieved pressure on Cotton to join the majority continued:

MR. ENDECOTT: I speak in reference to Mr. Cotton. I am tender of you, Sir. . . . Mrs. Hutchinson hath spoken of her revelations as you have heard. . . . Do you witness for her or against her?

MR. COTTON: This is that I said, Sir, and my answer is plain. If she doth look for deliverance from the hand of God by his providence, and the revelation be in a word or according to a word, that I cannot deny.

At this, John Endecott, always easily swayed by the last man to have spoken to him averred: "You give me satisfaction."

But Deputy Governor Dudley roared: "No, no, he gives me none at all." And when Cotton tried to save himself by equivocation, Dudley expostulated: "Sir, you weary me and do not satisfy me," adding irritably, "I . . . am sorry that Mr. Cotton should stand to justify her."

Fanatic Hugh Peter who, along with his fellow minister Thomas Weld of Roxbury, had been one of the most active promoters of Anne Hutchinson's prosecution, concurred: "I can say the same . . . and I think that is very disputable which our brother Cotton hath spoken."

John Cotton remained firm.

Obviously, the Devil was at work. Several members of the court decided that some good old-fashioned scare tactics were in order, the kind the Puritans had seen firsthand while they were growing up in England. Forty-three-year-old Increase Nowell of Charlestown, an assistant since the founding of the colony in 1630, and currently serving as secretary for Massachusetts, had previously proclaimed Anne's revelations "a devilish delusion." Deputy Governor Dudley now had a similar thought: "I am fully persuaded that Mrs. Hutchinson is deluded by the Devil, because the spirit of God speaks the truth in all his servants."

John Cotton refused to change his position, leading John Winthrop to turn full attention back to Anne Hutchinson, declaring: "Mr. Cotton is not called to answer to anything but we are to deal with the party now standing before us." The governor seemed on the verge of pronouncing censure, when Anne Hutchinson's friend William Coddington interrupted with the futuristic complaint that the court was allowing no freedom of speech or due process of law:

Sir, another thing you lay to her charge is her speech to the [ministers]. Now I do not see any clear witness against her, and you know it is a rule of the court that no man may be a judge and an accuser too. . . . I do not for my own part see any equity in the court in all your proceedings. Here is no law of God that she hath broken nor any law of the country that she broke and therefore deserves no censure.

Changing the subject completely, the aristocratic twenty-six-year-old Roger Harlaakenden spoke out for the first time, commenting that if only Anne had behaved herself as women are supposed to, she would not be facing her present difficulties, and could even hold small meetings if she chose.

So many serious subjects were swirling around the courtroom that a creature complaint roused absolutely no reaction. "We shall all be sick with fasting," whined the highly disciplined sixty-one-year-old deputy governor, cold, hungry, and restless after hours on a hard bench in the crude meetinghouse.

Without even a pause for acknowledgment, the hearing went right on. Coddington continued to demand civil liberties. Several of the ministers took out their personal pique at being compared adversely with John Cotton. And Cotton, chastened, remained silent. John Winthrop had been quiet for a long time, but in his private record of the proceedings let posterity in on the thoughts rushing through his mind as he prepared to pronounce judgment on Anne Hutchinson—in his dual role as her chief prosecutor and judge: "See the impudent boldness of a proud dame, that Attila-like makes havoc of all that stand in the way of her ambitious spirit; she had boasted before that her opinions must prevail, neither could she endure a stop in her way. . . . The Court did clearly discern where the fountain was of all our distempers."

At this point in his personal record, John Winthrop labeled the activities of Anne and her disciples a terrifying replica of the Anabaptist uprising at Munster, 1534-36—exactly one hundred years before Anne, in his view, embarked on her Massachusetts mission of anarchy, chaos, and destruction. He warned: "The tragedy of Munster . . . gave just occasion to fear the danger we were in . . . so as the like hath not been known in former ages that ever so many wise, sober, and well-grounded Christians should so suddenly be seduced by the means of a woman, to stick so fast to her, even in some things wherein the whole current of Scripture goeth against her."

Unfortunately for Anne, she would hear the Anabaptist "tragedy of Munster" used over and over as justification for silencing her and all Hutchinsonians. The Anabaptists were the left wing of the early-sixteenth-century Reformation, who practiced adult rebaptism of true believers, rejected the idea that infants were born in Original Sin, insisted on separation of the church (the community of the redeemed) and the state (the instrument used to punish sinners), and refused to take up arms, even for a "just war." (The refusal of Anne's Boston followers to rally to the support of the Pequot War was, of course, considered an ominous similarity by the governor and his colleagues.) They considered women believers the equals of men. Striving to attain the good life for good men and women, they forced civil and religious officials to renounce all claim to control of individuals who were true believers. Unhappily, hostile reports of these idealistic, anarchistic Anabaptists—virtually the only information available to John Winthrop and his cohorts—portrayed the Munster rebels as monsters intent mainly on institutionalizing polygamy, easy divorce, and sexual promiscuity.

In 1534, Protestants and Catholics had dropped their usual hostility to each other to join in strong measures against Anabaptists rebelling at Munster. In response, radical Anabaptists took over completely, forcing opponents to flee, so that the population dwindled to about 1700 men, 6800 women, and several thousand children. Following a year of terrorism and turmoil, the Roman bishop formerly in control regained power in Munster, and by 1536 put all Anabaptist leaders to death, burning the men and burying the women alive. Due to the population ratio then obtaining at Munster, the majority of these martyrs were female.

Among other things, this was a strong object lesson to New England Puritan authorities of the seventeenth century that women must be kept out of the political-religious arena completely.

Roger Clap, who arrived in 1630 with the Winthrop fleet and who witnessed the trials of Anne Hutchinson, wrote an account for his four surviving sons and two surviving daughters to warn them: "Dear Children, beware of false teachers, though they come unto you in sheep's clothing as some of the Anabaptists do. . . . One of them says . . . 'that the miseries and death that came by Adam's fall extendeth not unto all eternity.' " Under these circumstances, Anne probably should have been grateful that she was neither tortured nor directly put to death.

About to pronounce sentence on Anne Hutchinson, Governor Winthrop allowed Rev. Hugh Peter of Salem and Assistant Israel Stoughton of Dorchester to make final statements:

> MR. PETER: I profess I thought Mr. Cotton would never have taken her part.
>
> MR. STOUGHTON: I say now this testimony doth convince me in the thing, and I am fully satisfied the words were pernicious, and the frame of her spirit doth hold forth the same.

With the stage thus set, Governor Winthrop summed up the proceedings and asked for a vote:

> The court hath already declared themselves satisfied . . . concerning the troublesomeness of her spirit and the danger of her course amongst us, which is not to be suffered. Therefore, if it be the mind of the court that Mrs. Hutchinson for these things that appear before us is unfit for our society, and if it be the mind of the court that she shall be banished out of our liberties and imprisoned till she be sent away let them hold up their hands.

Only William Coddington and William Colburn of Boston voted against the sentence of banishment and imprisonment. Deputy William Jennison of Watertown announced that he had decided not to vote one way or the other. And John Cotton, lacking the stomach to be a minority of one among his fellow ministers, abandoned Anne to her fate and voted with the majority.

Isolated and abandoned though she was, Anne fought spiritedly to the very end. The governor, exhilarated by his successful struggle to save the colony, lost his usual self-control. Emulating the despotic English kings whom everyone in court had fled, he now intoned: "Mrs. Hutchinson, the sentence of the court you hear is that you are banished from out of our jurisdiction as being a woman not fit for our society, and are to be imprisoned till the court shall send you away."

Anne protested: "I desire to know wherefore I am banished."

The governor thundered: "Say no more, the court knows wherefore and is satisfied."

Significantly, the sentence, as officially recorded, is carefully detailed (except for the omission of Anne's own first name):

> Mrs. _____ Hutchinson (the wife of Mr. William Hutchinson), being convented for traducing the ministers and their ministry in this country, she declared voluntarily her revelations for her ground, and that she should be delivered and the court ruined, with their posterity, and thereupon was banished, and the meanwhile was committed to Mr. Joseph Weld until the Court shall dispose of her.

Following Anne's hearing that Wednesday, November 8, 1637, the famous Pequot War soldier Captain John Underhill was stripped of all office and disfranchised for signing the Wheelwright petition. He was a married man whose sensationally reported dalliances with much younger girls gave proof for those who were digging for such evidence that Anne's followers were a bunch of libertines.

But beating the anti-Hutchinsonians at what they did best—reading the Bible "legalistically"—he wrote very tenderly and respectfully of his wife in his own memoir, *Newes from America*, and told the reader "instance Abraham" (Sarah, the barren wife of the patriarch Abraham, suggested that he conceive a child by her maid Hagar, Genesis 16). In an era when women produced children every eighteen to twenty-four months, Helena Underhill gave birth to only two children, born six years apart: Elizabeth, baptized February 14, 1636, and John, Jr., baptized April 24, 1642.

In any case, following the punishment and disfranchisement of Captain Underhill, the court finally adjourned—until the following Wednesday, when Anne's activities produced an unusual sequel: the placing of the college, which the General Court had already voted to establish, in Newtown (renamed Cambridge as of May 2, 1638) rather than in Boston. "The college is ordered to be at Newtown," read the official record, and in his memoirs Rev. Thomas Shepard of Newtown explained:

> The Lord having delivered the country from war with Indians and Familists (who arose and fell together), he was pleased to direct the heart of the magistrates (then keeping Court or-

dinarily in our town, because of these stirs at Boston) to think
of erecting a school or college, and that speedily, to be a nursery
of knowledge in these deserts, and supply for posterity. And
because this town, then called Newtown, was, through God's
great care and goodness, kept spotless from the contagion of the
opinions, therefore, at the desire of some of our town, the
deputies of the Court, . . . for that and sundry other reasons,
determined to erect the college here. . . . The Lord put it into
the heart of one Mr. Harvard, who died worth £1600, to give
half his estate to the erecting of the School.

Reinforcing the contention that the heresies of Anne Hutchinson
and her followers prompted the establishment of Harvard at Cambridge rather than at Boston, Edward Johnson, New England's
early eyewitness historian—the very title of his book reflected un-
bridled ebullience: *The Wonder-Working Providence of Sions
Savior in New England*—wrote a long, convoluted poem around the
idea that the inhabitants of Newtown-Cambridge, "they no antinomians are."*

Twelve days after sentencing Anne Hutchinson, the General
Court carried out a virtual coup d'état against the Hutchinsonians,
ordering them, on Monday, November 20, to surrender their guns,
powder, and ammunition at the house of Captain Robert Keayne (a
wealthy Boston merchant who nonetheless had kept himself free of
the taint of Hutchinsonianism, perhaps because his wife, Anne, was
the sister of Elizabeth Wilson, wife of Anne Hutchinson's *bête
noire*, pastor John Wilson). The order, prepared in the dark, hidden rooms of secrecy and issued precipitately, with no warning,
again made ominous reference to the rebellion at Munster a hundred years before:

---

*For some mysterious reason, at the actual time of the controversy sur-
rounding her, Anne Hutchinson and her followers were denounced as
"Familists," but by the following decade, in retrospect, were labeled "Antinomians," a pejorative sixteenth-century epithet taken from the Greek,
anti (against) and *nomos* (law), i.e,, contemptuous of the law on which
society depends.

Whereas the opinions and revelations of Mr. Wheelwright and Mrs. Hutchinson have seduced and led into dangerous errors many of the people here in New England, insomuch as there is just cause of suspicion that they, as others in Germany, in former times, may, upon some revelation, make some sudden eruption upon those that differ from them in judgment, for prevention whereof it is ordered that all those whose names are underwritten shall (upon warning given or left at their dwelling houses) before the 30th day of this month of November, deliver in at Mr. Keayne's house at Boston, all such guns, pistols, swords, powder, shot, and match as they shall be owners of, or have in their custody, upon pain of ten pound for every default to be made thereof; which arms are to be kept by Mr. Keayne till this Court shall take further order therein. Also, it is ordered, upon like penalty of ten pound, that no man who is to render his arms by this order shall buy or borrow any guns, swords, pistols, powder, shot, or match, until this Court shall take further order therein.

The list of fifty-eight men disarmed in Boston was headed by the rakish soldier Captain John Underhill. William Hutchinson was third on the list, following the surgeon Thomas Oliver, perhaps "tainted" by working professionally with Anne Hutchinson in crisis cases. Mentioned by name in the court order but, of course, not on the list herself, Anne was nevertheless represented (in addition to husband William) by her son Richard, brother-in-law Edward, and her sons-in-law John Sanford and Thomas Savage. Interestingly, among friends and neighbors on the list was the Charlestown-Boston ferryman and entrepreneur Thomas Marshall, whose job was turned over to an employee chosen by the colony and required, by law, to give all revenue to the newly established college at Cambridge.

In addition to the fifty-eight Boston men disarmed, there were seventeen from other towns: five from Salem, three from Newbury, five from Roxbury, two from Ipswich, and two from Charlestown—giving substance to Rev. Thomas Weld's complaint that Anne Hutchinson had a colony-wide following, her "tainted" supporters spreading what he was pleased to call "the infection."

Fearful that insurrection might follow these harsh measures, the General Court, at this same session of November 20, further "ordered that the powder and ammunition of the countries now at Boston should be delivered half to Newtown and half to Roxbury, to be appointed by Mr. Dudley and Mr. Harlaakenden."

Almost at once, thirty of the seventy-five men who were ordered disarmed decided that recantation was the better part of valor and had their gun-toting privileges restored, as did another group of five who denied supporting the trouble-causing Wheelwright petition, insisting that their names had been added without their consent or knowledge. The remaining forty stalwarts protested loudly, agitated furiously, "but at last, when they saw no remedy, they obeyed."

Following this veritable coup d'état, a large number of the Boston church attempted retaliation against Governor Winthrop. But the church elders would have none of it. John Winthrop succeeded in calming the situation with a speech declaring that always he had only the public interest in mind and had thus carried out all his obligations under the official oath of office to which he had solemnly sworn. "For his part, he was persuaded," he said, that the sentencing of Anne and her followers was "most for the glory of God and the public good." Like Anne—whose words the governor had seized on at her hearing as proving the case against her—the governor was determined to make himself heard and his words accepted. Therefore, again like Anne, he revealed that he had acted in partnership with God, on the basis of direct communication.

In a burst of compassion for Anne Hutchinson, the General Court had decided that the snow-filled winter season was unsuitable for banishing a woman.* They would wait till spring. Furthermore, the court granted her enough time to return to Boston, there to make provision for care of her seven children still at home: Francis, seventeen; Samuel, thirteen; Anne, ten; Mary, nine; Katherine, seven; William, six; Susanna, four; and Zuriel, one. Expenses for

---

*Anne Hutchinson was in exclusive company when she was banished from Massachusetts in this controversy. Only three were so punished: her brother-in-law, Rev. John Wheelwright; William Aspinwall, accused of writing the Wheelwright petition; and Anne herself.

detaining her at the Roxbury home of Joseph Weld, brother of Rev. Thomas Weld, were ordered "to be defrayed by her husband." (It was customary for the prisoner or the prisoner's family to pay all expenses of food and shelter.)

Ruggedly wild Roxbury was a hard two-mile journey over scrawny Boston Neck, a long, ridiculously narrow isthmus running between the Charles River and the Atlantic Ocean and connecting the settlement at Boston with the land to the south. Here, members of the General Court congratulated themselves, Anne Hutchinson should be relatively inaccessible to her family, friends, and supporters; the clamor of her society-shaking ideas muffled if not silenced completely.

At the same time, the brothers Weld—Joseph, the jailer, and Thomas, the minister—could, between them, keep an eye on her day and night.

13

"YOU HAVE RATHER
BEEN A HUSBAND
THAN A WIFE"

There was no doubt about it. Anne Hutchinson was irrepressible. Even safely tucked away in remote Roxbury, well out of earshot of her loyal followers, "she thought it now needless to conceal herself any longer," a worried Governor Winthrop marveled. Repeatedly, the governor saw her behaving as the darling of "Satan [who never] would lose the opportunity of making choice of so fit an instrument." The evidence of this devilish connection was all around him. First of all, "she began now to discover all her mind to such as came to her, so that her opinions came abroad and began to take place among her old disciples, and now some of them raised up questions—which the elders finding to begin to appear in some of their churches they took much pains both in public and private to suppress." Secondly, the governor confided to his journal, he still felt a sense of disbelief that a woman-led faction—"the root of all was found to be in Mistress Hutchinson"—should have attempted to censure him.

At the same time, Rev. John Cotton, the governor's recently recruited ally, was finding neither inner nor outer peace. Anne and her followers had "abused" him, he protested, making him their "stalking horse" by their insistence that Anne's ideas were exactly the same as his. Indeed, nothing could be further from the truth, he proclaimed: "Mistress Hutchinson seldom resorted to me. . . . And when she did come to me, it was seldom or never . . . that she tarried long." Giving her the short shrift he was now convinced she deserved, he huffed: "I rather think she was loath to resort much to me, or to confer long with me, lest she might seem to learn somewhat from me."

Furthermore, the minister was decidedly uncomfortable that, because of Anne, the colony had had to pass an alien exclusion law. Thanks to this selfsame law, he worriedly observed, no new recruits were coming into Utopia at New England. Just recently, in fact, he had been "informed that some godly passengers who hither arrived out of England were refused to sit down among us." All things considered, therefore, John Cotton let it be known that he "had thoughts of removal, yet not with Ms. Hutchinson." She now stood revealed as that most divisive of all spoilers, he claimed, a New World Separatist. If he went anywhere, he asserted, it would have to be to the newly founded colony at New Haven, whose churches were part of the Established New England Church.

The very thought that they might lose the renowned John Cotton sent additional shivers down the spines of John Winthrop and the magistrates, already suffering the icy blasts of one of New England's worst winters. Supporters back in England were certain to see the minister's departure as a sure sign of the Bay Colony's failure and cut off all future funds. (Puritans in England regularly sent money to preserve New England as a place of refuge should they ever lose every last hope of reform in the motherland.) Posthaste, John Winthrop and his colleagues went to work, finally persuading Cotton to remain in new Boston.

While all this was going on, Anne, under house arrest in Roxbury—several times John Winthrop referred to her as "the prisoner"—had few friendly visitors, though her husband and family made the trip whenever the weather cooperated. All winter long, there had been killing ice and snowstorms, packed with high winds, so that almost the only reason anyone went outside for days on end was to cut wood, for warmth near the fire and for cooking. Even at that, a frightening story made the rounds about thirty

Bostonians who had left home in supposedly good weather to gather wood, only to lose fingers and toes—and at least one life—to frostbite.

Hard as it was on her not to see her family more often, Anne could thank the ill winds for blowing the Massachusetts ministry off course. Various ministers had planned to visit her frequently, either to shut her up or to make her see the light. But in almost four months, only the two local ministers had managed to visit her fairly regularly: gentle John Eliot, the Indian Apostle, and vituperative Thomas Weld, second only to John Winthrop in denunciations of her. Sporadically, they were joined by Thomas Shepard, the young Newtown-Cambridge minister who had himself once toyed with Familism, but who now behaved with the fanaticism of the reconverted, and Rev. Hugh Peter of Salem, rapidly donning the mantle of the colony's leading Puritan extremist.

At least the two Roxbury ministers could congratulate themselves on brilliant foresight. Before Anne's arrival as house prisoner at brother Joseph Weld's house, they had cast three of Anne's sympathizers out of the local church: Henry Bull, a poor servant in his late twenties; Philip Sherman, twenty-seven, vocation unknown; and Thomas Wilson, a miller, age unknown.

The weather was treacherous, the ministers were resolute, but something was different about Anne. She was not her usual self, a stubbornly brilliant mind in a bouncily healthy body; she was pregnant and menopausal, and her body was behaving in strange, unfamiliar ways. The only thing that kept her going was knowing, from her experience as a midwife, that women her age experienced similar feelings. That being the case, her only salvation might be to plunge deeper and deeper into her private studies of the Bible.

Quite unintentionally, her ministerial visitors further helped her take her mind off her personal distress. Furious that somehow she was loosing on Massachusetts a steady stream of subversive ideas, even though she was forbidden to see any but her own family and certifiably pure ministers, they proceeded to collect what they called "the growing evils" spawned by her "secret opinions." By March their collection amounted to twenty-nine such opinions. For example, they pointed out, she refused to accept the immortality of the soul or the idea of afterlife on grounds that "the souls of all men by nature are mortal and die like beasts." She contended: "Every man consists of soul and body. Now Adam dies not except his soul and body die."

Obviously, banishing Anne from Massachusetts would not be enough, the ministers concluded. They must first call her to account "in a church way," looking to excommunication from the New England Church. The date they set was lecture day, Thursday, March 15, 1638. This time they could hold the hearing in the Boston church-meetinghouse, now made completely harmless and impotent, since all of Anne's strongest sympathizers and supporters had been disfranchised and disarmed. In addition, many members had decided to pull up stakes and leave the colony forever, including Anne's husband, William (his name had been third on the list of those disarmed following the November hearing at Newtown-Cambridge). Together with nineteen Bostonians similarly punished, he had signed an agreement to go south to Aquidneck (now the island of Rhode Island in Narragansett Bay), a fertile area extending fifteen miles north to south, where they planned to build new homes and settle, at the invitation of Roger Williams who helped them purchase the land from the sachems Canonicus and Miantonomo.

Before her excommunication hearing, Anne mercifully was allowed to return to her own home in Boston, balm to her troubled mind, heart, and body, even though William was not there.

The November General Court hearing for banishment and the March church trial for excommunication had distinct similarities and distinct differences. The chief defendant was the same, again she was alone in the limelight, and the purpose of both hearings was to silence her in such a way that would-be transgressors would be frightened. For this particular hearing, however, the church-meeting house was under religious control. And most of Anne's inquisitors this time would be ecclesiastics, not magistrates—except for Governor John Winthrop, Deputy Governor Thomas Dudley, and Treasurer Richard Bellingham who were specifically excused from the concurrent meeting of the General Court at Cambridge in order to attend the Boston hearing. Roles were reversed at this hearing, so that the clergy were the persecutors, with the few magistrates present acting in support positions.

Four months, plus extreme measures against Hutchinsonians, had taken their toll. The once overwhelmingly sympathetic and supportive Boston congregation now remained silent, even though gathered in their own church—with the exception of Anne's son Edward Hutchinson and her son-in-law Thomas Savage. Some former followers who remained in Boston were intimidated, afraid that to speak for Anne was to lose their hard-worked land and income. Others were overwhelmed by the ministerial weight of authority behind John Winthrop and John Cotton, in contrast to the visible solitariness of Anne Hutchinson. They had cheered Anne on the first time she had similarly occupied center stage all by herself, at the November General Court at Newtown-Cambridge. But the harsh repercussions afterward weakened their stamina for further resistance.

The meeting was called for 10:00 A.M., two hours earlier than usual. Anne, fighting back the best way she could, arrived late, substituting actions for words to show contempt for the religious rite preceding the hearing. Anne's medical colleague, surgeon Thomas Oliver—close to seventy, he had been second man on the list of those disarmed and disfranchised, but was restored to his position and privileges on recantation—was now one of the ruling elders of the Boston congregation. Trying to persuade the assembled ministry to overlook her insultingly late entrance into the hall, he explained that there were medical reasons: She had come late "not out of any contempt or neglect . . . , but because she had long been under durance, she is so weak that she conceives herself not fit nor able to have been here so long together."

Speaking out to give seating directions was Boston's other ruling elder, Thomas Leverett, John Cotton's longtime protector whom Anne had known back in old Boston. He requested that all members of the Boston congregation sit together so that they might be distinguished from the others present and so that their votes of approval or condemnation for each item might easily be counted.

After this, the hearing got down to business. For hours on end there was theological disputation over Anne's twenty-nine alleged errors, in which she more than held her own.* Then toward the end of the day the hearing turned into a kind of contest to see which inquisitor could come up with the best all-purpose denunciation of Anne Hutchinson, the woman who did not yet know her proper place in society, and refused to learn that place from the men who were her superiors.

On behalf of the four ministers who had by turns subjected Anne to proselytizing and interrogation during her Roxbury house arrest, Thomas Shepard of Cambridge called her "a very dangerous woman to sow her corrupt opinions to the infection of many."

These words were not strong enough for Rev. Peter Bulkley of Concord—the minister John Cotton had snubbed back in the days when Cotton tended to be more sympathetic to Anne. Bulkley got right down to the putrid, poisonous core of the matter: "I desire to know of Mrs. Hutchinson whether you hold . . . that foul, gross, and abominable opinion held by Familists of the community of women."

Vehemently, Anne responded, "*I hold it not*" (italics in place)—undoubtedly wondering why a loyal, loving, and pregnant wife and mother of twelve, who had used her abundant energy and time stolen from sleep to succor women and upgrade their role in the community, should be so accused.

But the denunciations went right on. Wholeheartedly aligning himself with Anne's opponents was forty-one-year-old John Davenport, the Oxford-educated minister of New Haven who was visiting Boston, staying at John Cotton's house. Somehow, Davenport equated Anne's rejection of resurrection—"I do not think the body that dies shall rise again," she said earlier—with acceptance of the libertine doctrine of free love. If resurrection is not acknowledged, then neither is marriage, he asserted, so that "if there be any union

---

*Cotton Mather, the brilliant grandson of John Cotton and himself a minister, dismissed these errors in his *Magnalia*, the ecclesiastical history of New England, in 1702, as "needless now to repeat; they are dead and gone; and for me beyond hope of resurrection; . . . 'tis enough to say they were of an Antinomian and Familistical tendency." Cf., *Magnalia Christi Americana*, vol. 2, p. 512.

between man and woman, it is not by marriage but in a way of community." In a word, Anne, having been convicted at her November trial of attempting to subvert church and state, now stood accused of undermining those most basic of all human relationships, marriage and family.

Mastering all her dignity to rebuff this twisting of her beliefs, Anne retorted: "If any such practice or conclusion be drawn from it, then I must leave it, for I abhor that practice."

Once again, Rev. Thomas Shepard of Cambridge spoke out, warning any wavering members of the congregation, "especially simple women of her own sex," to ignore Anne who, using her "fluent tongue and forwardness in expression," had "often boasted of of the guidance of God's spirit and that her revelations are as true as the Scriptures."

Anne found these accusations particularly painful, coming as they did from Thomas Shepard, in whom she thought she had once detected glimmerings of sympathy. Treating his own wife as "a meet yoke-fellow," he had seemed to understand that women suffered at least as much as men, working side by side with their husbands in the untamed wilderness.

After sitting through hours of contempt, anger, and innuendo, all directed at Anne, her eldest son, Edward Hutchinson, and son-in-law Thomas Savage (married to her oldest daughter, Faith) spoke up in her defense—to no avail. Taking it on himself to answer their objections, Anne's old idol John Cotton cut all remaining ties with Anne, insulting her, her son, and her son-in-law with one strong unfeeling statement:

I do admonish you both . . . to consider how ill an office you have performed to your mother this day to be instruments of hardening her heart and nourishing her in her unsound opinions by your pleading for her and hindering the proceedings of the church against her which *God hath directed us to take* . . . and which God might have . . . made more effectual to her had not you intercepted the course and now instead of loving and natural children you have proved vipers to eat through the very bowels of your mother to her ruin. [Italics purposely have been added to Cotton's revelation of the directive from God.]

Next, New England's most renowned minister turned to the
women present at the hearing:

> Let me say somewhat to the sisters of our own congregation,
> many of whom I fear have been too much seduced and led aside
> by her; therefore, *I admonish you* . . . to look to yourselves
> and to take heed that you receive nothing for truth which has
> not the stamp of the word of God from it. I doubt not but some
> of you have also received much good from the conference of this
> our sister and by your converse with her: and from her it may
> be you have received help in your spiritual estates . . . , but
> *let me say this to you all and to all the sisters of other congrega-
> tions. Let not the good you have received from her make you to
> receive all for good that comes from her*; for you see she is but a
> woman and *many unsound and dangerous principles are held
> by her*, therefore whatsoever good you have received, own it
> and keep it carefully, but if you have drunk in with this good
> any evil or poison, make speed to vomit it up again and to re-
> pent of it and take care that you do not harden her in her way
> by pitying her, or confirming her in her opinions. . . . [N.B.,
> italics were used in the document apparently to indicate em-
> phasis on Cotton's part.]

Warming to his subject, Cotton turned directly to, and on, Anne
Hutchinson, and cleverly began his diatribe with compliments, with
the result that the criticism and condemnation that followed stand
out in dishearteningly bold relief. First the flattery:

> You have been an instrument of doing some good amongst us.
> You have been helpful to many, to bring them off from their un-
> sound grounds and principles. . . . And the Lord has endowed
> you with good parts and gifts fit to instruct your children and
> servants and to be helpful to your husband in the government of
> the family. He has given you a sharp apprehension, a ready ut-
> terance and abilities to express yourself.

Then came the flood of denunciation, including accusations of
free love, and the community of women:

Let me warn you and admonish you . . . to consider seriously how . . . these unsound tenets of yours . . . and the evil of your opinions do outweigh all the good of your doings. Consider how many poor souls you have misled and how you have conveyed the poison of your unsound principles into the hearts of many which it may be will never be reduced again. . . . You cannot evade the argument that was pressed upon you by our brother Bulkley and others that the filthy sin of the community of women, and all promiscuous and filthy coming together of men and women, without distinction or relation of marriage will necessarily follow, and though I have not heard, neither do I think, you have been unfaithful to your husband in his marriage covenant, yet *that will follow upon it*, for it is the very argument . . . against the Resurrection . . . which the Anabaptists [instigators of the Munster Rebellion of 1534–36] and Familists bring to prove the lawfulness of the common use of all women, and so more dangerous evils and filthy uncleanness and other sins will follow than you do not imagine or conceive.

Anne, calling Cotton's attention to her weakened state, asked, and was granted, leave to answer immediately, instead of waiting for him to finish his statement. Without elaboration, she exclaimed, "All that I would say is that *I did not hold any of these things before my imprisonment*." (Italics already in place.)

Unmoved, Cotton returned to the attack, embellishing his accusations with age-old platitudes; for example, that Anne, by her speech and behavior had "set an open door to an epicurism and libertinism, [and] if this be so, then come let us eat and drink for tomorrow we shall die, then let us neither fear hell nor the loss of heaven." He warned her pointedly not to sully "the hearts of young women with such unsound and dangerous principles, . . . which you have drawn them to."

At 8:00 P.M., after a very long day with no time off for food, rest, or natural relief, Boston's pastor John Wilson adjourned the meeting till the following Thursday. Anne was not allowed to return to her own home, but neither was she forced to go back to her jailer, Joseph Weld, in Roxbury. Instead, she stayed for the week with John Cotton and his wife, Sarah. With John Davenport also a guest at the Cottons', Anne was subjected to seven days of unrelenting arguments as to why she must return to the fold, subdued and subordinated.

On March 22, 1638, Anne made her final appearance before most of the colony's ministers, a few magistrates, "and the face of the country." Feeling sick, exhausted, and fatalistic about her future (she had, after all, already been pronounced *persona non grata* and banished from the colony, and her husband at that very moment was setting up a new home in Rhode Island), Anne agreed to read a recantation of her former views: "I spoke rashly and unadvisedly. I do not allow the slighting of ministers, nor of the Scriptures, nor anything that is set up by God."

So far, so good. This proud, haughty woman had obviously been "reduced" to the meekness and mildness expected of women. But then in the next breath, she stunned her hearers with a Delphic enigma (using "man" the first time to refer to masculine beings, and leaving it to her inquisitors whether to interpret the second reference to "man" as being to males only or to all humans, in accordance with seventeenth-century usage): "It was never in my heart to slight any man, but only that man should be kept in his own place and not set in the room of God."

One by one, the ministers rose to object. Rev. Thomas Shepard of Cambridge called her a "heretic," her tale-bearing shipmate Zechariah Symmes of Charlestown protested she had not shown sufficient "humiliation," and Thomas Eliot who had visited her almost daily during her Roxbury confinement added that he was "not satisfied." Pastor John Wilson of Boston, who never made pretenses to being diplomatic or magnanimous, blurted out exactly what he thought of this woman who had, by holding meetings at her own home, tried to substitute her own preaching for his sermons: "I must needs say . . . that the cause or root of these your errors was . . . above others that you might be extolled and admired and followed after, that you might be a great prophetess and undertake to expound Scriptures and to interpret other men's sayings and sermons after your mind."

Deputy Governor Dudley chimed in with a generalized objection:

"Mrs. Hutchinson's repentance is only for opinions held since her imprisonment. For her form of recantation, her repentance is in a paper . . . not in her countenance. None can see it there I think."

But it was Rev. Hugh Peter of Salem who incisively cut to the heart of the ministers' quarrel with Anne. Angrily he recalled the time he had had a conversation with her about the Woman of Ely, a female preacher back in England whom Anne "did exceedingly magnify . . . to be a woman of 1000." This was too much. Anne was not only reinterpreting the Bible for her own purposes, she was making this holiest of all writings the butt of parody. (Ecclesiastes 7:28: "One man among a thousand have I found; but a woman among all those have I not found.") In no uncertain terms, therefore, the Reverend Mr. Peter denounced her for not knowing her place as a woman:

> I would commend this to your consideration, that you have stepped out of your place, you have rather been a husband than a wife, a preacher than a hearer, and a magistrate than a subject, and so you have thought to carry all things in church and commonwealth as you would, and have not been humbled for this.

Agreeing totally, Governor Winthrop lamented that "divers sisters of the Congregation have built upon her experience." And Thomas Shepard worried aloud that "all those women and others have been led by her and doted so much upon her and her opinions."

Again, Pastor Wilson spoke out frenziedly, citing Anne's partnership with the Devil:

> I look at her as a dangerous instrument of the Devil, raised up by Satan amongst us. . . . Whereas there was much love and union and sweet agreement amongst us before she came, yet since, all union and love have been broken and there have been censurings [Winthrop's and his own near-censures by the Boston church] and judgings and condemnings one of another. . . . The misgovernment of this woman's tongue has been a great cause of this disorder which has . . . been . . . to set up herself and to draw disciples after her, and therefore she

says one thing today and another thing tomorrow. . . . Therefore, we should sin against God if we should not put away from us so evil a woman, guilty of such foul evils.

At this point, a distraught John Cotton attempted to recede well into the background. He told everyone present why Pastor John Wilson should take over the formal expulsion of Anne Hutchinson. He tried to explain that when they were dealing with "point of doctrine," he, as Boston teacher, was in charge. However, "now she is dealt with in point of practice and so it belongs to the pastor's office to instruct." He would not pass sentence, he said, but he let his denunciation of his once adoring disciple hang heavily in the damp stagnant air: "God has let her fall into a manifest lie . . . , and therefore as we received her in amongst us, I think we are bound upon this ground to remove her from us and not to retain her any longer, seeing she doth prevaricate in her words, as that her judgment is one thing and her expression is another."

Feeling completely vindicated, Rev. John Wilson took over, vindictively sentencing Anne Hutchinson to hell and hopelessness:

Forasmuch as you, Mrs. Hutchinson, have highly transgressed and offended and forasmuch as you have so many ways troubled the church with your errors and have drawn away many a poor soul and have upheld your revelations, and forasmuch as you have made a lie, etc., therefore . . . in the name of the Church I do not only pronounce you worthy to be cast out, but I do cast you out and . . . deliver you up to Satan that you may learn no more to blaspheme, to seduce and to lie. Therefore, I command you in the name of this church as a leper to withdraw yourself out of the congregation; that as formerly you have despised and condemned the holy ordinances of God and turned your back on them, so you may now have no part in them nor benefit by them.

A formal answer was neither expected nor permitted from Anne. But her reaction verged on the obscene, a horrified Governor Winthrop observed: "She [was] not affected with any remorse." Instead, "her spirits which seemed before to be somewhat dejected, revived again and she gloried in her sufferings."

In little more than three short years, Anne Hutchinson had come to tower over Massachusetts, so that the colony and church were well rid of her, John Winthrop maintained, excoriating her as "this American Jezebel,"* who was guilty of "undervaluing the ordinances of Magistracy and Ministry":

> She had . . . insinuated herself into the heart of much of the people (yea of many of the most wise and godly) who grew into so reverent an esteem of her godliness and spiritual gifts as they looked at her as a prophetess raised up of God for some great work now at hand . . . , so as she had more resort to her for counsel about matter of conscience and clearing up men's spiritual estates, than any minister (I might say all the elders) in the country.

As far as Anne Hutchinson's female followers were concerned, John Winthrop assured himself, at least, that "if their modesty had not restrained them, [they] would have born witness against her."

This female silence during the proceedings made all the more astonishing two incidents that occurred as Anne left the meeting-house. First, in words loud enough for John Winthrop to hear distinctly, "One standing at the door said, 'The Lord sanctify this unto you,' to whom she made answer, 'The Lord judgeth not as man judgeth.' " Second, young Mary Dyer, whose life Anne had helped save during a difficult stillbirth, rose from the bench on which she was seated and in plain view accompanied Anne outside.

Two or three days later, Anne received from the governor the official warrant ordering her to leave Massachusetts before the end of the month.

Denounced as liar, leper, and Devil's helper, she once again packed her belongings and gathered her children for a journey to a land frighteningly unknown but promisingly untried—and presumably beyond the jurisdiction of John Winthrop's government and Pastor Wilson's church. Pregnant and not quite forty-seven, she had had more than her share of personal persecution and repeated rejection during her three and a half years in Massachusetts.

---

*In the Bible, Jezebel was a willful queen who led Israel into idol worship. I Kings, II Kings, Revelation.

14

"A DEAR SAINT"

For six days Anne and her children traveled the sixty-five miles from Boston to Aquidneck—by canoe over rivers and streams, on foot over Indian paths still a foot-and-a-half deep in snow despite the lateness of the season—occasionally finding along the way a wigwamlike shelter or simple hut dug into the ground for warmth, whose inhabitant providentially invited them to stay the night. On the seventh day she was finally reunited with her husband, William, who was living in a primitive cabin nothing like the Hutchinson home in Boston.

Creature comforts aside, her first few months in Aquidneck were sheer misery. Governor Winthrop refused to let up in his persecution, instead keeping her under constant surveillance. So much so, that she confided to Roger Williams of nearby Providence Plantation that she very much longed for the return of Henry Vane and that "if he come not to New, she must to Old England."

Roger Williams quoted this remark in a letter dated April 16, 1638, to John Winthrop, written in response to the Massachusetts governor's wild recounting of the story of "a monster" expelled from the womb of "comely" young Mary Dyer, "notoriously infected with Mrs. Hutchinson's errors and very censorious and troublesome."

The sharp-eared governor had been alerted to Mary Dyer's stillbirth "the very day [March 22, 1638] Mistress Hutchinson was cast out of the church. . . . Mistress Dyer accompanied her, which a stranger observing asked another what woman that was. The other answered that it was the woman who had the monster." The governor ordered an immediate investigation, which revealed that Anne Hutchinson and her friend Jane Hawkins, "a rank Familist also," had precipitately buried the fetus on advice of John Cotton more than five months before. Five days after Anne had left Massachusetts, the governor supervised the exhumation of Mary Dyer's stillborn daughter:

> It had a face, but no head, and the ears stood upon the shoulders and were like an ape's; it had no forehead, but over the eyes four horns, hard, and sharp; . . . it had two mouths, and in each of them a piece of red flesh sticking out; it had arms and legs as other children; but, instead of toes, it had on each foot three claws, like a young fowl, with sharp talons.

To the gruesome description, Governor Winthrop added the omen-filled detail that when the baby had died in Mary Dyer's body, "about two hours before the birth, the bed whereon the mother lay did shake, and withal there was such a noisome savor." To his many listeners and correspondents in old and New England, he never failed to point out the connection between this "monster" delivered of Mary Dyer and the "monstrous errors" of Anne Hutchinson.

Roger Williams understood very well the reason for the governor's news release on Mary Dyer, responding: "I also humbly thank you for that sad relation of the monster, etc. The Lord speaks once and twice: He be pleased to open all our ears to His Discipline."

Unhappily, the governor's stonyhearted reaction to Mary Dyer's personal tragedy reached Anne when she was at her lowest ebb physically. She was very sick, suffering the complications of late-age pregnancy exacerbated by standing trial twice, two days each time; added to four months of constant ministerial badgering while she was under house arrest; as well as her first long separation from her husband and the necessity to dismantle their Boston home without him; and the jouncing journey to Aquidneck. "Six weeks before her delivery, [perceiving] her body to be greatly distempered and her spirits failing, and in that regard doubtful of life," she made up her mind to send for the local preacher, twenty-eight-year-old John Clarke who shared her religious philosophy and was one of the original planters of the new colony. Clarke "considered that her condition was both doubtful and dangerous, and . . . he was somewhat unwilling to meddle, at least before her delivery," he explained in a letter to John Cotton back in Boston, requesting "some medicines proper for the occasion."

If received, the medicine did no good—Anne suffered a painful miscarriage accompanied by much loss of blood—but Cotton did much harm to Anne, using Clarke's subsequent description of her delivery to sermonize that "it might signify her error in denying inherent righteousness."

Worst of all, John Winthrop, hearing Cotton's sermon, proceeded to badger John Clarke with letters asking for additional details, writing them down in his journal with uncontrolled voyeurism, and then apparently, with no discernible sympathy for Anne, repeating them orally to everyone with whom he came into contact.

John Clarke admitted, though no one paid much attention, that he had not been present during the actual crisis:*

> After . . . it was brought to light, . . . I was called to see it, where I beheld, first unwashed (and afterwards in warm

---

*John Clarke signed his name, adding the designation "physician," which twentieth-century historians have erroneously taken to mean "medical doctor." Moreover, they have compounded this error by repeatedly calling him *Dr.* Clarke, rather than *Mr.* Clarke, as did John Winthrop in his journal. *Journal*, vol. 1, p. 277. There is no evidence extant that John Clarke received any medical training, cf. *Dictionary of National Biography, Dictionary of American Biography*, or his own writing, *Ill Newes from New England*, a long political-religious dissertation. His use of the word "ill" in the title is intentional. The second definition for "physician" in *Webster's Third International Dictionary* is "one who restores (as a troubled spirit or the body politic)." Likewise, in the *Oxford English Dictionary* the third definition is "a healer, one who cures moral, spiritual, or political maladies or infirmities."

water), several lumps, every one of them greatly confused, and if you consider each one of them according to the representation of the whole, they were altogether without form. . . . Of these several lumps there were about twenty-six . . . or twenty-seven, distinct and not joined together.

Expatiating on this same miscarriage, John Winthrop's friend and co-author Rev. Thomas Weld of Roxbury, brother of Anne's jailer, reported that Anne had brought forth "thirty monstrous births or thereabouts, at once, some of them bigger, some lesser, some of one shape, some of another; few of any perfect shape, none at all of them (as far as I could ever learn) of human shape."

Sick at heart and body, Anne found herself subjected to interminable moralizing on her miscarriage. The Reverend Mr. Weld reported the consensus of the Establishment: "See how the wisdom of God fitted this judgment to her sin every day, for look as she had vented misshapen opinions, so she must bring forth deformed monsters; and as those were public, and not in a corner mentioned, so this is now come to be known and famous over all these churches and a great part of the world."*

*Dishearteningly, Emery Battis in his 1962 book, *Saints and Sectaries: Anne Hutchinson and the Antinomian Crisis in the Massachusetts Bay Colony*, has used Anne's miscarriage, as reported by her hostile opponents, to hypothesize that she was experiencing "severe menopausal symptoms including neurotic manifestations. Under these conditions such aspects of the delusional system which Mrs. Hutchinson may hitherto have entertained inwardly could have been forced into open expression" (p. 346).

For some reason, he has felt called on to contradict the long-held assumption that though she may or may not have been pregnant during her November General Court hearing, she was certainly pregnant during her excommunication trial. I have reverted to this earlier assumption, based on her own expressions of illness during her trials, as well as John Clarke's report that she had consulted him "six weeks before her delivery." Since she arrived in Aquidneck by the middle of April, her due date could have been June 1. She could have conceived either before her November trial, immediately afterward when she may well have been allowed to return home for a night or two before going on to her house arrest at Roxbury, or during her confinement when in the words of John Winthrop, "the truth was that she was not put to durance but only a favourable confinement, so as all her family . . . resorted to her at their pleasure."

Hearing of the continued repercussions from her Massachusetts activities must have made Anne happy to be resident in Rhode Island. To Rev. Thomas Weld, reporting the controversy surrounding her, her new home was "the Island of Errors." To her, it was a place free from the persecution the Bay Colony was still visiting on outspoken women.

For example, at the very time Anne was undergoing excommunication by the church at Boston, her friend Jane Hawkins, the midwife, was being given two months to get out of the colony by the General Court meeting in Newtown:

> Jane Hawkins, the wife of Richard Hawkins, had liberty till the beginning of the third month, called May [1638], and the magistrates (if she did not depart before) to dispose of her: and in the meantime she is not to meddle in surgery, or physic, drinks, plaisters [a kind of adhesive bandage], or oils, nor to question matters of religion, except with the elders for satisfaction.

Approving this action, Governor Winthrop dismissed Jane Hawkins as a "rank Familist" and "notorious for her familiarity with the Devil." He based these accusations on her reputation as a

---

Dr. Theodore Barton, assistant clinical professor of obstetrics and gynecology at Harvard Medical School since 1957, and gynecologist and obstetrician at Boston Hospital for Women, a Harvard teaching hospital, assures me that Anne Hutchinson's menopausal abortion was indeed, as Emery Battis insists, a hydatidiform mole, but contrary to Battis's assumption could have been expelled as late as seven months after conception. Further, she need not have been neurotic because she was menopausal.

In any case, denigrating Anne's leadership activities and long-held ideas by labeling them the products of a menopausal neurotic hardly seems worthy of Emery Battis. More concerned with the male Hutchinsonians—interestingly, an appellation he uses over and over again—he has written an excellent study of the business climate of the colony and has provided invaluable charts on the men who comprised the Hutchinsonian movement. It is unfortunate, then, that his subtitle does not reflect the emphasis on business, and that he resorts to a pejorative psychoanalytic dismissal of Anne Hutchinson.

popular prophet back home in St. Ives, England, and her practice of midwifery in New England.*

In April 1638, just as Anne was settling in Aquidneck, the Boston church was casting out Judith Smith, servant of Anne's brother-in-law Edward Hutchinson. She was accused of "obstinate persisting" in "sundry errors." Eight months later, in December, John Winthrop was complaining that "the devil would never cease to disturb our peace." This time the Devil's agent was Mary Oliver of Salem. Winthrop compared her to Anne Hutchinson and found that "she was for ability or speech and appearance of zeal and devotion far before Mrs. Hutchinson, and so the fitter instrument to have done hurt, but that she was poor and had little acquaintance." When she refused to be silenced, she was imprisoned till she "submitted herself and acknowledged her fault in disturbing the church." She was excommunicated, as were three other Salem women late that same year: Jane Verin who refused to follow her husband's commands on the subject of church attendance, Marjorie Holiman, a servant, and Marjorie Reeves, a widow.

Around this same time in Aquidneck, Anne Hutchinson, finally on the way to recovery from her massive miscarriage, received an auspicious boost in morale. Her youngest sister, Katherine—born around the time of their father's death in 1611, and Anne's earliest disciple—settled in Providence, Rhode Island, with her husband, Richard Scott, a shoemaker. John Winthrop, certain that Katherine Scott's move spelled trouble, worried in his journal that "things grew still worse" in Rhode Island with the arrival there of "a sister of Mrs. Hutchinson . . . [who was] infected with Anabaptistry" (pro-

---

*Jane Hawkins, whose reputation for outspokenness in England had preceded her to New England, has been besmirched by historians reading literally the written deprecation by Anne Hutchinson's brother-in-law John Wheelwright: "She attended [Mrs. Hutchinson's] weekly lecture . . . where when Mrs. Hutchinson broached any new doctrine, she would be the first who would taste of it. And being demanded whether it were not clear to her, though she understood it not, yet would say, 'Oh yes, very clear.' "

It is extremely important to note, however, that John Wheelwright wrote his account of the Hutchinsonian controversy, in which he was a prime participant, in 1645, after he had, in 1643, sent letters of repentance to Boston and had, in 1644, had his sentence of banishment officially removed.

fessed by the rebels in the bloody Munster uprising of 1534–1536).

By March 1639, exactly one year after Anne had been banished from Boston, she was preaching publicly in Aquidneck—and advocating anarchy. Torn between rage and disbelief, John Winthrop observed: "Mrs. Hutchinson exercised publicly and she and her party (some three or four families) would have no magistracy." Anne was acting out her belief that talent had no gender. Having finally found a way to block interception, in the form of an ordained minister, between herself and God in the church, she saw no reason why she should be subservient to a political establishment. The individual, whether woman or man, should be self-controlled.

Supremely confident that hers was the only path to truth and justice, she tried sending a letter to the church of Boston, "but the elders would not read it publicly because she had been excommunicated." A relieved John Winthrop noted that God, demonstrating approval of this policy of no communication following excommunication, had caused a house-shaking earthquake when "Mrs. Hutchinson and some of her adherents happened to be at prayer."

Even so, Anne's following was growing and spreading. In Boston itself, the church had to excommunicate Phillipa Harding:

> for speaking evil of authority both in church and commonwealth, for having said in open court that Mrs. Hutchinson neither deserved the censure which was put upon her in the church, nor in the commonwealth. It was proved against her . . . that she had also spoken the like words of defamation both in her shop and other meetings, whereof . . . she was finally cast out of the church as a slanderer and reviler.

And just about the same period, twenty-one-year-old Reverend Robert Lenthall of nearby Weymouth "was found to have drunk in some of Mrs. Hutchinson's opinions. . . . The common sort of people did eagerly embrace his opinions." At a meeting of the General Court the magistrates and ministers called him in to explain, convinced him that he was disturbing the peace, and got him to retract his opinions "in writing . . . in the open court."

At Roger Williams's settlement at Providence, "also, the Devil was not idle," according to John Winthrop. There the problem was, once again, assertive women. They refused to follow God's ordinance, "the subjection of wives to their husbands." According to one husband, things had so far degenerated that "if they should restrain their wives, all the women in the country would cry out."

At Aquidneck, in the spring of 1639, Anne was on the verge of getting her wish for anarchy. Government though not totally abolished was reduced to a minimum. "The people . . . put out Mr. Coddington and the other three magistrates, and chose Mr. William Hutchinson only, a man . . . wholly guided by his wife, who had been the beginner of all the former troubles in the country, and still continued to breed disturbance." The speaker giving his opinion was John Winthrop, who added: "They also gathered a church in a very disordered way; for they took some excommunicated persons, and others who were members of the church of Boston and not dismissed."

While Anne was in virtual control of her own small settlement at Aquidneck, she was out of sight but far from out of mind in Boston. All through 1640 a man named Hugh Bewett went about publicly proclaiming that he was "free from original sin." At the end of the year the General Court ordered him banished. This was the same year that Massachusetts tried but failed to chasten Anne herself, sending a small delegation, three "men of a lovely and winning spirit . . . to see if they could convince and reduce her." Rev. Thomas Weld of Roxbury reported their mission, giving their words dignity and propriety, which he contrasted markedly with Anne's foulmouthed response:

When they came first unto her, she asked from whom they came, and what was their business. They answered, "We are come in the name of the Lord Jesus, from the Church of Christ at Boston, to labour to convince you of etc." [sic] At that word she (being filled with as much disdain in her countenance, as bitterness in her spirit) replied, "What, from the Church of Boston? I know no such Church, neither will I own it. Call it the Whore and Strumpet of Boston, no Church of Christ."

When they tried to convince William Hutchinson to disavow his wife's teaching, he retorted that "he was more nearly tied to his wife than to the church; he thought her to be a dear saint and servant of God."

Bolder than ever, Anne and her followers "broached new heresies every year. Divers of them turned professed anabaptists and would not bear any arms, and denied all magistracy."

Unable to deal with Anne to their satisfaction, the Massachusetts authorities found another way they hoped would wound her mortally. Hearing that her son Francis, now twenty-one, and her new son-in-law William Collins, a nonconformist minister from Barbados who had become "infected with [Anne's] heresies" (he was now married to her young daughter and namesake, Anne), were visiting Boston, the magistrates ordered them to appear before the governor and assistants. The two young men refused, were given stiff fines—partly to punish them, but mostly, John Winthrop admitted candidly, to compensate Massachusetts for all the expenses incurred because of Anne Hutchinson and her family and her followers: the synod, the trials, "and other occasions to the value of £500 at least"—and were thrown into prison until they could raise bond.

Obstinately refusing to recant, or to reject Anne's leadership, William Collins and Francis Hutchinson were finally released without paying a single penny. Keeping them in prison proved too "inconvenient" for the colony. They were ordered out of Massachusetts at once, and threatened with death should they ever return.

Interestingly, in the same year the colonial fathers were trying to stamp out all this female-fomented heresy, they included in their first written code of laws, the Massachusetts Body of Liberties of 1641, their tradition-shattering concession to women. Contrary to age-old European practice, no Bay Colony man was ever to beat his wife—unless she beat him first: "Every married woman shall be free from bodily correction or stripes by her husband, unless it be in his own defense upon her assault." This was a humane and progressive concession to women uprooted from their settled life in old England to wilderness living in New England. But, in a perverse rhyme, the author of this written code of laws, sixty-two-year-old Nathaniel Ward, pastor of the church at Ipswich, a graduate of the Puritan Emmanuel College, Cambridge, reflected official sentiment—that

women, childlike and troublesome, could hardly expect to share
responsibility with men:

> The world is full of care,
> Much like unto a bubble:
> Women and care, and care and women,
> And women and care and trouble.

In 1642, William Hutchinson died. Anne's beloved husband, best
friend, devoted partner. Without his constant comfort and enthusiastic support, she could no longer bear living under the abnormally long arm of Massachusetts persecution.

As soon as she possibly could, she set out—with six of her
children, her son-in-law William Collins, and several Rhode Island
families—for the Dutch settlement on Long Island, far away from
the jurisdiction of Massachusetts. Her little house was built on a
lonely site in Pelham Bay called Anne's Hoeck (*hoeck* means neck
or point in Dutch), located between a river eventually named
Hutchinson and an Indian trail. Tragically, in August or
September, 1643, Fate blinked momentarily. Anne, whose Boston
adherents had refused to supply men or money to fight native
Americans in the Pequot War of 1637, and whose colony at
Aquidneck had refused to bear arms, was massacred together with
all her family—except for ten-year-old Susanna—in a local war between the Dutch and Indians intent on killing all white settlers occu-
pying their ancient lands.

Unable to contain his vindictiveness, Rev. Thomas Weld of
Roxbury reported her murder to friends back in England:

Mistress Hutchinson, being weary of the Island, or rather the
Island weary of her, departed from thence—to live under the
Dutch. . . . And now I am come to the last act of her tragedy,
a most heavy stroke upon herself and hers. . . . There the Indians set upon them, and slew her and all her family. . . .

I never heard that the Indians in those parts did ever before
this, commit the like outrage upon any one family, or families,
and therefore God's hand is the more apparently seen herein, to

pick out this woeful woman, to make her and those belonging to her, an unheard of heavy example. . . . Thus the Lord heard our groans to heaven, and freed us from this great and sore affliction.

Anne had been murdered, but her ideas took on a life of their own. The theories that raised the anger of men boosted the expectations of women. Even the poet Anne Bradstreet, living at the center of Establishment politics—she was daughter of one lifelong magistrate, misogynist Thomas Dudley, and wife of another, Simon Bradstreet—was led to doubt the undoubtable and think the unthinkable. In a brief memoir addressed to her children, she wrote:

> Many times hath Satan troubled me concerning the verity of the Scriptures; many times by atheism how could I know whether there was a God. I never saw any miracles to confirm me, and those which I read of, how did I know but what they were feigned. . . . Some new troubles I have had since the world has been filled with blasphemy and sectaries [an epithet applied to Anne and her followers as dissenters from the Established Church of New England], and some who have been accounted sincere Christians have been carried away with them.

This was the same Anne Bradstreet whose collected writings began with a Prologue noting sadly the "despite . . . cast on female wits."

Symbolically, within three months of Anne's murder on Long Island, another Anne Hutchinson was born in Boston, the baby daughter of the eldest Hutchinson son, Edward, and his wife, the former Katherine Hamby.

AFTERMATH

Ironically, Anne Marbury Hutchinson who rejected the idea of afterlife achieved instant immortality following her murder.

In a convoluted scenario, Rev. Thomas Weld of Roxbury, one of her chief persecutors and brother of her jailer, Joseph Weld, had sailed for England on August 3, 1641, along with another of her inquisitors, the fanatic Rev. Hugh Peter of Salem. As official agents, their twofold mission was to tout the glories of life in Massachusetts—in order to attract more settlers—and to raise funds for the financially hard-pressed colony. Arriving just as Antinomianism was raging through England—promoting chaos and total disregard for the fundamental laws of society, charged critics of the sect—the two ministers immediately applied this same sixteenth-century pejorative to the Familist views for which Anne Hutchinson had been banished and excommunicated.

Within months of Anne's murder, Thomas Weld, using John Winthrop's extensive notes and documents on the Hutchinsonian controversy, published a tract, early in 1644, celebrating the victory of the "New England Way" of Congregationalism over Hutchinsonianism. Interspersing ponderous details with courtroom drama, vituperation, and gloating triumph, Weld as editor and Winthrop as "an eye and ear-witness of the carriage of matters" made the little book seethe, pontificate, and provoke—and go into three editions in the single year of 1644. The title: *A Short Story of the Rise, reign, and ruin of the Antinomians, Familists, and Libertines that inflicted the Churches of New England.* On the title page, Winthrop was given chief credit for the "ruin."

The Weld-Winthrop treatise descended on an England torn by civil war. Puritans, winning the upper hand in the struggle against the King, were already splitting into two factions—Congregationalism versus Presbyterianism—quarreling over what form their religion should take in replacing Anglicanism. The Rev. Robert Baylie of Glasgow, chief spokesman for the Presbyterians, expressed strong exception to the claim made in the "Short Story" that New England's treatment of Anne Hutchinson proved the supremacy of Congregationalism. On the contrary, he asserted, "to this day, many, if you will confer with them, they will assure that Mistress Hutchinson was much . . . wronged; that she was a most pious woman, and that her tenets, if well understood, were all true, at least very tolerable." In 1645, he published *A Dissuasive from the Errours of Time*, primarily attacking John Cotton, chief promulgator of Congregationalism, questioning his judgment for wandering "into the horrible errors of the Antinomians and Familists with his dear friend Mistress Hutchinson." In 1648, Cotton—four years before his death in 1652, at age sixty-seven—replied with a long rambling self-justification, "The Way of the Congregational Churches Cleared," trying to put great distance between his own views and those of Anne Hutchinson.

When the English Civil War and Cromwellian Interregnum came to a close in 1660 with the Restoration of the monarchy, King Charles II put two former participants in the Hutchinsonian controversy to death, one from each side as it quite coincidentally turned out. Hugh Peter, a fanatic foe of Anne Hutchinson, was publicly disemboweled and hanged from the scaffold for having preached enthusiastic sermons urging the death of the King's father, Charles I, in 1649. Similarly executed was Anne's powerfully placed supporter, ex-governor Henry Vane, accused of having handed over to Parliament the notes that brought death to Charles I's indispensable minister Thomas Wentworth, earl of Strafford, hanged in 1641. According to some particularly malicious gossip, Anne Hutchinson and Mary Dyer had returned to England with Henry Vane in August 1637; he "debauched them both and both were delivered of monsters."

It was not until 1676 that the first sympathetic account of Anne Hutchinson appeared, this time using the history of her persecution to revile the Puritans for their crusade in the late 1650s and early 1660s against the Quakers. The title of the book, published anonymously, tells all: *A Glass for the People of New England, in which They may see themselves and Spirits, and if not too late, Repent and Turn from their Abominable Ways and Cursed Contrivances.* A sentence describing Anne's banishment exemplifies the author's attitude—and also, since the author made no claim to being an eyewitness or contemporary of Anne Hutchinson, demonstrates that a full generation later, the details of her life and death continued to reverberate in both old and New England:

> So reader, thou mayest see the rage and envy of this professing generation [i.e., those who interpret the Bible literally, the "legalists" referred to by both Anne Hutchinson and her opponents]; for they banished and imprisoned this tenderly-bred woman in or towards winter, and what with fears and tossings to and fro, the woman miscarried, upon which they ground their abominable untruth. Many witnesses might be produced to prove this and to disprove their abominable, frequently told slanders, and also printed by priests and New England professors and their confederates here in England.

Around the same time, William Hubbard, a second-generation minister from Ipswich, Massachusetts, wrote *A General History of New England*, in which he included several chapters on and references to Anne Hutchinson, largely based on John Winthrop's account. In 1702, Cotton Mather, grandson of John Cotton, wrote his *Magnalia Christi Americana*, the ecclesiastical history of New England. Basing his version on the writings of both John Winthrop

and William Hubbard, he recounted Anne's trials and her miscarriage and murder under the same heading John Winthrop had used,
"Dux Foemina Facti," (A Woman as Leader of the Act). Determined
to clear his grandfather's name, and apologizing for the need to tell
her story in view of the fact that among her "relations at this day
there are so many worthy and useful persons," he managed to include, among all the quotes from John Winthrop, a thought of his
own: "A poison does never insinuate so quickly, nor operate so
strongly as when mother's milk is the vehicle wherein 'tis given." In
1765, Anne's great-great-grandson Thomas Hutchinson, wrote *The
History of the Colony and Province of Massachusetts-Bay*, in which
he included a judicious account of his ancestor's activities and, even
more important, an eyewitness record of her General Court hearing,
fuller and notably more sympathetic than the account given by John
Winthrop and Thomas Weld in the "Short Story." Further, he
reported an unexpected expression of toleration by John Winthrop
on his deathbed: "Some writers say, that upon [John Winthrop's]
deathbed, when Mr. Dudley pressed him to sign an order of banishment of an heterodox person, he refused, saying, he had 'done too
much of that work already.' "

There was no doubt, then; history would forever have to take
notice of Anne Hutchinson. She was, as she herself had said of her
personal hero, the Woman of Ely, "A woman of a thousand, hardly
any like to her."

Happily, her unfinished campaign to make life humane for both
women and men went right on, without interruption. Many old
Hutchinsonians became the new Quakers. In the words of eyewitness Roger Clap who had previously assailed Anne Hutchinson
as an instrument of the Devil: "Satan made another assault upon
God's poor people here, by stirring up the Quakers to come amongst
us, both Men and Women."

William Coddington, the wealthy businessman who testified for
Anne as a witness at her General Court hearing and voted against
her banishment, went into exile with her at Rhode Island and
adopted Quakerism in 1656. Among other followers who turned
Quaker was Nicholas Easton, tanner, who at Aquidneck preached

Anne's doctrine of direct communication with God. John Winthrop dismissed him as "a man very bold though ignorant." Also, Anne's sister Katherine Marbury Scott joined the Quakers, actively proselytizing. She was frequently subjected to whipping and prison.

In 1658, the General Court, in an emotionally stormy session, passed by one vote a law ordering Quakers banished on pain of hanging. Defying the law was Anne's most conspicuous disciple, Mary Dyer. Preaching "inner light," Mary Dyer rejected oaths of any kind, taught that sex was no determinant for gifts of prophecy, and contended that women and men stood on equal ground in church worship and organization. She was imprisoned twice, and, when she refused to recant or depart, was hanged in Boston on June 1, 1660.*

Five children survived Anne, three daughters and two sons. The youngest was ten-year-old Susanna, taken captive when her mother and siblings were massacred at their Pelham Bay home. In the peace treaty between the Dutch and the Indians in 1645, she was to be released on payment of ransom provided by New England friends of the Hutchinsons. After four years of captivity she was freed, though she expressed reluctance to return to white civilization. She married John Cole of Boston on December 30, 1651, when she was eighteen, and disappeared into posterity.

Anne's oldest daughter, Faith, was living in Boston at the time of the massacre, married to Thomas Savage who, after staunchly defending his mother-in-law at her excommunication trial, made peace with the church. Her next oldest daughter, Bridget, was living in Rhode Island where, in 1653, her husband, John Sanford, was elected "President of Rhode Island."

Her son Richard, living in Boston at the time, was the ancestor of

---

*Today, statues of both Anne Hutchinson and Mary Dyer adorn the front lawn of the Massachusetts State House. Anne Hutchinson stands directly outside the west wing, the work of Cyrus Dallin, given by the Anne Hutchinson Memorial Association and State Federation of Women's Clubs on June 2, 1922. On the other side of the State House, close to the street, is the statue of Mary Dyer, funded by Zenith Ellis of Fairhaven, Vermont, a descendant. Sculpted by Sylvia Shaw Judson of Lake Forest, Illinois, it was presented on July 9, 1959.

nineteenth-century feminist Abigail Jemima Hutchinson and her three brothers, who, billing themselves as "The Hutchinson Family," toured old and New England as a singing quartet promoting antislavery, peace, temperance, and women's rights.

Her oldest son, Edward, a leading businessman and pillar of Boston by the 1660s, came to a sad but praiseworthy end in 1675. He was killed on a mission of friendship to the Nipmuc Indians amid the wholesale slaughter, on both sides, that occurred during King Philip's War (Philip, sachem of the Wampanoag tribe, was the son of Massasoit who had befriended and aided the Pilgrims in early Plymouth).

Interestingly, Edward's daughter Anne Hutchinson, born shortly after her grandmother's murder, married Samuel, son of William and Mary Dyer, the Quaker martyr. He died early, however, and on September 22, 1679, at the age of thirty-four, she married a Daniel Vernon and was not heard from again.

No history-shaking offspring was conceived by the Hutchinson-Dyer coupling. But more than a century after the murder of Anne Hutchinson, Sr., Hannah Mather was born at Boston, in 1752—daughter of the marriage of Hannah Hutchinson, great-great-granddaughter of Anne Hutchinson (through her son Edward), and Samuel Mather, great-grandson of John Cotton, quondam idol-turned-deserter of Anne Hutchinson. Hannah Mather was also the granddaughter of Cotton Mather, denouncer of Anne Hutchinson and a prime mover in the Salem witch hunt of 1692, whose victims were mostly women, many of them outspoken.

Married in 1779 to Joseph Crocker, Harvard graduate and Taunton, Massachusetts, businessman, Hannah Mather Crocker behaved like a virtual reincarnation of her famous ancestor Anne Hutchinson. Insisting that "women have an equal right with the other sex to form societies for promoting religious, charitable, and benevolent purposes," she organized women into study groups. Further, she declared that both sexes shared equally in divine grace, and she asserted that from perfect understanding between men and women would emerge the extra measure of "sense and judgment" essential for preserving a free government. In 1818, she published privately her book, *Observations on the Real Rights of Women*, contending that "the wise Author of Nature has endowed the female mind with equal powers and faculties, and given them the same right of judging and acting for themselves, as he gave to the male sex."

Anne Hutchinson had failed to change the world immediately, in her own lifetime.

But the Establishment had failed to silence her—or to prevent her from showering the future with irrepressible ideas and ideals.

Notes

Notes are keyed to the two-part Select Bibliography, which contains full details on sources cited. Part one of the bibliography, sixteenth- and seventeenth-century works, will be found on pages 225–229; and part two, eighteenth-, nineteenth-, and twentieth-century works, on pages 229–234. Carefully authenticated reprints of early sources, which have the dual advantage of easily readable modern typesetting and of availability in general libraries and bookstores, have been used and cited wherever feasible, with the original date included to direct the reader to the appropriate section of the bibliography. To facilitate identification of the original author of a work appearing as part of a modern collection, the name of the original author, title of the work, and date of publication are given in the first chapter reference, along with the editor and title of the collection that appears in the bibliography, and relevant page(s).

Spelling and punctuation in both title and text have been modernized, except in a few instances where the original adds to the flavor of the times without detracting from twentieth-century comprehension. There is no particular danger of distortion since copies of the same document often turn up with completely different spelling and punctuation.

INTRODUCTION:
A WOMAN FOR ALL SEASONS

PAGE

1   "Liar": *The New York Times*, December 6, 1979; *Boston Globe*, February 29, 1980.

1   "PLAN TO ORDAIN WOMEN . . .": *The New York Times*, December 21, 1979.

1 "CATHOLIC CHURCH . . . ": *The New York Times*, December 26, 1979.

1 "IN THE RELIGIOUS LIFE . . . ": *The New York Times*, March 8, 1980.

2 "rather been a husband . . . ": Franklin B. Dexter, ed., "A Report of the Trial of Mrs. Anne Hutchinson Before the Church in Boston, 1638," p. 186.

3 "nor fitting for your sex": Thomas Hutchinson, ed., "The Examination of Mrs. Anne Hutchinson . . . 1637," p. 366.

3 "that filthy sin . . . ": Dexter, p. 178.

3 "conveyed an impression . . . ": George E. Ellis, *Life of Anne Hutchinson*, 1845, pp. 366–67.

3 menopausal neurotic: Emery Battis, *Saints and Sectaries*, 1962, pp. 269, 346.

4 "the community of women . . . ": Dexter, p. 171.

CHAPTER 1
"THOU ART A VERY ASS"

9 "Kings on a Queen . . . ": Mary Sidney Herbert, "To the Thrice Sacred Queen Elizabeth," 1599, in Mary R. Mahl and Helene Koon, eds., *The Female Spectator*, p. 69.

10 "I know I have the body . . . ": Queen Elizabeth I, speech to troops at Tilbury, summer of 1588.

10–11 Small wonder . . . : Louis B. Wright, *Middle-Class Culture in Elizabethan England*, 1958, pp. 476–480.

12 Self-seeking soul murderers . . . : Francis Marbury, "The Conference between me and the Bishop of London . . . ," c. 1590, in Frederick L. Gay, ed., "Note and Documents on Rev. Francis Marbury," pp. 283, 285.

13 erroneously accused . . . ": William Pierce, *An Historical Introduction to the Marprelate Tracts*, 1908, pp. 281–82.

13 "and none other . . . ": Gay, pp. 288–90.

13 tiny isolated Alford . . . : Reginald C. Dudding, *History of the Parish and Manors of Alford*, 1930, p. 159.

15 "That young maidens can learn . . . ": Richard Mulcaster, *Positions*, 1581, p. 173.

16 "The conference between me . . . ": Gay, p. 238.

17 "B. Marbury, where were you . . . ": Gay, p. 283.

17–18 "Sir, if your ears . . . ": Ibid., pp. 283–84.

18 "Thy proposition . . . ": Ibid., p. 284.

18–19   Anomalously . . . : Ibid.
    19   "B. Thou speakest of making ministers . . . ": Ibid., pp. 284–85.
19–20   "Thou takest upon thee . . . ": Ibid., p. 285.
    20   "How provest . . . ": Ibid.
    20   "Go to the purpose . . . ": Ibid., p. 286.
    20   "You may try him . . . ": Ibid.
    21   "What trial would you have . . . ": Ibid.
    21   "I thought where thou wouldst be . . . ": Ibid., p. 287.
21–22   "Mul. Sir, in the beginning . . . ": Ibid.
    22   "Thou art an overthwart . . . ": Ibid.

CHAPTER 2
"HERS TO OBEY"

    25   St. Martin in the Vintry . . . : John Stow, *The Survey of London*, 1603, pp. 214, 215, 222. (St. Paul's, originally a Saxon cathedral, was destroyed in the great fire of 1087. The conquering Normans dedicated a new cathedral on the site in 1241, which was completed about a century later in 1327. Its 450-foot spire dominated the London skyline. This cathedral would be destroyed in the London fire of 1666.)
    25   The 141-mile journey: Richard Mather, "Journal," 1635, in Alexander Young, ed., *Chronicles of the First Planters of the Colony of Massachusetts Bay . . .*, p. 448; Joan Parkes, *Travel in England in the Seventeenth Century*, 1925, pp. 12–31, 52–83, 152–53, and 192–99. (Richard Mather, traveling from Warrington—20 miles from Liverpool—to Bristol, wrote that his party covered 119 or 120 miles in seven days, April 16–23, 1635.) Also highly informative is the permanent exhibition at the London Museum.
    26   Marbury coat of arms ("Sable, a cross . . . "): Meredith B. Colket, Jr., *The English Ancestry of Anne Marbury Hutchinson and Katherine Marbury Scott*, 1936, p. 18.
    26   Royal Exchange: Stow, pp. 69–70, 104, 173, 180.
26–27   rector's living quarters: Wallace Notestein, *The English People on the Eve of Colonization, 1603–1660*, 1962, p. 64.
    27   Two- and four-wheeled carriages: London Museum.
    27   cries of hawkers, quoted from contemporaneous plays by Henry Thew Stephenson, *Shakespeare's London*, 1905, p. 79.
    28   cleanse the air: Ibid., p. 71.
    29   imported or English glass: London Museum.

29   Thames River: Stephenson, p. 63.

30   His prosperous parishioners: Stow, pp. 215–16.

30–31   the vestry: London Museum; Carl Bridenbaugh, *Vexed and Troubled Englishmen, 1590–1642*, 1968, pp. 244 ff.

31   Puritan relatives of: Colket, pp. 24–26.

31   Dredging up every insult . . . : Anthony Weldon, "James I," 1650, pp. 3–9, John Chamberlain, *Letters . . . 1597–1626*, p. 348.

32   her sister Mary: Ibid., pp. 32–34.

33   London women had been conspicuous: *The Marprelate Tracts*, 1588, 1589, ed., William Pierce, p. 152; William Pierce, *An Historical Introduction to the Marprelate Tracts*, 1908, p. 25.

34   "agrees as well . . . ": William Barlow, *The Summe and Substance of the Conference . . . at Hampton Court, January 14, 1603* [1604], p. 79.

34   never must midwives . . . : Ibid., pp. 8, 14, 18, 30–31.

34   "the women further . . . ": William Bradford, *Of Plymouth Plantation, 1620–1649*, p. 12.

35   Equally dismaying: Wallace Notestein, *A History of Witchcraft in England from 1588 to 1718*, 1968, pp. 105–106.

35   "the snares of the Devil . . . ": James I, King of England, *Daemonologie*, 1597, pp. xii, xiii, 29, 37, 68–69.

36   "Teach your wife . . . ": Doris Mary Stenton, *The English Woman in History*, 1977, p. 142.

36   "The more women, the more witches": William Perkins, *A Discourse of the Damned Art of Witchcraft. . . .* 1608, p. 637.

37   "kings are justly called gods . . . ": James I, speech to Parliament, March 21, 1610.

38   "How can your priests . . . ": Alexander Cooke, *Pope Joane*, 1610, pp. 127–28.

38   "Daniell Marberye . . . ": Colket, p. 33.

CHAPTER 3
"THE ENGLISH HUSWIFE"

39   "sole executrix" . . . "and dwell where they would choose": Francis Marbury, Will, 1610 (1611).

40   on her mother's side . . . : John Denison Champlin, "Hutchinson Ancestry and Descendants of William and Anne Hutchinson," 1914, pp. 164–69.

41   his parents' house . . . : Edward Hutchinson, Inventory, 1631
      (1632).

42   "she must have a quick eye . . . ": Gervase Markham, *The En-
      glish Huswife*, 1647, p. 4.

43   "must be of chaste thought . . . ": Ibid., p. 5.

44   receptiveness of newly developing sects: William Pierce, *An His-
      torical Introduction to the Marprelate Tracts*, 1908, p. 25;
      Keith Thomas, "Women and the Civil War Sects," 1965,
      passim.

44   "Woman of Ely": Franklin B. Dexter, ed., "A Report of the
      Trial of Mrs. Anne Hutchinson . . . 1638," pp. 184–85.

44–45 Of a population . . . : George E. Fussell and Kathleen R. Fus-
      sell, *The English Countrywoman*, 1953, p. xiii.

45   Familists preached . . . : Elizabeth I, "A Proclamation against
      the Sectaries of the Family of Love," 1580; John Etherington,
      A Brief Discovery of the Blasphemous Doctrine of Familism,
      1645, passim; John Knewstub, *A Confutation of monstrous
      and Horrible Heresies* . . . , 1579, passim; Hendrik Niclaes,
      Comoedia, c. 1575, passim; and *Evangelium regni*, 1575,
      passim.

45   Some took to direct action . . . : Wallace Notestein, "The En-
      glish Woman, 1580 to 1650," 1955, p. 94.

45   "When to their husbands . . . ": Elizabeth Carey, *The Tragedy
      of Miriam, the Fair Queen of Jewry*, 1613, in Anne Stanford,
      ed., *The Women Poets in English*, pp. 35–36.

46   "Both man and woman . . . ": Rachel Speght, "A Dream,"
      1621, Stanford, ed., p. 42.

46   "This is the fashion . . . ": quoted in Notestein, p. 75.

47–48 "Let not us women glory . . . ": Aemelia Lanier, "Eve's Apology
      in Defense of Women," 1611, in Mary R. Mahl and Helene
      Koon, eds., *The Female Spectator*, pp. 84, 85, 86.

49   Week after week . . . : Samuel Whiting (1597–1679), "Life of
      John Cotton," in Alexander Young, ed., *Chronicles of the
      First Planters of Massachusetts Bay* . . . , pp. 419–30.

49–50 "for some more than ordinary assistance . . . ": quoted in Mark
      Spurrell, *The Puritan Town of Boston*, 1972, p. 3.

50   "a town so famous for religion": Ibid., p. 7.

50   "one of England's glories": Whiting, "Life," Young, ed., p. 427.

50   "invention, elegance . . . ": John Norton, *Biography of John
      Cotton*, 1652, in Albert B. Hart, ed., *American History Told
      by Contemporaries*, 1897, vol. 1, p. 336.

50   "five hours long . . . ": Spurrell, p. 9.

51 "There were some scores of godly persons . . . " John Cotton, "The Way of the Congregational Churches Cleared," 1648, in Larzer Ziff, ed., *John Cotton on the Churches of New England*, p. 198. (This quote is not included in the excerpt from "The Way . . . Cleared" printed in David D. Hall, ed., *The Antinomian Controversy*.)

CHAPTER 4
"WHEN I WAS IN OLD ENGLAND"

53 ". . . How soon my Dear . . . ": Anne Bradstreet, *Works*, 1650, 1678, ed., Jeannine Hensley, p. 224.

53 "well beloved in England . . . ": John Cotton, "The Way of the Congregational Churches Cleared," 1648, in David D. Hall, ed., *The Antinomian Controversy*, p. 411.

54 John Cotton in his preaching . . . : Samuel Whiting (1597–1679), "Life of John Cotton," in Alexander Young, ed., *Chronicles of the First Planters of Massachusetts Bay . . .*, p. 423; Larzer Ziff, *The Career of John Cotton*, 1962, p. 42.

54 no church authority . . . : Reginald C. Dudding, *History of the Parish and Manors of Alford*, 1930, p. 98.

55 "pious subtlety": quoted by Larzer Ziff, *Career*, p. 49.

55 "Of all men in the world . . . ": Whiting, "Life," Young, ed., p. 426.

56 *The Arraignment of Lewd, Idle . . .* : Louis B. Wright, *Middle-Class Culture in Elizabethan England*, 1958, p. 486; Doris Mary Stenton, *The English Woman in History*, 1977, p. 141; Lu Emily Pearson, *Elizabethans at Home*, 1957, p. 287.

56 *The Worming of a Mad Dog . . .* : Wright, p. 489.

56 *Swetnam, the Woman-hater . . .* : quoted in Carroll Camden, *The Elizabethan Woman*, 1952, p. 263.

56–57 *Esther hath hanged Haman . . .* : C. Camden, pp. 259–60; Stenton, pp. 141–42; Wright, p. 488.

57 "January 25, 1620 . . . ": John Chamberlain, *Letters Concerning Life in England, 1597–1626*, ed., Elizabeth M. Thomson, p. 271.

57–58 "Our pulpits ring . . . ": Ibid.

58 *Hic Mulier . . .* : C. Camden, pp. 264, 270; Wright, p. 494.

58–59 *Haec Vir . . .* : quoted in Wright, p. 495.

59 "went to King James . . . ": Whiting, "Life," Young, ed., p. 426.

59 "When I was in old England . . . ": John Winthrop, "Short

Story," 1644, in David D. Hall, ed., *The Antinomian Controversy*, pp. 271-72. Also see Thomas Hutchinson, ed., "The Examination of Mrs. Anne Hutchinson . . . 1637," p. 383.

60 "The Lord saw that these waters . . . ": Thomas Shepard, "Memoir," c. 1646, Young, ed., pp. 539-40.

62 "heard early in the morning . . . ": quoted by Keith Thomas, *Religion and the Decline of Magic*, 1973, p. 162.

CHAPTER 5
"TO NEW ENGLAND...I MUST GO"

63 "a man of very mild temper . . . ": John Winthrop, *History of New England, 1630-1649*, James K. Hosmer, ed., vol. 1, p. 299. (Unless otherwise specified, all references to Winthrop's journal, *History of New England*, are taken from the version edited by James K. Hosmer.)

64 "the kind usage . . . ": William Wood, *New England's Prospect*, 1634, p. 115.

64 "since he came hither . . . ": Francis Higginson, "New England's Plantation," 1630, in Alexander Young, ed., *Chronicles of the First Planters of the Colony of Massachusetts Bay . . .*, p. 252.

64 a readily available feast . . . : Ibid.; Wood, pp. 54-57.

64 "Nature teaches bees . . . ": Larzer Ziff, *The Career of John Cotton*, 1962, pp. 60-62; Mark Spurrell, *The Puritan Town of Boston*, 1972, p. 7.

65 "If he should . . . ": John Winthrop, "Particular Considerations in the case of J. W.," printed in Robert C. Winthrop, *Life and Letters of John Winthrop*, 1869, vol. 1, p. 327.

66-67 at this worst of all times . . . : conversation and exhaustive tour to Mills Cross Hill (where the hollowed stone still stands) with Alford historian Geoffrey W. H. Hatfield, BE 17.

69 "a long and sore sickness . . . ": John Cotton, "Letter," 1633, Young, ed., pp. 435-36.

69 "You must fly . . . ": Cotton Mather, *Magnalia Christi Americana*, 1853, vol. 1, p. 263.

70 "The Lord carrying Mr. Cotton . . . ": Thomas Hutchinson, ed., "The Examination of Mrs. Anne Hutchinson . . . 1637," p. 384.

70 One time when a pregnant woman . . . : J. H. Adamson and H. F. Folland, *Sir Henry Vane*, 1973, p. 49.

71-72 "When I think of the sweet . . . ": John Cotton, "Poem," printed in Everett H. Emerson, *John Cotton*, 1965, p. 153.

72 Too many were leaving for New England . . . : John Winthrop, *History*, ed., Hosmer, vol. 1, pp. 127–28.

72 "things very unready . . . ": Richard Mather, "Journal," 1635, Young, ed., pp. 448–52.

73 "that she had never had any great thing done . . . " T. Hutchinson, ed., "Examination," 1637, p. 385.

73 "it was revealed . . . ": Ibid.

73 "she did slight . . . ": Ibid., p. 273.

73–74 miseries and terrors of the voyage . . . : See descriptions of voyages made around this same time, in the mid-1630s, by Richard Mather and Thomas Shepard, Young, ed., pp. 447–79 and p. 544.

74 "Corrupt" and "narrow": T. Hutchinson, ed., "Examination," 1637, p. 373.

74 "What would you say . . . ": Ibid., p. 385; John Winthrop, "Short Story," 1644, in David D. Hall, ed., *The Antinomian Controversy*, p. 263.

75 "had a revelation . . . ": T. Hutchinson, ed., "Examination," 1637, p. 385.

75 "I would remember . . . " and "I do not remember . . . ": Ibid.

PART TWO
"THE FOLLOWERS OF MS. HUTCHINSON"

77 "The Followers of Ms. Hutchinson": John Cotton, "The Way of the Congregational Churches Cleared," in David D. Hall, ed., *The Antinomian Controversy*, p. 398.

CHAPTER 6
"THE THIRD THIRD DAY
OF THE THIRD MONTH"

81 "satisfied that she held . . . ": Thomas Hutchinson, ed., "The Examination of Mrs. Anne Hutchinson . . . 1637," p. 370.

81 "in her answers . . . ": Ibid., p. 374.

81 "cunningly dissembled . . . ": John Winthrop, "Short Story," 1644, in David D. Hall, ed., *The Antinomian Controversy*, p. 263.

83-84 "The toil of a new plantation . . . ": Edward Johnson, *Wonder-Working Providence, 1628-1651*, p. 114.

85-86 "from the lips of an old lady . . . ": "Forefathers' Song," c. 1630, reprinted in *Annals of America*, vol. 1, pp. 21-22.

86 "even the most honored . . . ": Johnson, p. 78.

86 "some a foot long . . . ": William Wood, *New England's Prospect*, 1634, pp. 56-57.

87 "it would have been a strange thing . . . ": Roger Clap, *Memoirs from 1630*, p. 42.

88 "where there was so much of equality . . . ": Thomas Hutchinson, *The History of the Colony and Province of Massachusetts-Bay*, 1764, vol. 1, p. 381.

88 "man" as "human being . . . ": cf. *Webster's Third International Dictionary*, Unabridged, s.v. "man"; *The Oxford English Dictionary*, s.v. "man."

89 "the third third day . . . ": T. Hutchinson, *History*, vol. 1, p. 362.

89 "We were not willing . . . ": John Winthrop, *History*, 1630-49, ed., Hosmer, vol. 2, p. 331. Also see William Bradford, *Of Plymouth Plantation, 1620-1649*, p. 86.

90-91 "The Court taking into consideration . . . ": Nathaniel B. Shurtleff, ed., *Records of the Governor and Company of the Massachusetts Bay in New England, 1628-1641*, vol. 1, p. 126. (Hereafter cited as *Mass. Records*.)

92 The suggestion was too much . . . : John Winthrop, *History*, ed., Hosmer, vol. 1, p. 120.

93 "She hath wiped away . . . ": Anne Bradstreet, *Works*, 1650, 1678, ed., Jeannine Hensley, pp. 196, 197-98.

CHAPTER 7
"FIFTY, SIXTY, OR EIGHTY AT ONCE"

94 She took up the practice slowly . . . : John Winthrop, "Short Story," 1644, in David D. Hall, ed., *The Antinomian Controversy*, p. 267.

95 "The ground of my taking it up . . . ": Thomas Hutchinson, "The Examination of Mrs. Anne Hutchinson . . . 1637," p. 368.

95 "if any came to visit . . . ": Cotton Mather, *Magnalia Christi Americana*, 1853, vol. 1, pp. 275-76.

95-96 "a woman of a haughty and fierce carriage . . . ": Winthrop, "Short Story," Hall, ed., p. 263.

96   "the godly magistrates . . . ": Thomas Weld, "Short Story,"
        1644, Hall, ed., p. 208.

96   Mrs. Hett: John Winthrop, *History*, 1630-49, ed., Hosmer, vol.
        1, p. 230.

96   Dorothy Talbye: Ibid., p. 282.

96   "much pride and unnaturalness . . . ": Sidney Perley, *The His-
        tory of Salem, Massachusetts*, 1928, vol. 2, p. 52.

96-97 Ann Hopkins, "a godly young woman . . . ": John Winthrop,
        History, ed., Hosmer, vol. 2, p. 225.

97   "When I remember . . . ": Thomas Hutchinson, *The History of
        the Colony and Province of Massachusetts-Bay*, 1764, vol. 1,
        p. 405.

97   "threescore . . . ": Winthrop, "Short Story," Hall, ed., p. 264.

97   "fifty, sixty . . . ": Weld, "Short Story," Hall, ed., p. 207.

97   "As soon as she . . . ": Winthrop, "Short Story," Hall, ed.,
        p. 263.

97-98 "She did much good . . . ": John Cotton, "The Way of the Con-
        gregational Churches Cleared," 1648, Hall, ed., p. 412.

98   "this woman hath learned . . . ": Winthrop, "Short Story,"
        Hall, ed., p. 263.

98   "the pretense . . . ": Ibid., p. 264.

98   "the custom was . . . ": Weld, "Short Story," Hall, ed., pp.
        207-8.

99   "I sent some sisters . . . ": Cotton, "Way Cleared," Hall, ed.,
        p. 413.

99   "Midwives . . . not only have familiarity . . . ": Ibid., p. 437;
        Robert Baylie, *A Dissuasive from the Errours of the Time*,
        1645, p. 65.

99   "For a person that is distracted . . . ": quoted in George Dow,
        Every Day Life in the Massachusetts Bay Colony, 1935, pp.
        183-84.

100   "For sharp and difficult travail . . . ": Ibid., p. 185.

100   Native Americans had long relied . . . : Ibid., pp. 191-95.

100   Among the abuses to be outlawed . . . : Thomas R. Forbes, *The
        Midwife and the Witch*, 1966, pp. 146-47.

101   "That any but a lawful minister . . . ": William Barlow, *The
        Summe and Substance of the Conference . . . at Hampton
        Court, January 14, 1603* [1604], p. 8.

101   "the community of women . . . ": Franklin B. Dexter, ed., "A
        Report of the Trial of Mrs. Anne Hutchinson . . . 1638," p. 171.

101   "Some being tainted . . . ": Weld, "Short Story," Hall, ed.,
        p. 202.

101   "some of the magistrates . . . ": Ibid., pp. 207, 208.

102 "began to raise sedition amongst us . . . ": Ibid., p. 213.

102 "Mistress Hutchinson's opinions . . . ": Ibid., pp. 205–6.

102 "She would comment . . . ": Winthrop, "Short Story," Hall, ed., p. 264.

102–103 "To be obedient . . . ": Hendrik Niclaes, *Comoedia*, c. 1575, p. 12.

103 "It was a wonder . . . ": John Winthrop, "Short Story," 1644, Hall, ed., p. 264.

104 a syllogism . . . : paraphrase of Winthrop, "Short Story," Hall, ed., pp. 262–66; and Thomas Dudley quoted in T. Hutchinson, "Examination," 1637, p. 370.

104 "partly in respect . . . ": John Winthrop, *History*, ed., Hosmer, p. 150.

CHAPTER 8
"GRAND MISTRESS OF THEM ALL"

108 "Mr. Wilson cannot yet persuade . . . ": Robert C. Winthrop, *Life and Letters of John Winthrop*, 1869, vol. 2, p. 86.

108 "the son and heir . . . ": John Winthrop, *History*, 1630–49, ed., Hosmer, vol. 1, pp. 161–62.

109 Roger Williams . . . : Ibid., pp. 116, 149, 154, 162, 179.

110 women . . . among his most devout followers: Ibid., p. 168.

110 "The married women . . . ": Thomas Hutchinson, *The History of the Colony and Province of Massachusetts-Bay*, 1764, vol. 1, p. 363. Also see William Hubbard, *A General History of New England*, c. 1680, pp. 204–5.

110–111 "Whereas Mr. Roger Williams . . . ": Nathaniel Shurtleff, ed., *Mass. Records*, 1628–41, vol. 1, pp. 160–61.

111 "At a general meeting . . . ": James K. Hosmer, *The Life of Young Sir Henry Vane*, 1888, p. 32.

112 "foul, scandalous invectives . . . ": John Winthrop, *History*, ed., Hosmer, vol. 1, pp. 84–88.

112 "a more firm and friendly uniting of minds . . . ": Ibid., p. 170.

112–113 "that strict discipline . . . ": Ibid., p. 171.

113 "The snake was the devil . . . ": Ibid., pp. 83–84.

114 "Henry Vane . . . ": Ibid., p. 180.

114 "to congratulate his election . . . ": Ibid.

115 "Besides the quarter courts . . . ": Hubbard, p. 234.

115 "Come along with me . . . ": Edward Johnson, *Wonder-Working Providence*, 1628–51, p. 127.

115-116   "a little nimble-tongued woman . . . ": Ibid., p. 134.
116   Anne's leadership, describing her . . . : Ibid., pp. 128, 186.
116   "all sit till doomsday . . . ": Thomas Weld, "Short Story," 1644, in David D. Hall, ed., *The Antinomian Controversy*, p. 206.
116   "We must look . . . ": John Wheelwright, *His Writings Including His Fast-Day Sermon, 1637, and His Mercurius Americanus, 1645*, ed., Charles H. Bell, p. 211.
117-118   Other prosperous merchants and their wives . . . : Emery Battis, *Saints and Sectaries*, 1962, pp. 101-3.
118   Richard Hawkins . . . : Keith Thomas, *Religion and the Decline of Magic*, 1973, p. 163.
118   "disclaiming Mr. Williams's opinions . . . ": Ola E. Winslow, *Master Roger Williams*, 1957, p. 123.
119   "dangerous errors . . . ": John Winthrop, *History*, ed., Hosmer, vol. 1, pp. 195-96.

CHAPTER 9
"GUILTY OF SEDITION AND ALSO OF CONTEMPT"

121   "Your opinions . . . ": Thomas Hutchinson, "The Examination of Mrs. Anne Hutchinson . . . 1637," p. 369.
122   no new members joined the Boston church: John Cotton, "The Way of the Congregational Churches Cleared," 1648, in David Hall, ed., *The Antinomian Controversy*, p. 414. Also see editor James K. Hosmer's footnote in John Winthrop, *History, 1630-49*, vol. 1, p. 209.
122   "Some of the church of Boston . . . ": John Winthrop, *History*, ed., Hosmer, vol. 1, 196-97.
122   "My wife hath said . . . ": T. Hutchinson, "Examination," 1637, p. 388.
123   "while the glass was turned up twice": Edward Johnson, *Wonder-Working Providence, 1628-1651*, p. 135.
123   "whose spirit they knew not . . . ": John Winthrop, *History*, ed., Hosmer, vol. 1, pp. 196-97.
123   "so as he could be content . . . ": Ibid., p. 197.
123   "How this was taken . . . ": Ibid., pp. 198-211.
124   "in writing for the peace sake . . . ": Ibid., p. 201.
125   "the governor expressed himself . . . ": Ibid., p. 203.

125 "Before [Henry Vane] came . . . ": Ibid., p. 204.

125 "Mr. Wilson made a very sad speech . . . ": Ibid.

126 "as great as between heaven and hell": John Winthrop, "Short Story," 1644, Hall, ed., p. 248.

127 "to exercise as a private brother": Ibid., p. 291.

127 For example: "We must all . . . ": John Wheelwright, "A Fast Day Sermon," 1637, Hall, ed., pp. 158, 163, 166.

127 "brethren and sisters": Ibid., p. 171.

127 "valiant men": Ibid., pp. 158-59.

128 "the said officer . . . ": Nathaniel Shurtleff, ed., *Mass. Records*, vol. 1, 1628-41, p. 186.

128 "Groundless and presumptuous": John Winthrop, *History*, ed., Hosmer, vol. 1, p. 210.

128 "guilty of sedition": Ibid., p. 211.

128-129 "remonstrance . . . ": complete text printed in George Ellis, *Life of Anne Hutchinson*, 1845, pp. 371-75.

129 "accounted as legal preachers . . . ": John Winthrop, *History*, ed., Hosmer, vol. 1, p. 213.

129 "dealt with Mrs. Hutchinson . . . ": Cotton, "Way Cleared," Hall, ed., p. 399.

129-130 "Fierce speeches . . . ": John Winthrop, *History*, ed., Hosmer, vol. 1, p. 219.

130 "not finding how . . . ": Ibid., p. 216.

130 "Mr. Wilson, the minister, in his zeal . . . ": Thomas Hutchinson, *The History of the Colony and Province of Massachusetts-Bay*, 1764, p. 54 (footnote). The author noted that he was quoting the "MS Life of J. Wilson," a source that disappeared long ago without a trace.

130 "to keep out all such persons . . . ": John Winthrop, *History*, ed., Hosmer, vol. 1, p. 219.

131 "a man . . . having the spirit . . . ": Christopher Hill, *The World Turned Upside Down*, 1974, p. 83.

131 "Divine slaughter": Thomas Shepard, "Memoir," 1644, Alexander Young, ed. *Chronicles of the First Planters of the Colony of Massachusetts Bay . . .*, p. 549.

131 "not one man . . . ": John Winthrop, "Short Story," Hall, ed., p. 254.

131 "quarrel being as ancient . . . ": Johnson, p. 148.

131 "God permitted Satan . . . ": Roger Clap, *Memoirs from 1630*, p. 37.

132 "there was no lawful authority . . . ": John Winthrop, *History*, ed., Hosmer, vol. 1, p. 221.

132 "no man could tell . . . ": Ibid., p. 209.

132 "Such as knew . . . ": Ibid., pp. 216–17.

133 "That though women might meet . . . ": Ibid., p. 234.

134 "the magistrates should . . . ": Ibid., p. 171.

CHAPTER 10
"THE APPLE OF THEIR OWN EYE"

135 "was dissolved until a new be called . . . ": Nathaniel Shurtleff,
     ed., *Mass. Records*, 1628–41, p. 205.

135 "by reason of the great snows and frosts . . . ": John Winthrop,
     History, 1630–49, ed., Hosmer, vol. 1, p. 138.

135 "her wonted meetings . . . ": John Winthrop, "Short Story,"
     1644, in David D. Hall, ed., *The Antinomian Controversy*, p.
     248.

136 "he would have desired . . . "; "He had known other monstrous
     births . . . ": John Winthrop, *History*, ed., Hosmer, vol. 1,
     pp. 267–68.

136 "If any child be dead born . . . ": quoted in Thomas R. Forbes,
     The Midwife and the Witch, 1966, p. 147.

136 "Mr. Cotton had in public view . . . ": John Winthrop, "Short
     Story," Hall, ed., p. 248.

137 "almost in every family . . . ": John Cotton, "The Way of the
     Congregational Churches Cleared," 1648, Hall, ed., p. 433.

137–138 "Sad Boston, 1637 . . . ": Robert C. Winthrop, *Life and Letters
     of John Winthrop*, 1869, vol. 2, pp. 178–79.

138 "Business would not permit me . . . ": Ibid., p. 179.

139 "on other occasions . . . ": John Winthrop, "Short Story," Hall,
     ed., p. 263.

139 "a young man, coming alone . . . ": John Winthrop, *History*,
     ed., Hosmer, vol. 1, p. 238.

140 "a spacious plain . . . ": Edward Johnson, *Wonder-Working
     Providence, 1628–1651*, p. 201.

140 "one of the neatest . . . ": William Wood, *New England's Pros-
     pect*, 1634, p. 60.

140–141 "Whereas many complaints . . . ": Shurtleff, *Mass. Records*,
     p. 190.

141 "seditious libel": John Winthrop, "Short Story," Hall, ed.,
     p. 260.

141 "not one example . . . "; "If he had kept . . . ": Ibid., p. 259.

142 "one of the sergeants of Boston": Ibid., p. 261.

143 "in any other place . . . ": Ibid.
143 "very apt to meddle . . . ": Ibid., p. 262.
143 "so soon as any were set down . . . ": Johnson, p. 192.
143 "an honest poor man . . . ": John Winthrop, "Short Story,"
     Hall, ed., p. 262.
143 "the head of all this faction . . . ": Ibid.
144 "the governor thought not fit . . . ": John Winthrop, *History*,
     ed., Hosmer, vol. 1, p. 226.
144 "What an height . . . ": Thomas Weld, "Short Story," Hall,
     ed., p. 211.
144 "audaciously insolent . . . ": Ibid.

CHAPTER 11
"NOR FITTING FOR YOUR SEX"

149 "Mrs. Hutchinson, you are called here . . . ": Thomas Hutch-
     inson, ed., "The Examination of Mrs. Anne Hutchin-
     son . . . 1637," p. 366.
149 "I would entreat you . . . ": Ibid.
150 "I am called here . . . ": Ibid.
150 "Gov. I have told you . . . ": Ibid.
151 "fathers of the commonwealth": Ibid., p. 367.
151 "We do not mean . . . ": Ibid.
151–152 "I conceive . . . ": Ibid., p. 368.
152 "Suppose a man . . . "; "I think I may . . . "; "We do not
     call . . . ": Ibid.
152 "You have a plain rule . . . ": John Winthrop, "Short Story,"
     1644, in David D. Hall, ed., *The Antinomian Controversy*,
     p. 267.
153 "Mrs. H. I desire that . . . ": T. Hutchinson, "Examination,"
     p. 368.
153 "You say . . . ": Ibid.
153 "Your ministry is public . . . ": John Winthrop, "Short Story,"
     Hall, ed., p. 269.
153 "We are your judges . . . ": T. Hutchinson, "Examination,"
     p. 369.
154 "Yes, you are the woman of most note . . . ": John Winthrop,
     "Short Story," Hall, ed., p. 268.
154 "After she had stood . . . ": Ibid.
154 "I am not against . . . ": T. Hutchinson, "Examination," p. 369.

154   The colonial authorities "loved controversy . . . ": Charles F. Adams, *Three Episodes of Massachusetts History*, 1892, vol. I, p. 406.

154–155   "I am obnoxious . . . ": Anne Bradstreet, *Works*, 1650, 1678, ed., Jeannine Hensley, p. 16.

155   "that every time he read the Bible . . . ": Cotton Mather, *Magnalia Christi Americana*, 1702, vol. I, p. 378.

156   "whether that glorious estate of perfection . . . ": Thomas Shepard, "Memoir," 1644, in Alexander Young, ed., *Chronicles of the First Planters of the Colony of Massachusetts Bay . . .*, p. 507.

156   "I am loathe . . . "; "I desire to speak . . . ": T. Hutchinson, "Examination," p. 374.

156   "I am loathe to spend time. Therefore . . . ": Ibid.

156–157   "Mrs. Hutchinson, the court . . . ": Ibid., p. 376.

CHAPTER 12
"SAY NO MORE"

158   "here was sufficient . . . ": Thomas Hutchinson, ed., "The Examination of Mrs. Anne Hutchinson . . . 1637," p. 376.

158   "Mr. Wilson did then write . . . ": Ibid., p. 377.

158   "Let those that are not . . . ": Ibid.

159   "further casting dirt . . . ": Ibid., p. 380.

159   "reduce"; "profitable member": Ibid., p. 366.

159   "if they be allowed . . . ": John Winthrop, "Short Story," 1644, in David D. Hall, ed., *The Antinomian Controversy*, p. 274.

159   "I dare say . . . ": T. Hutchinson, "Examination," p. 380.

159   "How dare you . . . ": Ibid., p. 381.

159   "Mr. Peter takes upon him . . . ": Ibid., p. 381.

159–160   "came and sat down . . . ": Ibid., p. 380.

160   "I did not think . . . "; "that she had spoken . . . "; "If you put me in mind . . . ": Ibid., pp. 381–82.

160   "You say . . . ": Ibid., p. 382.

160   "weary of the clamor . . . ": John Winthrop, "Short Story," Hall, ed., p. 271.

160   "the Lord did reveal . . . ": Ibid., pp. 272–73.

160   "demanded how she did know . . . ": Ibid., p. 273.

160–161   "How did Abraham . . . ": T. Hutchinson, "Examination," p. 383.

161 "So to me . . . ": Ibid., p. 384.

161 throughout his political career . . . : John Winthrop, *History of New England, 1630-1649*, ed., James K. Hosmer, vol. 2, p. 238. In his private journal, John Winthrop recorded his speech summarizing the relationship between the colonial fathers and God: "The great questions that have troubled the country are about the authority of the magistrates and the liberty of the people. It is yourselves who have called us to this office, and being called by you, we have our authority from God, in way of an ordinance, such as hath the image of God eminently stamped upon it, the contempt and violation whereof hath been vindicated with examples of divine vengeance."

161 "You have no power . . . ": John Winthrop, "Short Story," Hall, ed., p. 273.

161 "to deliver his judgment . . . ": Ibid., p. 273.

161 "Though the word revelation . . . ": T. Hutchinson, "Examination," p. 386.

162 "I desire . . . "; "Do you believe . . . ": Ibid.

162 "Good Sir, I do ask . . . ": Ibid., p. 387.

162 "I should desire to know . . . ": Ibid.

162 "By a providence of God . . . ": Ibid.

162 "The case is altered . . . ": Ibid.

162 "Mr. Endecott . . . ": Ibid.

163 "You give me satisfaction": Ibid.

163 "No, no . . . "; "Sir, you weary me . . . ": Ibid.

163 "I can say the same . . . ": Ibid., p. 219.

163 "a devilish delusion": Ibid.

163 "I am fully persuaded . . . ": Ibid.

163 "Mr. Cotton is not . . . ": Ibid.

163 "Sir, another thing . . . ": Ibid., p. 389.

164 Changing the subject . . . : Ibid., p. 390.

164 "We shall all be sick . . . ": Ibid.

164 "See the impudent . . . ": John Winthrop, "Short Story," Hall, ed., p. 275.

164 "The tragedy of Munster . . . ": Ibid., pp. 275-76.

165 "Dear Children, beware . . . ": Roger Clap, *Memoirs from 1630*, p. 34.

166 "Mr. Peter . . . ": T. Hutchinson, "Examination," p. 391.

166 "The court hath already declared . . . ": Ibid.

166 "Mrs. Hutchinson, the sentence . . . "; "I desire to know . . . "; "Say no more . . . ": Ibid.

167 "Mrs. _____ Hutchinson": Nathaniel Shurtleff, ed., *Mass. Records, 1628-41*, p. 207.

167   "instance Abraham": John Underhill, *Newes from America*, 1638, p. 6.

167   "The college is ordered . . . ": Shurtleff, *Mass. Records*, 1638–41, p. 208.

167–168   "The Lord having delivered . . . ": Thomas Shepard, "Memoir," 1644, in Alexander Young, ed., *Chronicles of the First Planters of the Colony of Massachusetts Bay . . .* , pp. 550–51.

168   "they no antinomians are": Edward Johnson, *Wonder-Working Providence, 1628–1651*, p. 203.

169   "Whereas the opinions . . . ": Shurtleff, *Mass. Records*, 1628–41, p. 211.

169   The list of fifty-eight . . . : Ibid., p. 208.

169   In addition to the fifty-eight . . . : Ibid., pp. 211–12; Thomas Weld, "Short Story," 1644, Hall, ed., p. 202.

170   "ordered that the powder . . . ": Shurtleff, *Mass. Records*, 1628–41, p. 209.

170   "but at last . . . ": John Winthrop, *History*, ed., Hosmer, vol. 1, p. 241.

170   "For his part . . . ": Ibid., p. 257.

171   "to be defrayed . . . ": Shurtleff, *Mass. Records*, 1628–41, p. 212.

CHAPTER 13

"YOU HAVE RATHER BEEN A HUSBAND THAN A WIFE"

172   "she thought it now needless . . . "; "Satan . . . "; "she began now to discover . . . ": John Winthrop, "Short Story," 1644, in David D. Hall, ed., *The Antinomian Controversy*, p. 300.

172   "the root of all . . . ": John Winthrop, *History*, 1630–49, ed., Hosmer, vol. 1, pp. 256–57.

172   "abused"; "stalking horse": Ibid., p. 259.

173   "Mistress Hutchinson seldom . . . ": John Cotton, "The Way of the Congregational Churches Cleared," 1648, Hall, ed., p. 434.

173   "informed that some godly passengers . . . ": Ibid., p. 414.

173   "had thoughts of removal . . . ": Ibid., p. 415.

173   killing ice and snowstorms . . . : John Winthrop, *History*, ed., Hosmer, vol. 1, p. 258.

174   "the growing evils"; "secret opinions": Ibid., p. 259.

175 "the souls of all men . . . ": Franklin B. Dexter, ed., "A Report of the Trial of Mrs. Anne Hutchinson . . . 1638," pp. 164–65.

175 Aquidneck . . . at the invitation of Roger Williams . . . : John Clarke, *Ill Newes from New England*, 1652, pp. 22–25.

176 "not out of any contempt . . . ": Dexter, p. 162.

177 "a very dangerous woman . . . ": Ibid., p. 164.

177 "I desire to know . . . ": Ibid., p. 171.

177 *"I hold it not"*: Ibid.

177 "I do not think the body that dies . . . ": Dexter, p. 170.

177–178 "if there be any union . . . ": Ibid., p. 171.

178 "If any such practice . . . ": Ibid.

178 "especially simple women . . . ": Ibid., p. 173.

178 "a meet yoke-fellow": Thomas Shepard, "Memoir," 1644, in Alexander Young, ed., *Chronicles of the First Planters of the Colony of Massachusetts Bay . . .* , p. 520. John Cotton, who, it must be conceded, may have been attempting to shift attention away from himself, later wrote that of all colonial ministers "she esteemed best of Mr. Shepard." Cotton, "Way Cleared," Hall, ed., p. 413.

178 "I do admonish you both . . . ": Dexter, pp. 176–77.

179 "Let me say somewhat . . . ": Ibid., p. 177.

179 "You have been an instrument . . . ": Ibid., p. 178.

180 "Let me warn you . . . ": Ibid.

180 "All that I would say . . . ": Ibid.

180 "set an open door . . . ": Ibid., p. 179.

180 "the hearts of young women . . . ": Ibid.

181 "and the face of the country": Ibid., p. 180.

181 "I spoke rashly . . . ": Ibid., p. 182.

181 "It was never in my heart . . . ": Ibid.

181 "heretic"; "humiliation"; "not satisfied": Ibid., pp. 183–84.

181 "I must needs say . . . ": Ibid., p. 185.

182 "Mrs. Hutchinson's repentance . . . ": Ibid., p. 184.

182 "did exceedingly magnify . . . ": Ibid.

182 "I would commend . . . ": Ibid., p. 186.

182 "divers sisters . . . ": Ibid., p. 187.

182 "all those women . . . ": Ibid.

182–183 "I look at her . . . ": Ibid., p. 188.

183 "point of doctrine"; " . . . point of practice . . . "; "God has let her . . . ": Ibid., p. 189.

183 "Forasmuch as you . . . ": Ibid., pp. 190–91.

183 "She [was] not affected . . . ": John Winthrop, "Short Story," Hall, ed., p. 310.

183 "her spirits . . . ": John Winthrop, *History*, ed., Hosmer, vol. 1, p. 264.

184 "this American Jezebel . . . ": John Winthrop, "Short Story," Hall, ed., p. 310.

184 "She had . . . insinuated herself . . . ": Ibid., p. 308.

184 "if their modesty . . . ": Ibid., p. 307.

184 "One standing at the door . . . ": Ibid.

CHAPTER 14
"A DEAR SAINT"

185 For six days Anne and her children traveled . . . : Cf. Samuel Groome, *A Glass for the People of New England, 1676*, pp. 14-15; John Clarke, *Ill Newes from New England*, 1652, pp. 24-25; John Winthrop, *History*, 1630-49, ed., Hosmer, vol. 1, pp. 264-65, 269.

185 "if he come not . . . ": *Winthrop Papers*, 1638-44, vol. 4, p. 25.

185 "a monster": John Winthrop, "Short Story," 1644, in David D. Hall, ed., *The Antinomian Controversy*, p. 282.

185 "comely": Ibid., p. 280.

185 "notoriously infected . . . ": John Winthrop, *History*, ed., Hosmer, vol. 1, p. 266.

186 "the very day . . . ": John Winthrop, "Short Story," Hall, ed., p. 281.

186 "a rank Familist also": John Winthrop, *History*, ed., Hosmer, vol. 1, p. 266.

186 "It had a face . . . ": Ibid., p. 267.

186 "about two hours before . . . ": Ibid., p. 268.

186 "I also humbly thank . . . ": *Winthrop Papers*, vol. 4, p. 25.

187 "Six weeks before . . . ": John Winthrop, *The History of New England from 1630 to 1649*, ed., James Savage, vol. 1, p. 272.

187 "considered that her condition . . . ": Ibid., p. 273. Editor James Savage has quoted the letter from John Clarke in a footnote.

187 "it might signify . . . ": Ibid., p. 271.

187-188 "After . . . it was brought to light . . . ": Ibid., p. 272.

188 "thirty monstrous births . . . ": Thomas Weld, "Short Story," 1644, ed., p. 214.

188 "See how . . . ": Ibid., pp. 214-15.

188 "the truth was . . . ": John Winthrop, "Short Story," Hall, ed., pp. 303-4.

189   "the Island of Errors": Weld, "Short Story," Hall, ed., p. 218.

189   "Jane Hawkins, the wife of . . . ": Nathaniel Shurtleff, ed., *Mass. Records*, 1628-41, p. 224.

189   "rank Familist"; "notorious for . . . ": John Winthrop, *History*, ed., Hosmer, vol. 1, p. 266; John Winthrop, "Short Story," Hall, ed., p. 281.

190   "She attended . . . ": John Wheelwright, *His Writings Including His Fast-Day Sermon, 1637, and His Mercurius Americanus, 1645*, p. 198.

190   "she was for ability . . . ": John Winthrop, *History*, ed., Hosmer, vol. 1, pp. 285-86.

190-191   "things grew still worse . . . ": Ibid., p. 297.

191   "Mrs. Hutchinson exercised . . . ": Ibid.

191   "but the elders . . . "; "Mrs. Hutchinson and some . . . ": Ibid.

191   "for speaking evil . . . "; quoted in Ola E. Winslow, *Meeting-House Hill*, 1952, p. 184.

191   "was found to have drunk . . . "; "in writing . . . ": John Winthrop, *History*, vol. 1, p. 293.

191-192   "also, the Devil . . . ": Ibid., p. 286.

192   "The people . . . put out Mr. Coddington . . . "; "They also gathered . . . ": Ibid., p. 299.

192   "free from original sin": Ibid., vol. 2, p. 17.

192   "men of a lovely and winning spirit . . . ": Weld, "Short Story," Hall, ed., p. 215.

192   "When they came first . . . ": Ibid.

192-193   "he was more nearly tied . . . ": John Winthrop, *History*, vol. 1, p. 331, footnote by editor James Hosmer, quoting the official report submitted by John Oliver, one of the three men of the Massachusetts delegation.

193   "broached new heresies . . . ": John Winthrop, *History*, ed., Hosmer, vol. 2, p. 39.

193   "infected with . . . "; "and other occasions . . . ": Ibid., pp. 39-40.

193   "inconvenient": Ibid., p. 40.

193   "Every married woman . . . ": "The Massachusetts Body of Liberties, 1641," in Edmund S. Morgan, ed., *Puritan Political Ideas*, #80, p. 194.

194   "The world is full of care . . . ": quoted in Samuel Eliot Morison, *Builders of the Bay Colony*, 1962, p. 234.

194-195   "Mistress Hutchinson, being weary . . . ": Weld, "Short Story," Hall, ed., p. 218.

195   "Many times hath Satan . . . ": Anne Bradstreet, *Works*, 1650, 1678, ed., Jeannine Hensley, pp. 243-44.

195 "despite . . . cast . . . ": Ibid., p. 16. For fuller quote, see chapter 11, p. 208.

AFTERMATH

197 "an eye and ear-witness . . . ": "Introduction to a Short Story," 1637–48, quoted in David D. Hall, ed., *The Antinomian Controversy*, pp. 199–200.

197 "to this day . . . ": Robert Baylie, *A Dissuasive from the Errours of the Time*, 1645, p. 64.

197 "into the horrible errors . . . ": Ibid., p. 57.

198 "debauched them both . . . ": quoted in Winifred Rugg, *Unafraid, A Life of Anne Hutchinson*, 1930, pp. 224–25.

198 "So reader, thou mayest see . . . ": Samuel Groome, *A Glass for the People of New England, 1676*, p. 139.

198 "relations at this day . . . ": Cotton Mather, *Magnalia Christi Americana*, 1702, vol. 2, p. 516.

198 "Some writers say . . . ": Thomas Hutchinson, *The History of the Colony and Province of Massachusetts-Bay*, 1764, vol. 1, p. 129.

199 "A woman of a thousand . . . ": Franklin B. Dexter, ed., "A Report of the Trial of Mrs. Anne Hutchinson . . . 1638," pp. 184–85.

199 "Satan made another assault . . . ": Roger Clap, *Memoirs from 1630*, p. 34.

200 "a man very bold . . . ": John Winthrop, *History*, 1630–48, ed., Hosmer, vol. 2, p. 41.

201 oldest son, Edward . . . : John G. Palfrey, *History of New England*, 1865, vol. 3, pp. 158–59, 162.

201 "women have an equal right . . . ": Hannah Mather Crocker, *Observations on the Real Rights of Women*, 1818, p. 19.

202 "the wise Author of nature . . . ": Ibid., p. 2.

Select Bibliography

SIXTEENTH AND
SEVENTEENTH CENTURIES

Please note: Materials cited in this category were originally published or produced during the lifetime of Anne Marbury Hutchinson (1591–1643), as well as during the periods immediately preceding her birth and following her death.

Aubrey, John. *Brief Lives*. 1667–1697. Edited from the original manuscripts by Oliver Lawson Dick. London: Secker & Warburg, 1968.

Auden, W. H. and Norman Pearson, eds. *Elizabethan and Jacobean Poets*. New York: Penguin Books, 1978.

Barlow, William. *The Summe and Substance of the Conference . . . at Hampton Court, January 14, 1603* [1604]. Gainesville, Fla.: Scholars' Facsimiles and Reprints, 1965.

Baxter, Richard. *Autobiography, 1615–1691*. Abridged by J. M. Lloyd Thomas. Edited by N. H. Keeble. London: Dent, 1974.

Baylie, Robert. *A Dissuasive from the Errours of the Time*. London: Samuel Gellibrand, 1645.

Bradford, William. *Of Plymouth Plantation, 1620–1649*. Reprint. Edited by Samuel Eliot Morison. New York: Random House, Modern Library, 1952.

Bradstreet, Anne. *Works*. 1650–1678. Reprint. Edited by Jeannine Hensley. Cambridge: Harvard University Press, Belknap Press, 1967.

Camden, William. *The History of the Most Renowned and Victorious Princess Elizabeth, Late Queen of England*. 1615. Reprint. Edited by

Wallace T. MacCaffrey. Chicago: University of Chicago Press, 1970.

Chamberlain, John. *Letters Concerning Life in England, 1597–1626.* Reprint. Edited by Elizabeth McClure Thomson. New York: G. P. Putnam's Sons, 1965.

Chambers, E. K., ed. *The Oxford Book of Sixteenth Century Verse.* London: Oxford University Press, 1961.

Charters and General Laws of the Colony and Province of Massachusetts Bay. Boston: T. B. Wait, 1814.

Clap, Roger. *Memoirs from 1630.* Reprint. Freeport, N. Y.: Books for Libraries Press, 1971.

Clarke, John. *Ill Newes from New England, 1652.* Massachusetts Historical Society Collections. 4th series, vol. 2 (1854).

Clifford, Anne (1590–1676). *Diary.* Reprint. New York: George H. Doran, 1923.

Cooke, Alexander. *Pope Joane: A Dialogue betweene a Protestant and a Papist, Manifestly proving that a woman called Joane was Pope of Rome, against the surmises and objections made to the contrarie.* London: E. Blunt and W. Barret, 1610.

Dexter, Franklin B., ed. "A Report of the Trial of Mrs. Anne Hutchinson before the Church in Boston, 1638." Massachusetts Historical Society Proceedings. 2nd series, vol. 4 (1889), pp. 159–91.

Elizabeth I. "A Proclamation Against the Sectaries of the Family of Love." Richmond, 1580. Houghton Library, Harvard University, f STC 7758.5, #219.

Etherington, John. *A Brief Discovery of the Blasphemous Doctrine of Familism, first conceived and brought forth into the world by one Henry Nicolas of the Low Countries of Germany about an hundred years ago . . . .* London, 1645. Houghton Library, Harvard University, *EC65 Et365 645b.

"Forefathers' Song," c. 1630. Reprint. *Annals of America*, vol. 1, pp. 21–22. Chicago: *Encyclopaedia Britannica*, 1968.

Gay, Frederick L., ed. "Note and Documents on Rev. Francis Marbury." Massachusetts Historical Society Proceedings. 48 (1915): 280–91.

Groome, Samuel. *A Glass for the People of New England, 1676.* Reprinted in *Magazine of History*, 37, No. 3, Extra No. 147 (Tarrytown, 1929): 131–68.

Hall, David D., ed. *The Antinomian Controversy.* Middletown, Conn.: Wesleyan University Press, 1968. Excellent collection of important contemporaneous documents.

Harrison, G. B., ed. *The Letters of Queen Elizabeth I.* New York: Funk and Wagnalls, 1968.

Hart, Albert B., ed. *American History Told by Contemporaries.* Vol. 1. New York: Macmillan, 1897.

Hoby, Lady Margaret. *Diary, 1599-1605.* Reprint. Edited by Dorothy M. Meads. London: George Routledge & Sons, 1930.

Holy Bible. Authorized King James Version, 1611.

Hubbard, William. *A General History of New England.* c. 1680. Reprint. Boston: Charles C. Little and James Brown, 1848.

Hurault, Andre, Sieur de Maisse. *A Journal of all that was Accomplished by Monsieur de Maisse, Ambassador in England from King Henry IV to Queen Elizabeth, Anno Domini, 1597.* Reprint. Translated from the French and edited by G. B. Harrison. London: The Nonesuch Press, 1931.

Hutchinson, Edward. Inventory. Appraised February 18, 1631 (1632). Lincolnshire Archives Office, Lincoln, England.

Hutchinson, Lucy Apsley. "The Life of Mrs. Lucy Hutchinson" (born 1620). In *Memoirs of the Life of Colonel Hutchinson.* 1664-71: pp. 1-15. Reprint. London: J. M. Dent, 1965. Please note: Lucy Hutchinson, a strong-minded younger contemporary of Anne Hutchinson, was not related to Anne either by blood or marriage. Her brief memoir of growing up in the 1620s in England is, however, both interesting and informative.

Hutchinson, Thomas, ed. "The Examination of Mrs. Anne Hutchinson at the court at Newtown. November 1637." In Thomas Hutchinson, *The History of the Colony and Province of Massachusetts-Bay.* Vol. 2. 1767. Appendix, pp. 366-91. Reprint. Cambridge, Mass.: Harvard University Press, 1936.

James I, King of England. *Daemonologie.* 1597. Reprint. London: Curwen Press, 1924.

Johnson, Edward. *Wonder-Working Providence, 1628-1651.* 1st ed., 1653-54. Reprint. Edited by J. Franklin Jameson. New York: Barnes and Noble, 1959.

Knewstub, John. *A Confutation of monstrous and Horrible Heresies taught by H. N. and embraced of a number who call themselves the Family of Love.* London, 1579. Houghton Library, Harvard University, C 8725.75*.

Lechford, Thomas. *Plaine Dealing.* 1641. Reprint. Boston: J. K. Wiggin and J. P. Lunt, 1867.

Mahl, Mary R. and Helene Koon, eds. *The Female Spectator: English Women Writers before 1800.* Bloomington and London: Indiana University Press; Old Westbury, New York: Feminist Press, 1977.

Marbury, Francis. Will. January 30, 1610 (1611). Greater London Record Office, County Hall, London, England.

Markham, Gervase. *The English Huswife.* London: John Harison, 1647 (5th revision and printing).

The Marprelate Tracts, 1588, 1589. Reprint. Edited by William Pierce. London: James Clarke, 1911.

"The Massachusetts Body of Liberties, 1641." Reprint. Edmund S. Morgan, ed., *Puritan Political Ideas*, pp. 178–203. Indianapolis and New York: Bobbs-Merrill, 1965.

Moryson, Fynes. *An Itinerary*. London: John Beale, 1617.

Mulcaster, Richard. *Positions wherein those primitive circumstances be examined, which are necessary for the training up of children.* . . . London, 1581.

Niclaes, Hendrik. *Comoedia: A Worke in Ryme.* c. 1575. Houghton Library, Harvard University, 14433.7.150*.

———. *Evangelium regni. A joyfull message.* Amsterdam, 1575. Houghton Library, Harvard University, STC 18556.

Perkins, William. *A Discourse of the Damned Art of Witchcraft.* . . . Cambridge, England: University of Cambridge, Thomas Pickering, 1608.

Sharp, Jane. *The Midwives Book of the Whole Art of Midwifery Discovered.* . . . London: Printed for Simon Miller, at the Star at the West End of St. Paul's, 1671. (Available at the British Library, London.)

Shurtleff, Nathaniel B., ed. *Records of the Governor and Company of the Massachusetts Bay in New England.* Vol. 1, 1628–41. Reprint. Boston: William White, 1853.

Stanford, Anne, ed. *The Women Poets in English.* New York: McGraw-Hill, 1972.

Stow, John. *The Survey of London.* 1603. Reprint. London: J. M. Dent, 1970.

Tusser, Thomas. *Five Hundred Points of Good Husbandry . . . Mixed . . . with the Book of Housewifery* (or sometimes, *Points of Huswifery*). London. Numerous editions between 1561 and 1638.

Underhill, John. *Newes from America.* 1638. Massachusetts Historical Society, Collections. 3rd series, vol. 6 (1837), pp. 1–28.

Weldon, Anthony. "James I." 1650. In *Characters from the Histories and Memoirs of the Seventeenth Century*, edited by David Nichol Smith. London: Oxford at the Clarendon Press, 1963.

Wheelwright, John. *His Writings Including His Fast-Day Sermon, 1637, and His Mercurius Americanus, 1645.* Edited by Charles H. Bell. Vol. 9. Boston: The Prince Society, 1876.

Winthrop, John. *History of New England, 1630–1649.* 2 vols. Edited by James Kendall Hosmer. New York: Barnes and Noble, 1959.

Winthrop, John. *The History of New England from 1630 to 1649.* 2 vols. Edited by James Savage. Boston: Phelps and Farnham, 1825. N. B. John Winthrop's journal, *The History of New England*, as edited by James Savage, is unexpurgated and therefore preferable to the two volumes edited by James K. Hosmer. However, the Hosmer edition is more generally available in libraries.

Winthrop Papers, vol. 3, 1631–1637; vol. 4, 1638–1644. Boston: Massachusetts Historical Society, 1943, 1944.

Wood, William. *New England's Prospect*. 1634. Reprint. Edited by Alden T. Vaughan. Amherst: University of Massachusetts, 1977.

Young, Alexander, ed. *Chronicles of the First Planters of the Colony of Massachusetts Bay, from 1623–1636 . . . collected from original records and contemporaneous manuscripts*. Boston: Charles C. Little and James Brown, 1846.

Ziff, Larzer, ed. *John Cotton on the Churches of New England*. Cambridge, Mass.: Harvard University Press, Belknap Press, 1968.

EIGHTEENTH, NINETEENTH, AND TWENTIETH CENTURIES

Adams, Brooks. *The Emancipation of Massachusetts*. 1887. Reprint. Boston: Houghton Mifflin, 1962.

Adams, Charles Francis. *Three Episodes of Massachusetts History*. 2 vols. 1892. Reprint. New York: Russell and Russell, 1965.

Adamson, J. H., and H. F. Folland. *Sir Henry Vane: His Life and Times, 1613–1662*. Boston: Gambit, 1973.

Augur, Helen. *An American Jezebel*. New York: Brentano's, 1930.

Bailyn, Bernard. *The New England Merchants in the Seventeenth Century*. New York: Harper Torchbook, 1964.

Bainton, Roland H. *Women of the Reformation in Germany and Italy*. Boston: Beacon Press, 1974.

Bancroft, George. *History of the United States*. Vol. 1, 10th ed. Boston: Charles C. Little and James Brown, 1842.

Banks, Charles Edward. *The Planters of the Commonwealth, 1620–1640*. Boston: Houghton Mifflin, 1930.

Battis, Emery. *Saints and Sectaries: Anne Hutchinson and the Antinomian Controversy in the Massachusetts Bay Colony*. Chapel Hill: University of North Carolina Press, 1962.

Black, J. R. *The Reign of Elizabeth, 1558–1603*. London: Oxford University Press, 1959.

Bolton, Reginald P. *A Woman Misunderstood: Anne, Wife of William Hutchinson*. New York: Printed for the author, 1931.

Bridenbaugh, Carl. *Vexed and Troubled Englishmen, 1590–1642*. New York: Oxford University Press, 1968.

Burton, Elizabeth. *The Pageant of Elizabethan England*. New York: Charles Scribner's Sons, 1958.

——. *The Pageant of Stuart England*. New York: Charles Scribner's Sons, 1962.

Callender, John. *An Historical Discourse on the Civil and Religious Affairs of the Colony of Rhode-Island and Providence Plantations in New England in America from the First Settlement, 1638*. Boston: S. Kneeland and T. Green, 1739.

Camden, Carroll. *The Elizabethan Woman*. Houston: The Elsevier Press, 1952.

Carroll, Peter N. *Puritanism and the Wilderness: The Intellectual Significance of the New England Frontier, 1629–1700*. New York and London: Columbia University Press, 1969.

Chambers, E. K. *The Elizabethan Stage*. Vol. 3. Oxford: Clarendon Press, 1965.

Champlin, John Denison. "Hutchinson Ancestry and Descendants of William and Anne Hutchinson." New York Genealogical and Biographical Record, vol. 45 (1914), pp. 164–69.

Clark, Alice. *Working Life of Women in the Seventeenth Century*. London: Frank Cass, 1919, 1968.

Clark, Peter, and Paul Slack. *English Towns in Transition, 1500–1700*. London: Oxford University Press, 1976.

Clasen, Claus-Peter. *Anabaptism: A Social History, 1525–1618*. Ithaca: Cornell University Press, 1972.

Cohn, Norman. *The Pursuit of the Millennium*. London: Paladin, 1978.

Colacurcio, Michael J. "Footsteps of Anne Hutchinson: The Context of *The Scarlet Letter*." ELH 39 (1972): 459–94.

Coleman, D. C. *Industry in Tudor and Stuart England*. London: The Macmillan Press, 1975.

Colket, Meredith B., Jr. *The English Ancestry of Anne Marbury Hutchinson and Katherine Marbury Scott*. Philadelphia: The Magee Press, 1936.

Collinson, Patrick. *The Elizabethan Puritan Movement*. Berkeley and Los Angeles: University of California Press, 1967.

Creighton, Charles. *History of Epidemics in Britain*. Vol. 1, pp. 664–1666. New York: Barnes and Noble, 1894, 1965.

Crocker, Hannah Mather. *Observations on the Real Rights of Women, with Their Appropriate Duties Agreeable to Scripture, Reason, and Common Sense*. Boston: Printed for the author, 1818.

Curtis, Edith. *Anne Hutchinson*. Cambridge, Mass.: Washburn and Thomas, 1930.

Dow, George. *Every Day Life in the Massachusetts Bay Colony*. Boston: The Society for the Preservation of New England Antiquities, 1935.

Drake, Samuel Adams. *The Making of New England.* New York: Charles Scribner's Sons, 1886.

Dudding, Reginald C. *History of the Parish and Manors of Alford.* 1930.

Dunbar, Seymour. *A History of Travel in America.* New York: Tudor Publishing Co., 1937.

Earle, Anne Morse. *Margaret Winthrop.* New York: Charles Scribner's Sons, 1896.

————. *The Sabbath in Puritan New England.* New York: Charles Scribner's Sons, 1891.

Ellis, George E. *Life of Anne Hutchinson. The Library of American Biography,* edited by Jared Sparks, vol. 6, pp. 169–376. Boston: Charles C. Little and James Brown, 1845.

Emerson, Everett H. *John Cotton.* New York: Twayne, 1965.

Felt, Joseph B. *The Ecclesiastical History of New England.* Boston: Congregational Library Association, 1855.

————. *A Memoir, or Defence of Hugh Peters.* Boston: C. C. P. Moody, 1851.

Forbes, Thomas Rogers. *The Midwife and the Witch.* New Haven: Yale University Press, 1966.

Fussell, George E., and Kathleen R. Fussell. *The English Countrywoman: A Farmhouse Social History, A.D. 1500–1900.* London: Andrew Melrose, 1953.

Hawthorne, Nathaniel. *Tales, Sketches, and Other Papers.* "Mrs. Hutchinson," in *Hawthorne's Works,* vol. 12, pp. 217–26. Boston: Houghton Mifflin, Riverside Press, 1883.

Hill, Christopher. *Antichrist in Seventeenth-Century England.* London: Oxford University Press, 1971.

————. *The World Turned Upside Down.* Baltimore: Penguin, 1974.

Hosmer, James K. *The Life of Young Sir Henry Vane.* Boston: Houghton Mifflin, 1888.

Hufeland, Otto. "Anne Hutchinson's Refuge in the Wilderness." In *Anne Hutchinson and Other Papers,* pp. 3–20. White Plains, N. Y.: Westchester County Historical Society, 1929.

Hutchinson, Thomas. *The History of the Colony and Province of Massachusetts-Bay.* Vol. 1. 1764. Reprint. Edited by Lawrence Shaw Mayo. Cambridge, Mass.: Harvard University Press, 1936.

Jenkins, Elizabeth. *Elizabeth the Great.* London: Panther, 1958.

Koehler, Lyle. "The case of the American Jezebels: Anne Hutchinson and Female Agitation during the Years of Antinomian Turmoil, 1636–1640." *William and Mary Quarterly,* 3rd series, vol. 31 (1974), pp. 55–78.

Lawrence, Robert Means. *New England Colonial Life.* Cambridge, Mass.: Cosmos Press, 1927.

Mather, Cotton. *Magnalia Christi Americana.* 2 vols. 1702. Reprint. Hartford: Silas Andrus and Son, 1853.

McGrath, Patrick. *Papists and Puritans under Elizabeth I.* New York: Walker and Co., 1967.

Miller, Perry. *Errand into the Wilderness.* Cambridge, Mass.: Harvard University Press, Belknap Press, 1967.

———. *Nature's Nation.* Cambridge, Mass.: Harvard University Press, Belknap Press, 1967.

———. *The New England Mind: The Seventeenth Century.* Boston: Beacon Press, 1961.

———. *Roger Williams.* New York: Atheneum, 1970.

Morgan, Edmund S. "The Case against Anne Hutchinson." *New England Quarterly,* vol. 10 (1937), pp. 635-49.

———. *The Puritan Dilemma: The Story of John Winthrop.* Boston: Little, Brown, 1958.

———. *Roger Williams: The Church and the State.* New York: Harcourt, Brace and World, 1967.

———. *Visible Saints.* Ithaca: Cornell University Press, 1968.

Morison, Samuel Eliot. *Builders of the Bay Colony.* Boston: Houghton Mifflin, 1962.

———. *The Founding of Harvard College.* Cambridge, Mass.: Harvard University Press, 1935.

Mullett, Charles F. *The Bubonic Plague and England.* Lexington: University of Kentucky Press, 1956.

Notestein, Wallace. *The English People on the Eve of Colonization, 1603-1660.* New York: Harper Torchbook, 1962.

———. "The English Woman, 1580 to 1650." In *Studies in Social History,* edited by J. H. Plumb, pp. 71-107. London: Longmans, Green and Co., 1955.

———. *A History of Witchcraft in England from 1588 to 1718.* New York: Thomas Y. Crowell Co., 1968.

Osgood, Herbert L. *The American Colonies in the Seventeenth Century.* Vol. 1. 1904. Reprint. Gloucester, Mass.: Peter Smith, 1957.

Palfrey, John Gorham. *History of New England.* 3 vols. Boston: Little, Brown, 1865.

Parkes, Joan. *Travel in England in the Seventeenth Century.* London: Oxford University Press, 1925.

Pearson, Lu Emily. *Elizabethans at Home.* Stanford: Stanford University Press, 1957.

Perley, Sidney. *The History of Salem, Massachusetts.* 3 vols. Salem: Sidney Perley, 1928.

Pierce, William. *An Historical Introduction to the Marprelate Tracts.* London: Archibald Constable, 1908.

Plowden, Alison. *Tudor Women: Queens and Commoners.* New York: Atheneum, 1979.

Pope, Charles H. *The Pioneers of Massachusetts, 1620-1650.* Boston: Printed for the author, 1900.

Root, Waverley, and Richard de Rochement, *Eating in America, A History.* New York: William Morrow, 1976.

Rowse, A. L. *The England of Elizabeth: The Structure of Society.* New York: Macmillan, 1951.

Rugg, Winifred King. *Unafraid, A Life of Anne Hutchinson.* Boston and New York: Houghton Mifflin, 1930.

Rutman, Darrett B. *Winthrop's Boston.* Chapel Hill: University of North Carolina Press, 1965.

Savage, James. *A Genealogical Dictionary of the First Settlers of New England, Showing Three Generations of Those Who Came before May 1692.* 4 vols. Boston: Little, Brown, 1860-1862.

Schelling, Felix E. *Elizabethan Drama, 1558-1642.* Boston and New York: Houghton Mifflin, 1908.

Shrewsbury, J. F. D. *A History of Bubonic Plague in the British Isles.* Cambridge: Cambridge University Press, 1970.

Spurrell, Mark. *The Puritan Town of Boston.* Boston, Lincolnshire, England: Richard Kay Publications, 1972.

Stenton, Doris Mary. *The English Woman in History.* New York: Schocken, 1977.

Stephenson, Henry Thew. *Shakespeare's London.* New York: Henry Holt and Co., 1905.

Tawney, R. H. *Religion and the Rise of Capitalism.* New York: Mentor, 1954.

Thomas, Keith. *Religion and the Decline of Magic.* Middlesex, England: Penguin, 1973.

———. "Women and the Civil War Sects." In Trevor Aston, ed., *Crisis in Europe, 1560-1660.* New York: Basic Books, 1965.

Thornton, John Wingate. *New England and the English Commonwealth.* Boston: Printed for the author, 1874.

Wigmore, John H. *Law of Evidence.* Brooklyn: The Foundation Press, 1935.

Wilson, F. P. *The Plague in Shakespeare's London.* London: Oxford University Press, 1963.

Wilson, Violet A. *Society Women of Shakespeare's Time.* Port Washington, N. Y.: Kennikat Press, 1970.

Winslow, Ola Elizabeth. *Meetinghouse Hill, 1630-1783.* New York: Macmillan, 1952.

———. *Master Roger Williams.* New York: Macmillan, 1957.

Winthrop, Robert C. *Life and Letters of John Winthrop.* 2 vols. Boston: Little, Brown, 1869.

Wright, Louis B. *Middle-Class Culture in Elizabethan England.* Ithaca: Cornell University Press, 1958. (See especially chapter 13, "The Popular Controversy over Woman," pp. 465–507.)

Ziff, Larzer, *The Career of John Cotton.* Princeton: Princeton University Press, 1962.

Index

235